Spring Winds of Beijing

Spring Winds

of

Beijing

Gail Copeland

Glenbridge Publishing Ltd.

Library of Congress Catalog Card Number: LC 92-73014

International Standard Book Number: 0-944435-20-3

Printed in the U.S.A.

To Buddy, Ted, Kyle, Michael, Mom, and Sandy.

and

To Beijingshimin:
They are the bravest and the best.

CONTENTS

ILLUSTRATIONS

ACKNOWLEDGMENTS

This book was very much a cooperative effort in spirit. With that in mind, there are certain people to whom I would like to express my appreciation. Among them are several people in China whose names I dare not mention. They are always in my thoughts and in my prayers.

I am especially grateful to my Chinese history professor, Dr. Edward Lazzerini. His question—"Why don't you go write about China?"—gave me courage and sent me on my way to do just that.

Special thanks go to my aunt, Nelle Coleman, who purchased a word processor so that I could write with greater ease, and to Stanley and Ting Hung who stuffed me with Chinese delicacies as I wrote. The late Joseph J. Davies, Jr. was a guiding force in the early stages of this book, and Marge Davies continued that force by reading every word that I wrote with a critical but encouraging eye.

Wuer Kaixi graciously and gently offered me the use of his calligraphy skills. Dr. Alsace Yen made significant contributions to the translation of the June 4, 1989, memorial. Wen Hong translated the vast majority of the documents and patiently endured my assistance.

Donna LaBorde deserves a gold star for typing the manuscript as do Ginger Gauthe, Susan Guidry, and Rod Guidry for handling my film with the greatest professional care. Glenda and Lanvil Gilbert were a source of special encouragement to me, as were my sister-in-law, Patricia Bender, and my partner, Cliff Miller. Anna and Jaisan Fu, Fu Imo, Ge Xun, Lu Jin, Huang Yuangeng, and Man Yuanlong were not only generous with their assistance and encouragement, but also inspired me to fulfill their expectations.

Asia Watch, Human Rights in China, and Inside Mainland China were invaluable sources of information, which allowed me to verify the facts that I had gathered and put the pieces of the puzzle together. Most important, these groups work diligently to expose and combat injustice in The People's Republic of China.

It has been a pleasure to work with both Mary and James Keene. They are delightful people and a thoroughly professional team. As an editor, Jim is a writer's dream.

Peter Miller is my favorite literary agent in the world. He is a beloved friend as well.

Finally, I would like to express my deep gratitude to my husband, Buddy; my children, Ted, Kyle, and Michael; my mother, Virginia; and my sister, Sandy for their love and unselfish support. With extreme patience and boundless understanding, they have tolerated my idiosyncrasies and endured my absences—both literal and as a state of mind.

PREFACE

From the moment I first stepped on Chinese soil in 1982, I felt connected to China. It was not a feeling I had anticipated when my husband, a banker, told me we would be going there with a delegation of Louisiana bankers. "China!" Just saying the word conjured up ethereal images of mist-covered mountains, jade-green rivers, and long-bearded sages.

I knew so little about the country. By the time our departure date arrived, I had barely scratched the surface of China's four thousand years of history. In my ignorance, even reading about the cities we would visit had left me more confused than enlightened. The names sounded so strange and were difficult to remember. Was Guangzhou a city in the province of Guangdong, or was it the other way around? Anyway, why didn't the Chinese just call it Canton, like everyone else?

From a Westerner's perspective, China can be quite perplexing, and many times things seem to be upside down and inside out. Last names come first and first names come last. The meal does not begin with soup, but ends with it. Dragons are not monsters to be slain, but harmless, warm-hearted creatures. To add to the Westerner's confusion, China is a country where ancient continually collides with modern, making you wonder, at times, which century you are in. I thought it unreasonable to travel in a country without being able to say, "hello, goodby, thank-you, please, and you're welcome" in the native tongue. Therefore, I concentrated my efforts on learning those few words in Chinese. A phrase book and cassette helped me as I stumbled over words that began with q, x, and z and looked entirely unpronounceable in print. As I mumbled them to myself, I could not wait to try them out to see if they would accomplish their intended purposes. I was overjoyed and duly impressed with myself when I discovered that they actually worked. What impressed me even more was the response my modest vocabulary received from the Chinese people. There was always a friendly reply in Chinese from those who did not speak English, and those who could speak English praised me extravagantly, encouraging me to learn more.

Of course, there were times when my efforts with the language proved to be less than successful. One evening I wandered into a neighborhood bakery. Seeing a cake, which looked delicious, I pointed to it and pantomimed that I wanted to purchase a piece. After the transaction was completed, I said, "*Zai jian*" (goodby in Chinese), and walked out the door. When I reached the sidewalk, I remembered I had forgotten to say thank-you. Not willing to pass up an opportunity to use another one of my Chinese words, I went back to the store, stuck my head around the door, and said, "*Qing*." The salesclerks looked at me with puzzled expressions, as if they were waiting for me to say more.

When I just stood there smiling foolishly, they began to giggle. It only took a couple of seconds for me to realize what they found so humorous. Instead of saying "thank you," I had said "please."

I remember so clearly my first departure from China. As the plane rose up into the sky, I looked through the window and saw China disappearing below me. It filled me with such sadness to be leaving. It was then that I knew I must return. Like so many Westerners before me, I was captivated by China and her people, bewitched by her magnificent beauty and a culture that is equally magnificent in its richness and depth.

In 1983 and 1985 I did return. In my travels through China, I went up the Yangste River and down the Grand Canal. I went to two Autonomous Regions, over a dozen Provinces, more than twenty-five cities, and even a few villages. In 1987 I returned to China for another purpose: to study the Chinese language in Beijing.

Each time I returned, I found myself even more connected to China as I developed friendships with people from a cross section of Chinese society. My friends include teachers, students, doctors, workers, guides, bus drivers, soldiers, farmers, artists, businessmen, officials, and writers. Some I met casually, on street corners, in buses, in restaurants, and in shops. Others I met through formal introductions.

Once, I even received a proposal of marriage. It was in the fall of 1985. I had stopped on a street corner in Wuhan to photograph a food peddler who was battering and frying apple slices. An old man came over to watch as I took pictures, and gradually, a crowd gathered around us. The old man asked my nationality and if I had a husband and children. By that time, I had taught myself enough Chinese to handle a simple conversation. I answered his questions: "American, married, two sons, and one daughter." He then asked if my husband and children were also in Wuhan. When I replied that they were back in America, he laughed and said that I should stay in China and be his wife, assuring me that he would take much better care of me than my American husband who had allowed me to roam around a foreign country alone. The crowd all had a good laugh at his proposal, the peddler insisted on treating me to a serving of apples, and I promised the old man that if I ever left my American husband, I would head straight for his door.

When I was not actually in China, I was reading about China. I read about Chinese history, politics, language, culture, and literature. I took courses in Chinese history and language, as well as continuing to study independently. With each course taken and each book read, I felt there was still so much I needed to learn. Finally, I came to understand that I would always feel that way, for learning about China is like being served a banquet of ten thousand courses. There is so much to consume, it takes a lifetime just to taste it all.

I undertook the monumental and intimidating task of studying those subjects, not only to satisfy my curiosity, but because I wanted to write about China and about the Chinese people who had moved me by their kindness to me as a stranger and by their loyalty to me as a friend. When I learned in 1989 that I had been awarded a scholarship to study again in Beijing, I knew the time had come. At last I was ready to write about the people and the place I love. I decided I would stay on in China, after the term ended, to do research in preparation for the book I wanted to write. However, history intervened.

On April 15, 1989, Hu Yaobang died. Until his forced resignation in 1987, Hu had been the General Secretary of the Chinese Communist Party and successor to Deng Xiaoping. Even before Hu's death, there had been strong indications that China was nearing a point of crisis. With Hu's death, the crisis began.

Since many of my Chinese friends knew of my plans to write a book, they urged me to broaden the scope of my book to include what was happening in Beijing. They asked that I write of the things they wanted the American people to know, to tell of their dreams and desires for a better China.

In order to assist me with this book, many people took great personal risks. They allowed me to record conversations, take notes, met with me repeatedly to help me in obtaining information, discussed their feelings without reservation, and, after I left Beijing, they had letters to me smuggled out of China. It was their courage and their assurances that I was up to the task that inspired me to write this book. China being China, I have taken certain precautions to protect the people in this book. In addition to other measures, I have used pseudonyms for those who are not public figures and have even changed the names of some streets and places. Sadly, the repressive political climate in China makes this necessary. As one friend so aptly stated, "when you write the book, please remember that I am Chinese, and I must live in China for a long time."

GLOSSARY OF TERMS

Beida	Beijing University; short for Beijing *Daxue*
Danwei	Work unit
Dazibao	Big character poster
Fuwuyuan	Service person
Ganbei	Toast when drinking; literal translation, "empty cup"
Guandao	Official profiteering
Guanxi	Relationship, connections, political pull
Lao	Old; term used in front of surname when you are addressing a friend of approximately the same age
Laobaixing	Ordinary people; literal translation, "old one hundred names"
Man man zou	Walk slowly; take care
San Lou	Building #3
Shitang	Cafeteria; dining hall
Shiwuyuan	Room attendant
Shoupiaoyuan	Conductor; ticket seller on bus or trolley
Xiuxi	To rest; also refers to daily rest period from 1:00 to 2:00 p.m.
Yeyinglu	Nightingale Lane
Zenma ban	What's to be done

Pinyin is the translation used in the People's Republic of China. Pronunciation is as follows:

c = ts as in its. Cai = tsai
q = ch as in chair. Qing = ching
x = sh as in she. Xiuxi = shiu she
zh = j as in jar. Zhou = Joe

PART ONE
SETTLING IN

"I have a feeling we're not in Kansas anymore."
Dorothy, *The Wizard of Oz*

CHAPTER ONE

SAN LOU

At fifteen minutes after one o'clock on Thursday, April 6, 1989, the plane touched down. It had taken winning a scholarship to finance my trip, months of preparation, and no small amount of cooperation and sacrifice from my family, but I was back in Beijing. In my excitement at returning I had almost organized myself to death, packing and repacking, but the big payoff had finally come. At last, I was back in Beijing.

As I stepped from the plane, I breathed in the familiar, distinctive odor of the Beijing International Airport: part disinfectant, part Beijing dust, and part who knows what. A new odor was apparent as I rounded a corner. The walls and ceilings were getting a fresh coat of paint, probably in preparation for Gorbachev's upcoming visit in May for the Sino-Soviet Summit.

Grabbing a luggage cart, I sat down to await the clang and hum of the carousel that signals baggage is on the way. While I waited, I scanned the crowd in the lobby. On the other side of the glass panels, people craned their necks, eager for the first sight of friends or relatives they had come to meet. I had written to my friends to tell them a representative of the organization that had granted my scholarship would meet me.* However, there was always a possibility that my letters had not arrived in time and there might be a familiar face in the crowd.

Not recognizing anyone, I looked for my name on the signs held up by official greeters. Neither my English name nor my Chinese name was on any of the signs, and I began to worry that I might have to hoof it to the

---

*An agency of the Chinese government had awarded me a scholarship to study the Chinese language.

campus. The currency exchange window was closed, and I didn't have enough Chinese money to take a taxi all the way across town to the northwest section of Beijing.

The luggage arrived and I breezed through customs. Growing more anxious, I waited in the lobby, watching as the crowd thinned out. After several minutes I walked to the exit, wondering how I could get on a bus with my purse, a carry-on, a standard sized bag, and a huge, heavy-duty, Chinese-made "Long March" suitcase. A middle-aged man rescued me at the door.

Tentatively he asked, "Are you Kong Kailing,* the American who speaks Chinese?" When I replied that I was indeed Kong Kailing, the man smiled broadly and said, "Lao Kong, I almost didn't recognize you."

It was confusing. He had called me Lao Kong, and in Chinese "*Lao*" (old) is the form of address used for a close friend of approximately the same age. The man was a stranger and although I had not yet met anyone from the organization, it would have been unusual for someone from the organization to address me in such a familiar manner.

Noticing my look of bewilderment, the man laughed, saying "Lao Kong, you don't recognize me either. I am Lu Minghua's husband, Dong Dianfei."

It was embarrassing that I hadn't recognized my dear friend's husband. Yet, despite my friendship with Lu Minghua, it was understandable since Lao Dong and I had only met once. Lu Minghua and I had become friends when I first studied in Beijing in 1987. Being nearly the same age and having similar personalities, we had immediately felt as if we had known each other for years. A close bond had formed between us, and our friendship had deepened through our correspondence over the past two years.

Lao Dong explained that Lu Minghua was working and unable to come to the airport to greet me. As we stood talking, another man came up and asked my name. It was Mr. Jiang, an official from the organization. He had seen me waiting, but assumed I must be someone else since Lao Dong had come to meet me.

---

*In Chinese, the surname comes first and the given name last. Therefore, my Chinese surname is Kong and my given name is Kailing.

As we drove through the city, Mr. Jiang and Lao Dong chatted. I stared out the car window, thinking about my past visits to China. It was my fifth trip and each time I returned, I was astonished by the changes that had occurred since the previous visit. For ten years China had been in a constant state of change, and the fast pace of those changes had made them seem even more dramatic. In fact, the country was transforming so rapidly, that I sometimes wondered if China might go spinning out of control.

For thousands of years Chinese culture had placed its value on tradition and stability rather than progress and change. A Chinese friend had once described this reluctance to vary from the old ways by saying, "Change can be as fierce as a tiger. If one can manage to ride the tiger, to stay astride, he emerges as a hero. If he slips in one direction, he must cling to the tiger's tail. However, if he slips in the other direction, he will certainly be crushed in the tiger's powerful jaws."

There were changes: new hotels, new office buildings, old buildings that had been renovated, more up-to-date fashions, an influx of rock music, and an increase in taxis and cars. Those were the obvious changes. But it was the subtle changes that interested me; those that could not be seen from a car window, but would take time to discover.

Although there were new dormitories on campus, I was once again assigned to a room in good old *San Lou* (Building #3). Mr. Jiang paid for my tuition and room as a part of my scholarship. After he assisted me in going through the formalities of checking in at the school office and getting my student ID, we drove to *San Lou* and brought my luggage up to my room.

Apologizing for the meager sum, Mr. Jiang handed me an envelope containing one thousand four hundred yuan in Renminbi (RMB). The money was for incidental expenses and meal tickets, and although it only amounted to roughly three hundred and seventy-six US dollars,* it was more than a year's salary for many Chinese.

As he was leaving, Mr. Jiang told me a car would come for me on Saturday to take me to the Beijing Hotel for lunch with Mr. Liu, the head of his department. Thanking Mr. Jiang for the organization's generosity, I told him I looked forward to meeting Mr. Liu.

---

*This book was written chronologically. Therefore, the prices, wages, and ages referred to here are those that applied in 1989. The rate of exchange at that time was 3.72 yuan for US$1.00.

Lao Dong insisted that I must be tired from my long trip and advised me to get some rest. He reminded me that the cafeteria would be open for dinner at 5:40 and said he and Lu Minghua would come to visit later.

I was tired but much too excited to rest. When I was finally alone, I sat on the bed and took a good look around the room. The furniture was old, battered, and utilitarian, but certainly adequate since there was barely enough space left in the room for movement. Each half of the room had an institutional-style iron bed with a mattress around two inches thick. There were two pillows filled with grain husks, a cotton-stuffed quilt, a scratchy wool blanket, and a thin cotton bedspread stacked on the bed. A wooden desk and a straight-backed wooden chair were jammed against the foot of the bed. A small bookcase sat next to the desk against the side wall of the room. On the front wall of the room, an armoire stood facing the desk, leaving about three feet of space between the two pieces of furniture.

In addition to the furniture, each student was provided with a thermos, an ashtray, an enamel basin, and a lamp with a bulb of such low wattage it was probably measured in fractions. Between the two beds was a small night table, and on it an electric fan for the hot months. A fluorescent light fixture hung from the center of the high ceiling, buzzing and flickering the entire time it was on.

Since my roommate had not yet arrived, I had my choice of which side of the room I wanted. Having some experience under my belt, I knew the decision would not be based upon which bed was the most comfortable. Neither bed is ever comfortable. The deciding factor was the armoire. Both had bottom drawers, but in one, the clothes rod was disengaged at one end and the other end was attached by a flimsy piece of wire wrapped around a nail. My decision was made when I opened the other armoire and saw that its rod was attached at both ends.

Now I was ready for serious business. Unpacking a sponge, a wash-cloth, and a small bottle of pine-scented liquid cleaner, I set about cleaning my room. Actually, I was fighting a losing battle. *San Lou* had stood for over thirty years, and it's doubtful the rooms had ever been thoroughly cleaned. Also, it didn't help matters that dust is the one thing in Beijing that is in abundant supply the year round. After three decades of neglect, the pine-scented cleaner could not accomplish miracles, but it did make the dirt smell good.

When I had finished unpacking and cleaning, I went down to the first floor to get hot water. Since drinking water in China must be boiled to prevent contracting hepatitis, *San Lou* is equipped with a boiler. I would have to get cold drinking water from the massive water cooler in the cafeteria or buy chilled mineral water at the university store. I filled my thermos, and went back to my room to dine on tea and crackers, which I had brought from home. Although Mr. Jiang had given me money to buy meal tickets in the cafeteria, I planned to avoid eating there for as long as I possibly could.

The Chinese word for cafeteria is *shitang*, and it doesn't take much imagination to figure out the nickname that many English speaking foreign students have to describe the food. While most Chinese food is absolutely delicious, *shitang* food is far from gourmet fare. Granted, no college cafeteria is going to win five stars, but *shitang* food is in a class of its own.

First, there are the sanitary conditions. The utensils are dirty, the plates are dirty, the glasses are dirty, the tables are dirty, and the floors are dirty. Second, the menu board does not always seem to correspond with what is actually being served. In addition to the menu, there is a wooden and glass cupboard used to display the dishes for the day, or year, as the case may be. However, the contents of the dishes on display are not always easy to discern by merely looking. That brings us back to the menu board. If number seven says fish, you look at number seven in the cupboard, and although it doesn't exactly resemble fish, you decide it will do. You go to the window at the service area and order number seven. The *fuwuyuan* (service person) gets your plate from the kitchen and hands you something that looks neither like fish nor whatever was on the plate in the cupboard. There are three possible explanations for this. Perhaps she misheard the number. Maybe number seven is sold out and she just doesn't want to go through the hassle of asking you to decide on another selection. It is more likely that many *fuwuyuan* have a perverse sense of humor, and to make an otherwise dull job more interesting they switch dishes. The *shitang* only varies its menu to adapt to seasonal changes in vegetables, or shortages in a certain type of meat, so after a few days, you have memorized the menu and are not so easily fooled. The only recommendation for *shitang* food is that it is incredibly cheap. The most expensive entree is around four yuan or US$1.08.

Since I only planned to get cold water from the *shitang*, it was not necessary to get there until a few minutes before closing. I thought about taking a walk around the campus and the surrounding neighborhood, but cleaning and unpacking had left me exhausted. Fluffing my grain husk pillows, I settled down for a short nap.

I knew it would be difficult to sleep since it was well past the traditional 1:00 P.M. to 2:00 P.M. *xiuxi* (rest period). Every little noise in *San Lou* bounced off the concrete floors and walls, echoed down the hallways from one floor to the next, and came into the room through the transom window. The voice of the *shiwuyuan* (room attendant) periodically boomed over the intercom speakers at each end of the hallway on all four floors of the building as she paged students or made announcements. The sounds of music, conversation, and laughter drifted down from the rooms above and rose up from the courtyard below into the open windows behind my bed. Those noises mingled with the constant rat-a-tat-tat of jackhammers and the gong-like clashing of heavy steel bars that accompanied the shouts of orders being barked to workers at a nearby construction site. Nevertheless, I slept a sound, contented sleep.

Around eight o'clock, I awoke with a start. Having slept for three hours, I had missed the opportunity to get cold drinking water from the *shitang*. However, I was more concerned that Lu Minghua and Lao Dong had already come to visit. Since Chinese tend to knock very softly, their knock wouldn't have awakened me.

At nine o'clock, there was a light tap on the door. I opened the door with relief, and greeted my dear friend, Lu Minghua. Her face wore the same expression that I see so clearly in my mind whenever I think about her. Her eyebrows were slightly raised, her eyes sparkled with humor and intelligence, and her mouth was turned up at the corners in a sly little smile. When we first became friends, it was that expression that made me so frustrated with my limited ability to communicate in Chinese. I wanted to know what was going on behind those eyes, what she was really thinking. Alas, my Chinese wasn't up to the task. The letters we had exchanged over the past two years had brought my written Chinese up to a level where I could really appreciate her sharp wit and clever mind. Unfortunately, my spoken Chinese, while improved, still lagged behind.

We greeted each other warmly, and I went through the traditional Chinese routine of politeness, which I refer to as the "Three *Qings*." *Qing* means please, and it is customary when a guest arrives to say, "*Qing jin lai*" (Please come in), "*Qing zuo*" (Please sit down), and "*Qing he cha*" (Please drink tea).

Lu Minghua laughed at my formality, and nudging Lao Dong said, "Little Sister is too polite." Since Lu Minghua is a few years older than I, she calls me *Meimei*, younger or little sister. In turn, I call her *Jiejie*, elder sister.

As mothers usually do, we talked to each other about our children. As close friends usually do, we sometimes spoke in half sentences and sometimes spoke at the same time. Lao Dong complained that it was like listening to chattering monkeys, but the room rang with Lu Minghua's laughter and was warmed by our delight in seeing each other again.

When we finally gave Lao Dong a chance to talk, he asked if there was anything I needed. I wanted to purchase a bicycle. It would be easier to get around Beijing by bike, and it would give me independence. While it was possible to buy a used bicycle from one of the departing foreign students, it would probably be an inferior brand. It wasn't that I was looking for a status symbol; the inferior brands are truly inferior and begin to fall apart almost immediately.

Lu Minghua said it wouldn't be necessary for me to buy a bike. She and Lao Dong had already decided I would use their son's bicycle, a Flying Pigeon. I told them it was much too generous since a Flying Pigeon is one of the best brands, and the equivalent of lending someone your Mercedes. However, Lao Dong was insistent. He felt it would be foolish to buy a new bicycle for just a few months stay and told me he would bring the bicycle over on Sunday morning.

Lu Minghua added that after I had the bike, I was to return with Lao Dong to their apartment for Sunday dinner. She smiled and told me she would be preparing *jiaozi* because she remembered that the dumplings were my favorite Chinese food. I felt doubly honored since it is traditional to serve *jiaozi* on festive occasions.

Shortly after ten o'clock there was another knock at the door. My roommate had finally arrived. She was a twenty-year-old Japanese woman, and although she repeated her name for us three times in Japanese, we still couldn't say it correctly. Giggling at our feeble attempts at Japanese, she told us her Chinese teacher in Japan called her Jinjin. We decided she would be Jinjin to us as well.

Jinjin had only studied Chinese for six months, and while she had studied English in high school for two years, she had forgotten most of what she had learned. Since my Japanese was limited to greetings, farewells, and the standard courtesy words, we wondered how we would communicate. Fortunately, the girl was a walking bookstore. She had a Japanese-Chinese dictionary, a Chinese-Japanese dictionary, a Japanese-English dictionary, and an English-Japanese dictionary. We could fill in the gaps by writing, since much of written Japanese was based on Chinese characters. Sometimes it was a slow process, but using a combination of writing, the Chinese we had in common, the English she remembered, and the dictionaries, we could communicate.

Despite their insistence that I was once again being too formal, I went through the process of the "Chinese goodby" when Lao Dong and Lu Minghua rose to leave. In China, it is good form to first plead with the guests not to leave so soon, even if they stay until dawn. Then you go through the process of three farewells. The first is at the door to the room or apartment. The second is at the door of the building. The third, and final goodby, is after you have accompanied the guests a short distance down the road and said, "*Man man zou.*" It means walk or go slowly, but it is much like saying, "Take care."

As I walked with them to the main road of the campus, Lu Minghua scolded me gently, saying, "We are like family, so you shouldn't be so formal." She looked at my cotton blouse disapprovingly and added, "Especially since the night air is cool and you aren't wearing a sweater."

I insisted that it was a very special occasion which demanded the best manners. "We have not seen each other for such a long time, and it would not be proper if I failed to show my elder sister and her husband the appropriate respect."

Lu Minghua laughed warmly at my explanation and said, "Little Sister, perhaps you should have been born Chinese."

CHAPTER TWO

RED EYE DISEASE

Yeyinglu (Nightingale Lane) is the marketplace just down the street from the back gate of the university. There are clusters of closet-sized shops selling a variety of items: a large open-air market with vegetables, fruits, and live fowl; food stores; stalls where you can rent magazines to read on the premises; bicycle repair stands; small restaurants; a bookstore; a small department store and a tea shop. Street vendors peddle popsicles, soft drinks, cigarettes, snacks, clothing, shoes, straw hats, straw mats, cooking pots, basins, and book bags.

Yeyinglu bustles with activity and a symphony of sounds fills the air. Horns honk and bicycle bells tingle as drivers, riders, and pedestrians weave in and out on the congested street trying to maneuver through the traffic while avoiding collision. A policeman atop the round wooden traffic stand in the middle of the intersection blows on his whistle, first in short spurts then in long, attempting to bring order to the madness around him. Vendors call out the praises of their wares, and customers bargain and bicker in loud voices. Children shout and laugh as they run along the side of the road. Babies cry and mothers coo and click their tongues to comfort them. Friends and neighbors greet each other, stopping to chat under the shade of poplar trees. Teenage girls giggle and whisper secrets as they run across the street hand in hand. Ducks quack, chicks cheep, and a chicken squawks and flaps its wings as it is handed, feet bound, upside-down, to a customer who stuffs it in his net shopping bag, ties it to his handlebars, and peddles off with his family's dinner swinging to and fro as he rides.

The odors of *Yeyinglu* are both repulsive and enticing as they swirl together and float through the air. Diesel fumes from passing trucks and buses mix together with the stench of rotting vegetables piled against a wall to be used later for compost. The reek of open trenches in public toilets and manure in the streets from mule- and horse-drawn carts mingles with the fragrance of exotic spices, herbs, and teas. The air is heavy with the delicious aroma of seasoned mutton slices roasting on skewers, sweet yams baking over hot coals in a steel barrel, and crêpes topped with a swirl of egg and chili sauce simmering on a large metal disk in a shabby wooden pushcart. *Yeyinglu* is the center of the neighborhood and a mosaic of daily life in Beijing.

With list in hand, I headed for *Yeyinglu* early Saturday morning. I needed to finish my shopping and return to *San Lou* in time to shower before the car arrived to take me to the hotel for my luncheon date. At the heart of the market, I saw before me a new and improved *Yeyinglu* Department Store. The building now had a fancy facade and an elegant sign with shiny brass characters hung over the entrance. Even the bicycle parking lot had been spruced up with a freshly painted, ornate iron fence.

Out of curiosity, I checked with the parking lot attendant to see if the rates were still the same. The charge for parking a bicycle had skyrocketed from three fen* to five fen. I entered the department store to discover only the outside of the building was new and improved. The inside was a freeze frame from 1987; the selection and display of products exactly the same. However, closer inspection proved that inflation had struck inside as well as outside. By American standards, prices were still extremely low, but the increases were significant to Chinese whose average monthly income is from US$20 to US$40.

There had been numerous articles written in the Chinese press and U.S. press about the problem of inflation in China, and many of my Chinese friends had complained about the rising prices in their letters to me. While the government acknowledged that inflation was a serious problem in the overheated economy and admitted to figures which ranged from 20-26 percent, my friends in Beijing had put the real figure at 30-50 percent. For certain items it was even higher. With pork at US$1.07 per jin,** fish at

---

*One fen equals 1/100 of one yuan.
**A jin is half a kilogram.

US$1.60 per jin, and sesame oil at US$1.60 per jin, it was harder for Chinese families to make ends meet.

I braced myself for an encounter with the *fuwuyuan* of *Yeyinglu* Department Store. The *fuwuyuan* in government stores are legendary for their lack of interest in the customer and their nonchalant attitude toward making a sale. However, there are simple explanations for their indifference. Their pay is low, their jobs are exceedingly boring, advancement or other employee incentives rarely exist, and they man the front lines of the battlefield, with customers who are frustrated and angered by a shortage of certain goods, poor selection, and the inferior quality of many products.

While my first purchases were a breeze, detergent stumped me since I couldn't remember the Chinese word. Chinese is a logical language, so I was certain that "wash clothes soap" would do the trick. The *fuwuyuan* corrected me and said, "you want wash clothes powder," then recommended that I buy Panda brand. It was a few fen more than the other brand, but I decided if it was good enough to clean a panda, it could certainly handle my laundry needs.

I had purchased all the items on my list with the exception of straw mats for the floor, and those would have to be bought from a vendor. The vendors sell their goods in street stalls or from pushcarts. They are China's entrepreneurs, and as such, they are on the cutting edge of capitalism in China. Like businessmen the world over, they wheel and deal, cut or raise their prices according to supply and demand or the bargaining ability of a customer, and complain about overhead and taxes. They are islands of free enterprise and earn hundreds, even thousands of yuan a month. Their prosperity has also earned them the envy of some workers and intellectuals.[*]

The Chinese call it "Red Eye Disease" and the government has at times encouraged and at other times discouraged this envy.[**] The rate of unemployment in China has increased steadily over the past several years and

---

[*]In China, anyone with a secondary or higher level of education or a technical title higher than assistant engineer is classified as an intellectual. There were 22.8 million intellectuals in China in 1989 and only one third of those classified as intellectuals had received a college education.

[**]Red is the color assigned to envy in China.

is a problem the government seems unable to resolve through traditional methods of central planning. The free market system not only eases unemployment, but the taxes that are collected from the vendors have put much needed cash into government coffers. However, the success of these out-and-out capitalists is a real and constant threat to the Communist Party. Some workers and intellectuals have responded to the prosperity of the entrepreneurs, not with "Red Eye Disease," but by moonlighting in street stalls of their own to augment their low wages. Indeed, capitalism has proven it can be just as contagious as "Red Eye Disease."

While department stores and other government-owned shops have set prices, bargaining is not only accepted form in street stalls, it is expected. When a foreigner is involved, it is not uncommon for a crowd to gather, and the entire procedure becomes street theater. The vendor's first price is determined by whether the customer is Chinese or foreign, whether he appears to be affluent or of modest means, and whether he appears to be dimwitted or bright. If the customer is a foreigner, the vendor assumes he is affluent regardless of his economic status. I suspect he also assumes the customer is dimwitted. The vendor adjusts his price accordingly and states it. The customer responds with a figure which is not so low as to be insulting, but allows plenty of room for negotiation. When all is said and done, the vendor and the customer usually reach a fair price and everyone, including the spectators, has a good time.

I located the stall with the straw mats and found two large mats that were perfect. In the bargaining process, the vendor threw in a smaller mat which would fit nicely at the entrance to the door between the two armoires. The mats were about an inch thick and would really cheer up the room with its drab furnishings and whitewashed walls, grayed with age. They would serve an additional purpose as well. The Beijing dust, which constantly coats everything with a fine powder, would sift through the woven mats and provide a much cleaner surface for Jinjin and me to walk on than the bare concrete floors.

I knew that later that evening, I would mentally thumb through my purchases as I lay in bed awaiting sleep. I would savor them along with my other little victories of the day. Shopping, getting from one place to the other, crossing language and cultural barriers, and managing to keep myself, my things, and my room clean might be mundane and easy tasks in America. In China they are time-consuming, difficult, and challenging obstacles to be used as a measure of the day's success. However, for the Chinese who face a lifetime of such daily drudgery, it is an entirely different matter. Foreign television programs now come into their homes to show them the "good life" of supermarkets, shopping malls, and all the gadgetry of modern ease. In comparison, many Chinese view their lifestyle as one that not only depletes their energy and imagination, but fills them with frustration and dissatisfaction.

CHAPTER THREE

PRIVACY WAS NEVER A PRIORITY

The Beijing Hotel is located on Eternal Peace Avenue between *Wangfujing Dajie* (Prince's Palace Well Street) and *Nanheyan Dajie* (South Edge of the River Street). That is, right now it is between *Wangfujing* and *Nanheyan*. If the Chinese government keeps attaching wings to the hotel, it will devour the entire city in a few years time.

The older wings of the hotel are a bit shabby, but despite its less than posh appearance, I was glad Mr. Liu had selected the hotel for our luncheon. It has the comfort of an old, over-stuffed chair, and since it is in the center of the city, it is the most convenient place in town to meet friends. Besides, such an interesting assortment of people wander in and out. Every country on the globe seems to be represented at one time or another by wealthy tourists, scroungy backpackers, businessmen, journalists, students, diplomats, and perhaps even a spy or two. Just about everyone who comes to the city eventually finds his way to the Beijing Hotel.

Mr. Liu and Mr. Jiang were waiting for me in the ground floor restaurant, which specializes in Sichuan food. When I arrived, they ordered what amounted to a banquet: four cold dishes, eight hot dishes, and sea cucumber soup. I felt more than a twinge of guilt at the extravagance on my behalf. Official banquets have become a major bone of contention to the Chinese people who have grown weary of footing the bill for government officials who not only wine and dine foreign scholarship recipients, but other Chinese officials as well. Exposés on corrupt officials, who have a propensity for giving lavish banquets, have resulted in efforts to enforce controls limiting the number of courses allowed for specific events. As the waitress packed up the leftovers for my hosts to take home, I suspected Mr. Liu and Mr. Jiang had purposely exceeded the limit for this occasion.

My hosts were quite congenial, and as the meal drew to an end, Mr. Liu and Mr. Jiang gave me their business cards and promised they would keep in touch. Mr. Liu insisted that I must contact his department immediately if I had any difficulties, and Mr. Jiang told me the driver was waiting to take me back to the campus. However, I had plans of my own.

When I told Mr. Jiang I preferred to return to the university by bus, he didn't seem too optimistic about my chances of ever reaching the campus. Since my budget wouldn't allow for many taxis, I was determined to stick to public transportation and my borrowed Flying Pigeon. That called for a crash course in the bus routes of Beijing, and the best time to start was immediately. While I had used the subways and the buses in the past, it had always been with someone who knew the schedules and spoke fluent Chinese. Now, I was on my own, and if it meant getting lost during the learning process, so be it.

Mr. Jiang wrote down the bus numbers and the names of the stops where I should transfer. Since he was uncertain about the number of the last bus, he told me to check with the *shoupiaoyuan* (conductor). Handing me the list, Mr. Jiang once again tried to persuade me to use his department's car. I assured him I would be fine, then said, "When the inquiries come in, just tell my family I was last seen boarding bus #10 at *Wangfujing*."

Mr. Jiang laughed nervously and reminded me to watch out for pick-pockets on the bus. I had been cautioned before to be on the alert for pickpockets when riding buses, but the warning always seemed so absurd. While I'm not sure who coined the phrase "mingling with the masses," I suspect he had just stepped off a Beijing bus. Frankly, riding a public bus in Beijing is not only a contact sport, it is one of life's more intimate experiences. Passengers are crammed so closely together that I doubt a thief could pick his teeth, much less someone's pocket.

Although Mr. Jiang had suggested I board the bus at *Wangfujing*, I decided to walk down Eternal Peace Avenue to the next stop. It was a beautiful, crisp spring afternoon, and the walk would give me a chance to cut through Tiananmen Square. Beijingers say that Tiananmen Square is not only located in the heart of the city, it is the heart of the city. Throughout the history of The People's Republic of China, the vast one hundred acre square has been the site of parades, state funerals, and other government spectacles as well as dissident demonstrations. The Monument to the People's Heroes, a thirty-five meter granite obelisk, stands in the center of the square. On three sides, the square is bordered by massive buildings, which are products of the drab Socialist-Proletariat-Russian style of architecture: the Great Hall of the People on the west, the Museums of Chinese History and the Chinese Revolution on the east, and Mao's Memorial Hall in the southern section of the square. However, *Qianmen* (Front Gate) on the extreme southern edge of the square and *Tiananmen* (Gate of Heavenly Peace) on the north are purely Chinese in design. The Gate of Heavenly Peace, with its bright vermilion walls and five arched marble bridges leading to five arched gates, eclipses everything else on the square. Adding a touch of drama, a huge portrait of a rather benign and grandfatherly looking Mao Zedong surveys the square from the center of the gate.

Weather permitting, the square usually bustles with activity during the daytime as people fly kites, relax in the sun, stroll around, and weave through hordes of foreign and domestic tourists snapping photographs in all directions. On warm days, vendors hawk sesame seed popsicles and ice cream bars shaped like pandas from little metal coolers atop wooden pushcarts. Even on cold winter days honeymooners, rural officials, soldiers, peasants, and entire families pose proudly at the Gate of Heavenly Peace for their mandatory, once-in-a-lifetime photograph beneath the portrait of Mao Zedong.

As I passed the vermilion walls, bus #18 was approaching the stop on Eternal Peace Avenue. Trotting the last few steps, I got into position for the scramble to board, then checked Mr. Jiang's instructions once more. The bus would take me to *Shuangjing Zhuang* (Double Well Village), the last stop for #18. From there, I would transfer to the suburban line since the university is located in the Haidian District.[*]

When the bus arrived at Double Well Village, a young man stopped to listen as I asked the *shoupiaoyuan* which bus would take me to my campus on *Dazhi Dajie* (Great Knowledge Boulevard). Gao Jiuling, a student at

---

[*]The Haidian District, in the northwest section of Beijing, is one of the city's ten districts. Since many of the city's universities are located in the Haidian District, it could be accurately described as the university section of Beijing.

another university in Beijing, introduced himself and offered to accompany me to my campus so I wouldn't get lost. He was on his way to visit three friends from his home province who were students at my university. One, a Miss Wen, could speak English. Along the way, Mr. Gao suggested that I might be able to work out an arrangement with Miss Wen where she would help me with Chinese and I would help her with her English.

Our stop was only half a block from the front gate of the university, which was the entrance to the main road of the campus. We had quite a walk from there. The dormitories are set back from the main road, past the post office, the bank, the clinic and the library. The *shitang* for foreign students, a small store, the laundry, and the *shitang* for Chinese students are directly behind the dormitories. To the back of the campus, behind a small park and sports field, there are a series of buildings for classes, administrative offices, and the bookstore.

As we walked along the main road, Mr. Gao talked about his impressions of America. They were not firsthand impressions, but perceptions which had been formed by reading Hemingway and Twain; reading about Washington, Jefferson, and Lincoln; talking to Chinese students who had returned from the States; and becoming friendly with a few of the American students who had studied at his university.

Mr. Gao summed up his views on America by saying, "I think it must be wonderful place because the Americans I have met are such friendly and open people." He paused, then added, "I think Chinese like Americans very much for this reason."

Mr. Gao asked if I knew the word, *reqing*. I nodded and he said, "Americans are *hen reqingde*" (very warm and enthusiastic). It was a comment I had heard many times from Chinese. When I pointed out that Chinese are also *hen reqingde*, he smiled and said, "Perhaps you are right." However, I could tell that he did not totally agree with my observation. Having said as much in the past to other Chinese, I had frequently received the same reaction. It was not the warmth that they had questioned, but rather the enthusiasm. This response had been confusing to me until I came to understand that while I was referring to the enthusiastic nature of the Chinese people, they had in mind the state of their lives. In truth, I had met very few Chinese who managed to maintain any enthusiasm for their jobs or studies or their day-to-day existence.

As we neared the entrance to Building #8 where his friends lived, Mr. Gao stopped and said, "What I admire most about Americans is your openness. You know, in my country, it is not easy to be open, to express one's thoughts. Americans always express their thoughts and feelings so easily. It is a very appealing trait. We Chinese do not discuss our feelings. Our culture has taught us to keep our feelings locked inside our hearts, and with our government, it is also best to keep our thoughts locked inside." Shaking his head, he said softly, "It is very difficult, very difficult."

As he spoke, I was reminded of something a Chinese friend had once said to me. "If there are many people around, you must not say anything. If there are a few trusted friends around, you must be very cautious what you say. If you are alone, you must be very cautious what you think."

As if Mr. Gao had just noticed where we were, he said, "Ah, Building #8, shall we go in and see Miss Wen?"

The Chinese student dormitories on the campus look much the same as *San Lou*. As you enter, there is a small desk for the one telephone that all the students in the dormitory must share, and a window on the opposite wall so that the *shiwuyuan* can sit in her office and see who is entering or leaving the dorm. Each floor has a large room with two cement troughs along the side walls of the room. There are multiple faucets above the troughs and the students wash their clothes, dishes, faces, and brush their teeth in the troughs. Since very little light manages to seep in from outside and there is only one small bulb overhead, the rooms are always damp, dark, and musty.

At opposite ends of each floor, there are two latrines with squat style toilets inside small wooden cubicles. The doors to the cubicles are set flush to the ground but are only between three to four feet high. This design provides maximum privacy when squatting, but very little when zipping; especially if you are over four feet tall.

There are two major differences between the dormitories for Chinese students and those for foreign students. Foreign students have at least one shower room; two if the dormitory is coed. However, Chinese students must shower in a separate building, which serves as a communal bathhouse for all of the Chinese students on campus. It is shared with the majority of the university's employees since most do not have showers in their living quarters. To add to the inconvenience, the showers in the bathhouse only have hot water once a week. On the other hand, foreign students enjoy the luxury of taking a hot shower the other six days of the week.

The most significant difference between foreign and Chinese student dormitories is the number of students per room. Although the rooms in the Chinese student dormitories are not much larger than those in the foreign student dormitories, six to eight students share a room. The cramped living conditions make it extremely difficult for students to study, and since libraries on many campuses are also small and overly crowded, it is not uncommon to see students sitting under dim street lights on benches or curbs, studying late into the night.

Living in such close quarters all but eliminates even seconds of privacy. But then, privacy was never a priority in China; especially Communist China. If anything, the desire for privacy is looked upon as suspect if not downright sinister, and that attitude is best explained by the Chinese word for privacy: *yinsi*. *Yin* means to conceal or hide and *si* means selfish, illicit, or illegal. Yet, despite the cultural and official disregard for privacy, the individual Chinese does seem to seek out solitude. In any park in any Chinese city, it is not uncommon to hear a seemingly disembodied voice coming from a clump of trees or bushes reciting poetry, singing, or practicing a speech in English or some other foreign tongue.

Building #8 had six students to a room with triple level bunk beds against the two side walls of the room, a long table, which served as a desk, between the beds, and three armoires, and three bookcases at the other half of the room. When we arrived at Miss Wen's room, her five roommates were in, but she had gone to *Yeyinglu*. Introductions were made, and as an honored guest I was served tea in their one porcelain cup while the others drank from enamel cups. Since Miss Wen was not there, we spoke in Chinese, talking about the weather, my flight from the United States, and other topics suitable for polite chitchat. It soon became apparent that because of my age, the students assumed I was a teacher. Once they understood I had come to Beijing as a student, the conversation became more relaxed.

The students were curious about America, and most interested in the social and academic life of their counterparts in America. Specifically, they wanted to know about the relationship between American college students and their professors. For a student in China, the university he attends is his *danwei* (work unit). As a result, the faculty and university administration play not only a significant, but an intrusive role in a student's life.

In China, a person's *danwei* is as much a part of his identity as his name, and he is controlled by his *danwei* and the petty bureaucrats who are in charge. It is the most direct and constant contact a Chinese has with his government and, therefore, the Communist Party. It is through the *danwei* that the government directs and controls the political life of Chinese by implementing government directives and enforcing party policy and campaigns. To safeguard the Party's interests, each *danwei* has neighborhood committees: a battalion of old women, as nosy as your Great Aunt Myrtle, who are assigned to snoop around their neighborhoods minding everyone's business. They are a gray-haired Gestapo, called "Old Auntie" to their faces, but are known by less polite names behind their backs. They make the rounds by dropping in for tea or just suddenly appearing to interrogate their neighbors, checking up on everyone and everything in their neighborhood and watching who comes and goes at all times. Indeed, Big Brother is alive and well, living in a *danwei* under the assumed name of "Old Auntie."

In a system where the individual is of little importance, the *danwei* reigns supreme. A person is assigned housing by his *danwei;* studies or works at his *danwei;* receives medical care from his *danwei;* receives ration coupons from his *danwei;* must get approval to marry from his *danwei;* and his children attend school through his *danwei.* If a Chinese wants to move or change jobs, he cannot do so without the approval of his *danwei.*

As the lowest officials on the gigantic totem pole of Chinese bureaucracy, the *danwei* leaders are the vanguard of corruption in China. When a person crosses the path of those in charge, he had better cross their palms as well. After years of dealing with corrupt officials, Chinese have found that the best way to get something done is to go through the "back door." That requires *guanxi.* Literally, *guanxi* means relationship or connection, but "political pull" might be a more apt translation. It is necessary to establish *guanxi* by giving "gifts" or doing favors in order to wade through or circumvent the seemingly endless maze of Chinese bureaucracy. Gifts of famous brand cigarettes, expensive liquor, appliances, and/or even cold cash are necessary to prevent a person from being strangled by red tape. Even officials cannot escape the trap of *guanxi*. Lower officials have to use the same tactics to bribe middle level officials, and so on. I've often wondered if somewhere in China there is a gargantuan warehouse packed to the rafters with all the cigarettes and liquor that have been passed up the official ladder from one hand to the next.

Hong Xin, a bright-eyed nineteen-year-old student from Beijing, was the most outspoken of Miss Wen's roommates. She found it amazing that American professors do not intrude in their students' personal lives, politics, or extracurricular activities. I laughed to myself thinking how appalling this intrusion into their students' lives would be to American professors.

"In China," Hong Xin explained, "students must be very careful about their behavior, and it is especially difficult for female students. If we have more than one boyfriend, or smoke cigarettes, or drink beer, or associate with someone who is considered a 'bad element,' then our roommates or our classmates might tell our teachers. The teachers would put this information into our records, and when we are assigned jobs, any criticism would go against us."

I told Hong Xin and the others that American professors require their students to attend class, come prepared for class, do the work assigned them in a timely manner, and pass their exams. "That's it! You are graded according to the level of the work you present, not whom you date or how many boyfriends you have."

Hong Xin grinned and said, "I think the American system is much better." Her roommates all nodded in agreement.

It was almost time for dinner, and I had stayed longer than I had intended. Just as I rose to leave, Miss Wen returned from *Yeyinglu*. Mr. Gao introduced us and told her about his suggestion; however, Miss Wen was extremely shy, and I sensed she was not eager to participate in the tutoring joint venture.

Thanking the students for their hospitality, I gave each of them my business card with my room number written on the back and invited them to visit me anytime. Hong Xin volunteered to see me to the door.

Once we were outside, Hong Xin asked if she might bring her friend, Liang Zhenjiang, to meet me. She had noticed from my business card that I was in the food business, and she was certain that Liang Zhenjiang and I would have a great deal in common since he was also in business. I assured Hong Xin that she and Mr. Liang were welcome to visit me as often as they liked.

In perfect English, Hong Xin said, "Kong Kailing, I am very happy to have you as my new American friend," then giggled in delight at my look of surprise.

1. May 19, 1989—The Monument to the Martyrs of the Revolution on Tiananmen Square. The photograph is of Zhou Enlai. A headband calling for support of the hunger strike was placed on the figure of the woman on the extreme left.

2. May 18, 1989—Despite the discomforts and dangers of a hunger strike, students felt it was necessary to use this tactic to press for political reform.

3. May 18, 1989—This sign on Tiananmen Square stated, "Our entire family supports the students, loves the students."

4. May 17, 1989—People lined the streets and overpasses to show their support for those who were going to the square to demonstrate.

5. May 17, 1989—During the "Four Days of Freedom" (May 17–19), people from all walks of life joined in the demonstrations. These workers from the Minzu Fandian (Minorities Hotel) carried the banner, "The Minorities Hotel [staff] Has Arrived!"

6. May 17, 1989—Supporters of the students gathered on Tiananmen Square. The man in the center holds up a sign which states, "Express Support for the Hunger Strikers." These four characters were displayed throughout the city on vehicles, store windows, headbands, and armbands.

7. May 15, 1989—A *dazibao* written by members of the faculty of Beijing University. It appealed to the Party and to Beijing City government officials on behalf of the hunger strikers.

CHAPTER FOUR

FRIENDS

Not even a strand of Jinjin's hair was visible from under the cocoon of her comforter. Listening to her soft, baby-like snores, I envied her deep, peaceful sleep. I had awakened just as dawn broke. Jinjin's window was ajar, and the room was chilled and damp from the early morning dew. Having placed my comforter under my bottom sheet to add a layer of quilted softness to the hard, thin mattress, there was only a sheet and a worn cotton bedspread between the cold and me. The scratchy wool blanket I had rejected at bedtime lay folded at the foot of the bed. Longing for the warmth it would provide, I was caught in the dilemma of wanting to sit up so that I could reach the blanket, yet not wanting to move an inch, knowing the cold air would cost me the small amount of warmth I already had and probably snap me into full consciousness.

I had planned to sleep late since there was nothing to do until Lao Dong came for me at noon. Jinjin and I had stayed up until after two o'clock. Funny that two people who share only snatches of a common language and have a twenty-five year age gap could sit up half the night talking. However, as we talked, we discovered those were merely small inconveniences, outweighed heavily by our mutual fondness for each other. Plus, we found that we did have shared interests: Chinese music, Ella Fitzgerald's singing, Van Gogh's paintings, cats, and eating a heaping bowl of *jiaozi* accompanied by a cold bottle of Beijing Beer. It was our first opportunity to really get to know each other, and even after we had turned out the light, the two of us continued to talk until we both dozed off.

There was a slight moan from under Jinjin's comforter, and I thought perhaps I was saved. If she got up first, she could close the window and hand me my blanket. After a brief silence, her muffled snores continued. Taking a deep breath and counting to three, I grabbed the blanket, flipped it open, and pulled it up to my nose, then flopped back in the bed. I closed my eyes and promised myself that, if it meant counting every blasted sheep in Inner Mongolia, I would go back to sleep. But despite my promise, I was wide awake. There was nothing else to do but get up, shower, and go to visit Lao Pang, the mother of one of my Chinese friends in the States. Moving about the room as quietly as possible, I put on my robe and slippers and headed downstairs for the shower room.

The hallways were deserted since most sane people were still asleep. In the stillness of the morning, the flip-flop of my slippers on the concrete floor sounded as loud as clanging cymbals. I tried tiptoeing, but after tripping on the stairs and nearly losing my balance, I decided the sound of my enamel basin crashing to the floor as I fell down three flights of stairs might cause a bigger disturbance than my flip-flops.

The nice thing about showering in the morning was that you had the shower room entirely to yourself. The bad thing was that there was no hot water until seven o'clock in the evening. During the sweltering Beijing summers, a cold shower was refreshing, but on a chilly April morning, it seemed an invitation to pneumonia.

Loaded down with the package her son had sent from America and the gifts I had brought, I hurried across the campus, eager to see Lao Pang. She was a kind, soft-spoken woman who did *Taijiquan** with a sword every morning and had a passion for television dramas based on classical Chinese stories. Still an attractive woman at age seventy, Lao Pang was twenty-two years younger than her husband, whom everyone referred to as "The Professor." It is common to call people in China by their surname and job title, such as Teacher Wang, Driver Wang, Worker Wang, etc. However, The Professor is known simply by his title in both Chinese and English. This is something akin to being called The King. It acknowledges that while there are other professors, he stands above them as THE Professor.

Despite his advanced years, The Professor was feisty, had a brain that operated at full blast, and though retired from teaching, he remained a

---

*The form of Chinese exercise known in the West as shadowboxing.

leading expert in his field. Through the years, his many accomplishments have not only gained him fame, but have subjected him to the same political suffering that had frequently been inflicted on other intellectuals in China. Fortunately, he outlasted this torment and is now considered to be a national treasure.

Although I declined more than the customary three times, Lao Pang told the maid to prepare breakfast for me. In China, one must refuse three times before he can politely accept what is offered. I am not certain just how many times one must decline to have his refusal taken seriously, as I have not yet accomplished that feat. Little Ma, the maid, responded to my refusals with steamed buns, boiled eggs, and tea.

Little Ma is in her mid-twenties and came to Beijing from a small village in Hebei Province a few years ago. She does the housework, shopping, and most of the cooking in exchange for room and board and a salary of twenty yuan a month.* More wholesome than attractive, she has the red-cheeked, robust look of a young peasant woman on a Cultural Revolution era propaganda poster. Although rather shy and almost illiterate, she is a warm person who smiles easily and has a delightful disposition.

When we met two years ago, I was one of the few foreigners Little Ma had ever seen and the very first foreigner she had actually spoken with. She finds my light hair, fair skin, and larger than average size amusing. On the other hand, she finds my Chinese to be absolutely hilarious. Whenever I speak, Little Ma goes through the same routine. First she laughs, then repeats what I have said a couple of times, laughs again, and finally answers me. It is like conversing with a demented echo, and I once joked with her that she would surely perish if the building were on fire and I was the only one around to tell her. However, according to Lao Pang, Little Ma is fond of me and talks about her "American friend" frequently. Once, when I called Lao Pang from America, Little Ma answered the phone and was so thrilled to be speaking to an American who was actually in America at the time, she was reluctant to turn the phone over to Lao Pang. On her next visit home, she related her experience to everyone in her village, and achieved incredible face due to her international *guanxi*.

---

*Approximately US$5.40 a month at the time.

When my hosts were satisfied that I had eaten enough, the gifts were distributed and we chatted over a second cup of tea. Lao Pang and The Professor told me they had not been well. The Professor had slipped and bruised his hip badly and was having difficulty keeping up with his daily schedule. Usually he worked at his desk for a couple of hours in the morning, then rested in his chair until noon. After the customary afternoon *xiuxi*, a former colleague or student would read to him from technical journals and papers until he was ready for his evening meal.

In the winter, Lao Pang had been ill with a serious viral infection, and as a result, she tired easily. She was able to do her daily exercise, but with decidedly less vigor, and after doing the day's shopping with Little Ma, she had little energy left for other activities. People from the neighborhood were always dropping in to check on Lao Pang and The Professor, and while the visitors meant well, it was clear that it exhausted them to receive so much company. I made a mental note to make my visits short and not too frequent.

Little Ma walked me to the sidewalk, which gave me a chance to explain my plan. She agreed that the old couple needed more rest, but insisted I must stop by at least once a week. However, it was questionable whether Little Ma was insisting on the weekly visits for the benefit of Lao Pang and The Professor or for her own entertainment. Nevertheless, we agreed to the schedule and I told Little Ma goodby. Walking away, I could hear her laughing to herself and repeating my words.

I returned to *San Lou* to get a textbook, then went outside to study on a park bench. The morning was much too beautiful to be wasted by staying inside. I had intentions of brushing up for the placement examination, which would be given the next morning, but watching the activity around *San Lou* was more interesting than studying vocabulary lists. Two of the younger *shiwuyuan* were flirting with the taxi drivers parked nearby. Although the *shiwuyuan* were in their early twenties and the drivers only a few years older, they related to each other in the same way twelve-year-olds in America would relate to the opposite sex. One of the girls and one of the drivers were teasing back and forth with each other. When he got the better of her, she socked him lightly on the shoulder, then ran off giggling as he chased her to the steps of *San Lou,* where she allowed him to catch her. One of the older *shiwuyuan* had pulled a chair outside to sit in the sun, and while she clucked her tongue in disapproval of the couple's antics, her smile betrayed her pleasure in watching them. I wondered if perhaps, like myself, they reminded her of her own youth.

After sitting on the steps for a few minutes, the couple joined their friends and continued their game of flirtation. Their behavior was typical of the naiveté I had observed in many young Chinese. There seemed to be a prolonged adolescence that lasted into their twenties. For two generations, this sexual naiveté was a result of the Party's puritanical attitude toward sex. Perhaps this generation's naiveté is due, at least in part, to the law against early marriage, which requires men to be twenty-two and women to be twenty before they can obtain a marriage permit. Although illegal early marriages are a problem in the countryside, many couples in urban areas are forced by unemployment, low wages, and shortages in housing to wait even longer than the legal age to marry.

As the decade has drawn to an end, there has been a more casual attitude toward romance, and even sex in China. There is more contact between young men and women than there had been in the past, but as Hong Xin pointed out, it is still not acceptable for a young woman to have a series of boyfriends before she marries, or to have several boyfriends at one time. Steady dating is tantamount to an engagement, so couples will arrange to go out with a group of friends to determine their compatibility before agreeing to date. Once a firm relationship has been established there is much more sexual freedom for today's generation. A noted Chinese sociologist, Liu Dalin, claims his research shows as many as 30 percent of Chinese youth have premarital sex.

Up until quite recently, public displays of affection between the opposite sex were simply not tolerated; which must have made riding a bus, where couples were pressed against each other by the crowd, the best part of a date. After the Cultural Revolution, dancing was once again allowed, but usually it was "disco" dancing without body contact or couples held each other at arm's length. I remember my surprise in 1987 at seeing couples, holding each other closely, glide across the dance floor during a community party. My fifth grade teacher, Miss Reagle, a staunch Southern Baptist, always claimed that dancing was evil since it led to "other things."

No doubt Miss Reagle would blame the fox trot for the apparent erosion of China's puritanical attitude toward sex. It is now quite common to see couples holding hands as they walk, snuggling on park benches, or riding the buses locked together in an outright embrace.

While physical contact between opposite sexes was taboo, it was and is quite acceptable for members of the same sex. Although authors of guidebooks on China invariably refer to the Chinese people's dislike of physical contact, their comments always leave me wondering if they actually visited China. True, the Chinese are not social huggers and kissers, but they are demonstrative with friends. It is a relaxed, warm attitude, with no social stigma attached to members of the same sex holding hands or draping an arm around a friend.

The sound of my name pulled me away from my thoughts. Lao Dong was pedaling toward me on his bicycle, pulling his son's Flying Pigeon along beside him. After Lao Dong had raised the bicycle seat a couple of inches to accommodate my long legs, he showed me the fastest route to his apartment. We rode out the front gate of the Campus, down Great Knowledge Boulevard, and cut through an alley to the West Gate of his campus. At a leisurely pace, the trip took around ten minutes. Since we could have easily walked the distance, I decided Lao Dong had wanted to see for himself that I could ride the bike without breaking my neck or his son's Flying Pigeon.

Lu Minghua put me to work as soon as we walked through the door. It is customary for everyone to participate in cutting and rolling the dough for *jiaozi* and stuffing them, but Lu Minghua wanted to give me a combination cooking/language lesson as well. While gathering the ingredients for the stuffing, she told me the Chinese name for each item. First she minced spring onions, cabbage, and garlic. Then she unwrapped a large chunk of pork and scrutinized it for a moment before declaring that it was much too fatty. She explained that it was getting harder to find leaner cuts of meat, since the better cuts went to special shops where officials and those with *guanxi* shopped. She sliced off some of the leaner pieces to be cooked with bamboo shoots and mushrooms, then chopped the rest over and over with the cleaver until it resembled ground meat. After she had mixed the pork with the vegetables, salt, pepper, and a little sesame oil, she shoved the bowl into my hands, stuck a wooden spatula in it, and told me to get to work stirring.

The kitchen was tiny, about the same size as a walk-in closet. There was a small iron stove with two burners and an oven stuck against one wall. On the wall opposite the stove, there was a single sink and a small cupboard. On the wall next to the door, there was one shelf which held oils, spices, and condiments. There was barely enough space left in the room for two people to pass without bumping into each other. As we talked, I zigged and zagged to avoid Lu Minghua as she gathered the other ingredients of the dishes she was preparing, deftly stepping over and around her three cats who had decided to join in the action.

In an attempt to help, I offered to rinse out a bowl. Unaware that the faucet was quite temperamental and the slightest turn would produce a gusher, I managed to soak the two of us, the cats, and most of the room with one blast. Lu Minghua burst out laughing and chased the three cats and me out of her kitchen.

The cats and I joined Lao Dong in the main room of the apartment, which functioned as master bedroom, den, study, and guest dining room depending on the time of day. The cramped apartment had two other smaller rooms. One was a bedroom for their son, Little Heping; the other room, actually little more than a foyer, served as a combination entrance way and breakfast nook. It was furnished with a small table, where the family ate their meals, a refrigerator, and a small wooden chest. In addition, each apartment in the building had an enclosed terrace that was about three feet by five feet. The windows on the terraces were only screened, but some people had replaced the screening with glass and used the terraces for additional living space. Lu Minghua's was filled with pots of herbs and a sandbox for her three cats.

Lao Dong had prepared the dough for the *jiaozi*. It was rolled into long strips about an inch in diameter and then cut into small chunks. He showed me how to roll the dough into little circles by holding the dough in his left hand and turning it swiftly as he rolled it from the center to the outside with his right hand. Each piece of dough came out in a perfect circle which was filled with about a teaspoon of stuffing, then folded over into a half-moon shape. Lao Dong finished the process by crimping the edges of the dump-ling together between his thumb and index finger. I mastered the stuffing and crimping part so easily that I was eager to graduate to dough rolling. My first dozen attempts yielded squares. The second dozen came out as ovals. Lao Dong praised me and insisted I was making great progress. Lu Minghua came into the room to offer her encouragement, but when the third batch could not even be defined in geometric terms, she threw up her hands and demoted me to stuffing and crimping.

As we finished preparing the last of the *jiaozi*, Little Heping came in.* At fifteen, he was already two inches taller than Lao Dong, and his face was a perfect blend of the best features of both his mother and father. Lu Minghua was a little upset when he retreated to his room to listen to his stereo, but I assured her that American teenagers also show little interest in their parents' friends.

Lu Minghua said, "I don't understand it. Whenever there is a show on television about America, he talks about his American Aunt. He has been so excited since he found out you were returning to Beijing, but now that you are actually in our apartment, he is more interested in listening to his music than talking with us. She laughed and said, "It is very confusing to raise a teenager." I agreed, telling her it was an international confusion.

Little Heping did manage to pull himself away from the stereo long enough to join us for the scrumptious meal Lu Minghua had prepared. In addition to the *jiaozi,* we had sliced tomato and cucumber, thousand-day-old eggs, quail eggs, the pork dish, bean sprouts, noodles with eggs and spring onions, and a whole fish that was cooked in a rich, spicy Sichuan sauce. We washed it all down with cups full of the best tea in China, Dragon Well tea from Hangzhou.

It was apparent that Lu Minghua had spared no expense for the meal and although honored, I worried about the cost. I reminded her that we had agreed that since we were "family," we would dispense with all of the rituals of politeness. Providing a costly banquet certainly fit into the category of polite ritual. She giggled and said, "Okay, Little Sister, from now on, we talk plainly and eat plainly."

---

*Xiao (Little) is frequently used in China when addressing or referring to children, teenagers, and even young adults.

After we cleared away the food and returned the table to the entrance area, Little Heping went back to his stereo. Lao Dong pushed his chair against the wall, sat down with a sigh of contentment, and propped his feet up on a stool. Lu Minghua and I sat on the bed to talk and were immediately joined by the three cats. Within minutes Lao Dong was snoring and the cats were purring.

Lu Minghua pulled out a box of family photos to show me a picture of her mother, who had died a few months earlier. She had written to me of her grief and the sorrow she felt at not being able to see her mother more frequently through the years. When she was not teaching in the summer, she had to do research, and was only able to return home once a year for Spring Festival. The picture she showed me had been taken a year before her mother's death, the last time Lu Minghua had gone home. Age and illness had left her mother frail, shrunken, and unable to stand without support from a cane, but she had the same warm smile as Lu Minghua.

Rummaging through the box, Lu Minghua selected a handful of photographs. There were pictures of Little Heping as a chubby baby with pink cheeks and during different stages of his childhood. Taking out two more photographs, she handed me one of Lao Dong taken right after he graduated from college. He had been thin and serious-faced, but quite handsome. Lu Minghua looked at the second picture, then brushed her hand across it softly, wiping away imaginary dust. She sighed and said, "It's hard to believe I was ever this young."

The picture had been taken when she was only twenty. She had been absolutely lovely and slender as a reed. Her sweet, round face was framed by smooth black hair which was plaited neatly into two short braids. I knew what she was thinking as she looked at the picture. What woman can see herself captured in time, at the prime of her youth, without lamenting her fading beauty. When she had spoken of her youth, Lu Minghua had really meant her beauty. However, she would never use that word. Chinese don't compliment themselves, even in the past tense. In fact, it is not even proper to say thank you when others compliment you since that would imply that you agree with the compliment. Instead, the proper response is *"nali, nali."* The literal translation is "where, where," but the implied meaning is that certainly the compliment could not be directed at you since you are undeserving of such praise.

Lu Minghua looked at the photograph once more, and then put it down with another long sigh. She said, "Look at me now, I am old with a face full of wrinkles. I have too much meat around my middle and my face and hands have also become pudgy."

I shook my head, saying, "Elder Sister, you are not old! You were certainly beautiful then, but you are more beautiful now." She giggled, but before she could say a word, I said, "Remember, Elder Sister, we are family so I don't want to hear you say *nali, nali.*"

Cutting her eyes at me in an impish expression, she said, "Little Sister, why would you say such a silly thing? How can a middle-aged woman be more beautiful than when she was twenty?"

"It's simple, the wrinkles you complain about are from your smiles and they add richness and character to your face. As for the extra meat around your middle, it gives you presence."

Laughing, Lu Minghua said, "If I get any more presence, I am afraid my clothes will no longer fit!" Reaching over and patting my shoulder, she said, "Little Sister, you have earned another cup of tea."

Lao Dong, still fast asleep in his chair, continued to snore evenly as Lu Minghua poured our tea. Leaning toward him, she tapped him lightly on the knee and said, "Wake up, old man! Drink some tea with us." Then poking him affectionately, she said, "All you are good for is making noise."

Lao Dong stretched, rubbed his eyes and took the cup Lu Minghua offered him. He laughed softly and said, "You complain about me making noise! Didn't I tell you that the two of you sound like chattering monkeys!"

When we finished our tea, it was time for me to leave. It was nearing dinner time and I was beginning to get a headache in what is probably the language area of my brain. I had spent all afternoon conversing in Chinese, and although quite satisfied with myself for having muddled through, I was fading fast. Lu Minghua walked with me to the front door of the building, and as we walked down the stairs hand in hand, she gave me last minute instructions on bicycling in Beijing.

"Now remember, Little Sister, you must be quite cautious and ride very slowly. You must watch out for trucks and buses because they will run right over you!"

I nodded my head obediently and told her not to worry, assuring her

I had no intention of becoming another Beijing traffic statistic. As I rode off ever so slowly, Lu Minghua called after me, "Good, that's correct, go slowly." When I had passed through the gate of her campus and knew she could not possibly see me, I picked up the pace to my regular speed. It was my experience that riding a bicycle too slowly could get you in just as much trouble in Beijing as riding too fast.

Instead of taking the shortcut, I took the long way home, past *Yeyinglu,* to get the feel of the bicycle and really check it out. The only problem seemed to be the bicycle bell, which had rusted and wouldn't work. In case of impending doom I would just have to shout. Of course, the problem would be remembering to shout in Chinese.

The traffic was lighter than usual, which gave me a chance to readjust to bicycling in Beijing. Although there are traffic regulations for cyclists, they are usually ignored. There are signs that caution the cyclist not to carry a passenger or hold hands with another cyclist, and there is one huge billboard that reminds the rider to always use hand signals. It appeared that these signs had gone unread.

There is one rule that is not posted on any sign but is the absolute law of the road. In order to survive, the cyclist must never worry about whatever or whomever is behind him. If he looks over his shoulder to check out the rear, he is history. He must keep his eyes to the front so that he can dodge and swerve around other cyclists who change lanes without a warning or come ambling along from a side road and pull out in front of him. He must also stay on the alert for pedestrians who cross the street at will and have never been instructed to "Stop, Look, and Listen."

There was the smell of rain in the air, so I rode faster, hoping to reach the dorm before the rain started. By the time I was in my room, there was a distant rumble of thunder as the rain came pouring down. Jinjin was out for the evening with friends, so I tuned in Chinese music on the radio, then stretched out on the bed and listened as the sounds of rain hitting the pavement outside blended with the melancholy whine of an *erhu.*[*]

It had been such an enjoyable day, and being with Lu Minghua had been so comfortable. In one of her letters, she had used a Chinese idiom to

---

[*] A Chinese fiddle with two strings.

describe our relationship, "To seem like old friends at the first meeting." There were so many similarities in the way we think that we communicated easily despite my difficulties with the language. Many times she knew what I was trying to say even when my Chinese wasn't adequate. While I searched my mind or my dictionary for the right word, she would laugh, roll her eyes at me, then tell me what I was trying to say.

Sometimes, she would gently chide me, saying "Little Sister, you know that word. I have already taught it to you."

We had promised each other to take advantage of my stay in Beijing, to spend as much time together as possible. It was difficult to be away from my family, but I loved being in Beijing. I looked forward to my visits over the next few months with Lu Minghua, Lao Pang, and others who were dear to me. I wanted to savor each and every minute of my stay, knowing the time to leave Beijing would come too soon.

PART TWO
BEING THERE

"Any excuse will serve a tyrant."
The Wolf and the Lamb

CHAPTER FIVE

THE FLYING PIGEON CRASHES

As the bus Susan and I were riding neared *Xidan,* I thought about Democracy Wall. Politics and dissent in China had been on my mind since the previous evening when I had received a telephone call from my friend, Li Yuanli. He had called to ask if I had heard the news. Hu Yaobang* had died that morning, Saturday, April 15th.

So much had happened in China since the winter of 1978 when people gathered at a wall near the intersection of *Xidan* and Eternal Peace Avenue to post and read *dazibao* (big character posters) which called for political reform, and voiced the suffering so many had endured during the Cultural Revolution. Among those who had expressed their anger and frustrations by writing *dazibao* was a twenty-nine year old electrician, Wei Jingsheng. His most famous *dazibao*, or infamous from the government's perspective, was an essay called "The Fifth Modernization." In that essay, which he posted on December 5, 1978, Wei proposed that without the fifth modernization, democracy, the government's program of Four Modernizations** would never be achieved.

Not content with merely expressing his views in wall posters, Wei started an underground magazine, *Explorations*. While short-lived, his journal featured compelling essays on China's need for a Western-style democracy and the government's abuses of human rights. Unlike most of those who posted *dazibao* on Democracy Wall, Wei no longer espoused the

---

*Hu Yaobang had been Deng Xiaoping's designated successor and Secretary General of the Central Committee of the Chinese Communist Party until his forced resignation in 1987.
**Agriculture, Industry, Science and Technology, and Defense.

theories of Marx and Lenin as the salvation of China, but viewed Communism as a utopian fantasy, with its beneficial and practical applications best described by the idiom *hua bing chong ji* (painting a picture of a cake to appease one's hunger).

Deng Xiaoping not only allowed Democracy Wall to exist for a time, but also took political advantage of the people's criticisms of The Gang of Four, Mao Zedong, Mao's successor Hua Guofeng, and the strict Maoists within the Party. In fact, the movement assisted Deng in gaining control of the Party and advancing to the position of supreme leader of China. However, as the criticisms of the government grew bolder and Deng became a target himself, his tolerance vanished, as did Democracy Wall. Sadly, the immediate result of the Democracy Wall Movement was not an advancement of political reform, but additional political restriction. In 1980, Deng Xiaoping had the right to post *dazibao* removed from China's constitution.

Deng's crackdown on Democracy Wall began in January 1979 and lasted through that spring. In March, Wei Jingsheng was arrested and charged with a variety of crimes. It was hardly coincidental that his arrest came only four days after he had written an article that was severely critical of Deng Xiaoping: "Do We Want Democracy, Or Do We Want a New Dictatorship."

Although it seems unlikely that an electrician who worked at the Beijing Zoological Gardens would be privy to top secret military affairs, Wei was eventually tried on the charge of passing military secrets about the Sino-Vietnam War to a foreign journalist. However, it should be noted that, at the discretion of the government, even the most innocuous and readily available information can be considered a military secret in China. The verdict was never in question, and that Wei had previously been in the army was more than sufficient evidence to convict him on the charge of espionage. On October 16, 1979, he was sentenced to fifteen years in prison.

While Wei is presently an inmate at a labor reform camp near Tangshan in Hebei Province, originally he was sent to Qincheng, a maximum security prison approximately twenty miles north of downtown Beijing. There is double irony in the selection of Qincheng for Wei's incarceration, as he had written about the inhumane conditions in that prison, and Jiang Qing,

Mao's widow and the leader of the Gang of Four, was one of his fellow prisoners at Qincheng. While at Qincheng, Wei was not allowed to receive visitors, and rumors persist that he has been kept in solitary confinement throughout most of his imprisonment. It is also rumored that physical and mental torture along with extended periods of isolation have robbed him of his health, all of his teeth, and perhaps his sanity.

The bus slowed as it approached the intersection and I asked my friend Susan if she remembered seeing Democracy Wall. She had only been a child at the time, but the movement had created such a swirl of political and social controversy in China, that I thought she might remember the excitement of the time, if little else.

Her first response was a shrug, which left me wondering if she had understood me. It had seemed inappropriate to discuss Democracy Wall in Chinese on a crowded bus in Beijing, so I had spoken to her in English. As a waitress in a hotel bar, Susan understood phrases such as "scotch and water on the rocks," but she was decidedly less fluent in nonservice-oriented English.

After a brief silence, she asked, "When did this happen?" When I replied, she knitted her brow in concentration for a few seconds, then shrugged again. Thinking Susan was either uncomfortable discussing the topic or that she actually didn't know anything about it, I decided it was best to drop the matter. But a man standing behind Susan spoke up. He appeared to be in his early thirties and had the look of an intellectual. Although he spoke in rapid-fire Chinese, I understood enough to know that he was talking about Democracy Wall. Turning to me, the man said in English, "She was a child at the time and doesn't remember. But I remember. . . ."

The bus pulled to a stop, and the rest of his words were lost as those who were getting off the bus at *Xidan* pushed against those getting on. Susan grabbed my hand and pulled me through the crush, stopping briefly on the curb to give me time to adjust my backpack. When I looked up, I saw the man standing behind Susan, patiently waiting to complete his sentence. Seeing that he had my attention once again, he said, "I remember Democracy Wall well. It was a very exciting time."

Nodding to me in parting, he turned and walked away. I wanted to go after him, to ask him to say more, but I knew that he had said all he intended to say.

While it had hardly been an earth-shattering statement, that he had said anything at all was surprising. In the past, it had taken time to win a person's trust before he would volunteer even a vague opinion on such a controversial subject. Yet, even more surprising than his few words was the manner in which he spoke. There had been a wistful tone in his voice, as if he longed for that time to come again.

Susan grabbed my hand as we crossed Eternal Peace Avenue. When I mentioned Hu Yaobang's death, she nodded saying "Yes, he died of a heart attack." Removing her hand from mine and placing it on my forearm, she cupped my elbow with her other hand, as younger people sometimes do when they walk with their elders. She guided me through the street market on *Xidan*, past a construction site, and over a wooden plank placed atop a large section of sidewalk, which had been torn up to allow heavy duty equipment access to the site. After we stepped back onto solid ground, she took my hand again and with a look of distaste said, "I really don't like politics." Her pronouncement was by no means a revelation to me. Although we had spent much time together during my last stay in Beijing, our conversations had never once touched on the subject.

Susan and I had met in 1987 in the lobby bar of the Yellow Mountain Hotel where she worked. Of course, Susan is not her real name. Most Chinese who work in hotels and restaurants assume an English name to accommodate their foreign customers, or to use the less capitalistic term the government prefers, "foreign friends." Some take English names that approximate the sound of their Chinese names, while others, like Susan, select a name simply because they like it.

Our friendship had developed as a result of my frequent trips to the Yellow Mountain Hotel and Susan's slight crush on Matt, one of my classmates. Matt and I had discovered that the hotel was not only within easy bicycling distance of our campus, but also a comfortable place to study and write letters home. On my way to eat dinner at the hotel one evening, I happened to run into Susan on the street. She was on her way to the bus stop, having just finished working her shift. While we chatted, she recommended that I try one of the neighborhood restaurants since it had better food and was less expensive than the hotel. She pointed out a good café, and after some polite persuasion, agreed to join me for dinner.

Susan eventually got over her crush on Matt, but our friendship continued. When I called to tell her I had arrived in Beijing and was settled in, we agreed to spend her next day off shopping for an outfit for her and books for me.

Having expressed her disregard for things political, it soon became apparent what Susan did like. Clothes were her passion, and to her they were not merely something to wear but an art form. She was a true connoisseur with a keen sense of style, a genuine appreciation for quality, and a natural radar system that honed in automatically on the best items each store had to offer. While she dragged me through one crowded department store and clothing shop after another, I watched her in action as she pushed aside most of the articles with a flick of her hand and a toss of her head. The few that deserved closer attention were inspected thoroughly both inside and out. Lovingly, she stroked the material of one dress, a soft yellow silk of good quality, cut in a classic style. She held it out at arms length, then close to her body before she put it back on the rack, declaring the price was too much to pay for a simple dress. Susan had decided she could get more for her money by buying a suit, and she wanted one with a long jacket and a short skirt, in a material that was durable but not too heavy. She knew it would be expensive, but she had been saving her money for months, and I had offered to make a small donation to the cause.

I couldn't help but wonder how Susan would react to being turned loose on Fifth Avenue with plastic in hand. She was a born shopper, but so limited by what Beijing had to offer. For more than three decades, stylishness had been considered decadent, bourgeois behavior. Chinese, both male and female, had dressed in the same drab manner, wearing the baggy blue suits which Americans had come to know as the "Mao suit."* It had been an amazing sight to walk down a crowded street with thousands of people who were dressed identically. Only high ranking cadres had stood out in China's sea of blue cotton. They tended to wear black or gray Mao

---

*The suit was actually popularized by Sun Yatsen significantly before the Chinese Communist Revolution.

suits, which differed not only in color, but were of a finer cut and material than those worn by the common people.

In the 1980s, the government decided it was time for Chinese industry and consumers to re-enter the world of fashion. They started right where they had left off: 1950. Much of what was available was old-fashioned, often garish, poorly made, and ill-fitting. Susan, however, knew where to ferret out surplus items that had been made for export. They were of a far superior quality than those made for the domestic market.

Having made the rounds at *Xidan*, Susan was ready to go to the next shopping area. First, we stopped in the Foreign Language Bookstore to attend to my passion. Little was available on the first floor, so we started up the stairs to the second level. Halfway up the stairs, I came to an abrupt halt. Posted at the top of the staircase was a small sign stating, "Foreign Friends Are Forbidden Above the First Floor." Pulling on Susan's sleeve, I pointed to the sign, and told her it was the first time I had seen a sign restricting foreigners in a foreign language bookstore. Susan left me at the bottom of the stairs to go up and check things out. After a couple of minutes, she returned to tell me there were only textbooks and the like on the second floor. Having asked one of the clerks why foreigners were forbidden entry, she had received a typical Chinese response; "Because it's the rule." No doubt the clerk thought Susan was foolish, naive, or incautious to even question the sign.

After a quick bowl of noodles to fortify us for the journey, a series of bus rides took us from one shop to the next in Susan's quest for the perfect suit. Our last stop was *Wangfujing,* the major shopping street of Beijing. The corner of *Wangfujing* and Eternal Peace Avenue was crowded with shoppers, tourists, commuters, money changers, and clusters of beggars. The beggars were a fairly recent addition to the corner in front of the Beijing Hotel.

While beggars were a common site in old China, The Peoples Republic of China takes a dim view of people standing around on street corners with their hands out. The sight is especially distasteful to the government when the beggars can be readily observed by foreigners. Yet, despite the incompatibility of begging with the Four Cardinal Principles of Socialism, the government has failed to eradicate them. The population of beggars appears to have grown over the past few years, or, perhaps the beggars have become more visible. In 1988 the number of people who had come to urban areas to engage in the "profession" of begging had become so large that the government admitted to spending an annual average of fifty million yuan to transport the beggars back to their homes in the countryside.

In old China, mendicancy was considered one of China's more profitable "professions," and there were Beggars' Guilds just as there were Merchant Guilds. The guilds each had hundreds, sometimes thousands in their membership, and they controlled the professional beggars by collecting dues and subscriptions; negotiating "contracts"; providing legal counsel; arranging protests; and acting as a social organization for their members. Each city had a King of Beggars who headed the local guild, ruled over the other beggars, and more often than not, was the wealthiest man in town.

The beggars of today are not so sophisticated or well organized. Some are unemployed, able-bodied men and women who come to Beijing, Shanghai, Guangzhou, and other large cities hoping to find decent jobs despite their lack of residence permits. The maimed, blind, or otherwise disabled sit on sidewalks at busy corners, in front of subway and train stations, and other places where people congregate. Their tragic stories are written on pieces of cardboard or directly on the sidewalks so that passersby can read about the cause of their misfortune. Others beg because it is an easy way to make as much as a hundred yuan a day. The take can go even higher when they add picking pockets, changing money, petty theft, and prostitution to their repertoire.

Knowing that as a foreigner I was a prime target, Susan was on her guard as we walked past the group of beggars. When we turned on to *Wangfujing,* a woman with two small children caught my eye. All three were dressed in ragged clothing and covered with dirt. The children looked sickly and malnourished, and the smaller of the two had crusted lesions on his scalp. Seeing my expression of concern, the woman shoved the children in front of me, then stretched out her hand. Susan shooed her away, moving closer to me and taking my arm. As she hurried me along, she said, "Don't give them any money! That only encourages them to keep on begging."

The woman persisted, following us down *Wangfujing.* I felt a slight tug on my backpack, and looked over my shoulder to see the woman trying to open it. Susan also saw what was happening and reacted immediately. Turning on the woman, she slapped her hand away, and in a loud, harsh voice that seemed alien to her diminutive body, shouted *"Zou! Zou! Zou!"* (Go! Go! Go!).

After the woman retreated, Susan stayed behind me, guarding the backpack.Although I told her it wasn't necessary since the backpack was locked, she remained at her post, insisting that pickpockets would slice it open with a knife and steal my belongings.

Susan found exactly what she had been looking for in one of the boutiques on the top floor of the No. 1 Department Store. It was a pale gold suit of fine lightweight wool. However, it cost more than she was willing to pay. As much out of exhaustion as generosity, I upped my ante and paid half.

Famished and unable to face the series of bus rides that would take us back to our bicycles, I did further damage to my budget by treating us to dinner at the Palace Hotel and a cab to take us to the lot where we had parked our bikes. While it was the first time in her life that Susan had owned such an elegant suit, eaten in such an elegant restaurant, or ridden in a cab, she took it all in stride. Throughout the meal and the taxi ride, she assumed a demeanor of perfect nonchalance. It would appear that Susan is a woman who adapts easily to elegance—bourgeois to the bone.

It was dark when we said good night and headed off on our bicycles in opposite directions. As I neared the entrance to the back gate of the campus, I looked over my shoulder at a truck that honked as it came up behind me. Turning my head back to the front, I saw a bicycle with two men on it heading right for me. Just as I had feared would happen, it was not a warning in Chinese that came out of my mouth, but a rather nasty American expletive.

Clamping down on the brakes, I swerved to my left. So did they! In a panic, I swerved back to my right. So did they! With only inches separating us, it was inevitable; we were going to collide! I hit the ground first. My bicycle, their bicycle, and the two of them followed, falling on top of me.

The men were very young, and judging from the strong smell of beer, it was a clear-cut case of riding while intoxicated. They jumped up immediately, pulling the bikes off of me and helping me to my feet as they asked if I had been injured. They apologized in extremely polite, albeit slurred Chinese, then asked my nationality. When I answered, they became even more distressed, telling me they were especially fond of Americans. I assured them that nothing was broken, and joined in with my own apologies, saying, "It was probably my fault. Everyone knows that foreigners don't know how to ride bicycles!"

They laughed at my joke, finally convinced I was more or less intact. Dusting off my backpack, the seat of my bicycle, and myself, they offered a final round of apologies before I slowly pedaled away. With a clang, clang, clang, I rode through the back gate, grateful that the clanging sound was coming from the bicycle and not me. However, I was worried that the collision had done serious damage to Little Heping's Flying Pigeon. Pulling up to *San Lou* I stopped under a street lamp to assess the damage.

The metal shield over the chain was slightly bent, which I assumed was the source of the clanging. After straightening it with my hands, I rode the bike for several yards until I was certain the clanging had ceased. While greatly relieved that the Flying Pigeon had survived without any real damage, I was then less confident about my own condition.

As I limped into our room, Jinjin took one look at me and sucked in her breath. The sight of me was too much for her to deal with in Chinese. Aghast, she babbled away in Japanese. I was covered with dirt from head to foot, and had a few smears of blood on my arms where I had scraped the ground. In the shower, I discovered multiple bruises all over my body, one gash on my left shin, and a big, red lump the size of an egg next to my right knee.

Hobbling back into our room, I crawled into bed with a moan, while Jinjin gave me tea, cookies, and sympathy. Comforting me, she blamed the two tipsy Chinese cyclists for the collision. However, I knew who had to bear the full burden of responsibility for the accident. It was I who had violated the cardinal rule of bicycling in Beijing. No matter how briefly, I had looked back to see what was behind me.

CHAPTER SIX

SMALL LANE NEWS

Monday morning I looked up at the four flights of stairs that led to my classroom and thought it might as well be the Himalayas. Every square inch of me was either stiff, swollen, or bruised. Moreover, the parts of my body that were supposed to bend seemed unable to do so, while those that weren't seemed as if they might. At least I had all afternoon and evening to recover from the bicycle wreck. Yuanli and I had planned to meet that afternoon at the Beijing Hotel, but he had called to postpone our meeting until Tuesday.

My aches and pains aside, I was disappointed that it would be another day before I could talk with Yuanli. I wanted to know what the people in his neighborhood were saying about Hu Yaobang's death, and what he thought about the government's reaction. Certainly Hu's death had created an awkward situation for the Chinese government. Although forced to resign from his post as General Secretary, he had not been shunned by the Party. What sparked my curiosity most was how Hu's funeral would be handled. The question was, would they come to bury Hu or to praise him. From my limited information, it appeared that the government was de-emphasizing Hu's impact on China in spite of, or perhaps because of, his popularity with the people.

My eagerness for information made the difficulty in obtaining it all the more frustrating. The *China Daily*, the English language newspaper, was not available in the neighborhood and I had only skimmed the Chinese newspapers which were posted on campus. It took time, patience, and the assistance of a dictionary for me to read "newspaper Chinese." *San Lou* had a television room, but it was locked more than it was open. When it was open, the poor reception and my inferior Chinese left me with only bits and pieces of information. In any case, Chinese news broadcasts and newspapers aren't all that informative. The government controls the media, and, therefore, the media only report what the government wants the people to know. Frequently, what is left unsaid is more significant than what is actually said.

The alternative source of information is the system of *xiaodao xiaoxi* (small lane news). Chinese rely on this word-of-mouth system heavily and indulge in it habitually as do foreigners who live in China. Unlike broadcasts by Voice of America, BBC, etc., small lane news cannot be jammed; nor can it be removed from the newsstands as sometimes happens with foreign publications. Although based on rumor, innuendo, and speculation, small lane news is the only uncensored source of information readily available in China. That lack of censorship alone gives it more credibility than the spoon-fed government reports. Admittedly, ascertaining the validity of small lane news, or put simply, knowing when to believe and how much to believe is a tricky task. Sometimes a person will emphasize that what they are saying is, after all, only *xiaodao xiaoxi*. At other times, people repeat it with an "etched in stone" certainty. Unfortunately, the former approach doesn't assure the inaccuracy of the small lane news, just as the latter doesn't assure its accuracy.

After lunch I stopped at the bulletin board in front of the foreign student *shitang* to see if someone more fluent in newspaper Chinese had posted a notice about Hu's death. I knew it was a long shot since the notices posted by foreign students rarely delved into current affairs or controversial issues. However, there were those rare exceptions. As recently as the previous Friday, someone had posted a notice that was highly controversial.

The article, "Taxi Drivers or Mafia," had been signed "Beijing Foreign Students Free Press," and concerned the escalating battle between foreign students and taxi drivers. The "Beijing Foreign Students Free Press" had urged students to boycott taxis because the drivers were refusing to accept payment in RMB. Drivers were demanding Foreign Exchange Certificates (FEC) even from the students who held White Cards, the permits issued to certain foreigners that allowed them to use RMB.

The problem stems from China's dual currency system, which was modeled after the Soviet system. In addition to protecting China's less than abundant foreign exchange reserves, having the two currencies—one for foreigners (FEC) and one for Chinese (RMB)—allowed the Chinese government to control and isolate both groups. Only FEC can be exchanged for foreign dollars or used for the purchase of imported goods. Furthermore, FEC were also required in hotels and shops, which catered to foreigners and often sold items that were rationed or otherwise unavailable to the average Chinese. Since most Chinese did not have access to FEC, it was another means of keeping the foreign devils and Chinese separated, and providing select products to the hordes of foreign tourists and businessmen in China, along with the few privileged Chinese who had the *guanxi* to obtain FEC. While it is now possible to use RMB in lieu of FEC in most places, there is a hefty surtax added to the charge unless one has special *guanxi*.

The dual system was adopted on April 1, 1980. April Fool's date was an appropriate choice since by law the two currencies have equal value; however, every fool knows that a currency that can be converted into foreign dollars is worth more than one that cannot. This inequality of value has resulted in a thriving black market. The exchange rate on the black market ranges from 1.65-1.70 RMB for $1.00 FEC. An even higher rate is available for the exchange of foreign dollars for RMB. Although the official rate is 3.72 FEC/RMB to $1.00 US, the black market rate is between 6.50-7.00 RMB to $1.00 US. The exact rate depends on negotiation and the frequency of police crackdowns on the money changers in the area.*

There was no word on Hu's death from "The Beijing Foreign Student Free Press," and their "Taxi Drivers or Mafia" had not survived the weekend. Only notes from students who wanted to buy or sell used bicycles and furniture or arrange tutoring exchanges were posted on the bulletin board.

As I scanned the notices, I remembered there was yet another source of information: Hong Xin. We had seen each other on campus a couple of times, and each time she had greeted me with a big hello. I had reminded her of the open invitation to visit me, but she hadn't taken me up on the

---

*All rates of exchange are Beijing rates as of April, 1989.

offer. I wondered if she had simply been too busy with her studies, or if she didn't want to bother with the red tape she thought she would have to endure in order to visit a foreign student.

Actually, Hong Xin would only have to sign in and out of *San Lou* to visit me. Chinese who lived off campus were not even allowed past the gate except during visiting hours, between four in the afternoon until ten at night, and they had to sign in and out at the gate as well as the dormitory. Unlike Chinese visitors, foreigners had free access to the campus and could visit other foreigners or Chinese at will without being stopped at the gate or required to sign in. This double standard resulted in the standing joke among foreign students that a foreigner draped in bandoliers, brandishing an AK47 in each hand, and with a grenade clenched between his teeth could waltz past the gate guard without so much as a "who goes there," while a little old Chinese grandmother would be stopped at the gate and interrogated.

Throughout the decade, there had been a general thaw in the government's attitude toward Chinese mixing with foreigners. During the early 1980s, a Chinese had to report even the most casual conversation with a foreigner to his *danwei,* or risk having it reported by someone who had observed it. For Chinese to visit foreigners, or vice versa, required the Chinese to get approval from his *danwei.* The request alone was enough to get him pulled into the neighborhood Public Security Bureau office for questioning. Although things had loosened up considerably, as late as 1987, the *shiwuyuan* had refused to allow Yuanli to visit me in my room. Not only had she insisted that we meet in the hallway, she had held his *danwei* card at the desk. He had been so angered and unnerved by the whole process that he forgot to ask her for his card when we left, and we had to return to the dormitory to retrieve it. In 1987, another friend had been hassled by the gate guard. She had been quizzed so thoroughly as to why she wanted to visit me and how she had met me that she was frightened away and never attempted to visit me again.

While rigid interrogations were a thing of the past, Chinese visitors still had to sign the register, which listed their name, their *danwei*, the person they were visiting, the date and time, and the purpose of the visit. The register was a permanent record of one's contact with a foreigner, and proof of association with foreigners might haunt them in the future, just as it had others in the past.

Not knowing when or if Hong Xin would come to see me, I decided to drop in on her. At least I wouldn't have to sign in at Building #8, but would only be subjected to the curious stare of the *shiwuyuan*. I doubted anyone would ask her about my visit, but if they did, I was confident she would be able to handle any inquiries. While Chinese youth might be regarded as naive when it came to relations between the sexes, there was no such innocence regarding the art of subterfuge. Having been born during the Cultural Revolution, this generation had learned as toddlers how to conceal thoughts and actions, and had a keen sophistication when it came to knowing what to say and what not to say when being questioned by those within their *danwei* empowered by the Party to protect and ensure the political and spiritual purity of their charges.

While I was eager to talk to Hong Xin, I would have to wait until afternoon classes were finished. I couldn't go straight away, as it would be inconsiderate to disturb her and her roommates during *xiuxi*. The 1:00 to 2:00 p.m. rest period is not taken lightly in China. In fact, *xiuxi* is so important to the Chinese that it is guaranteed by the constitution, and with just cause. While Westerners eat diets that are high in protein and calories, the Chinese diet is low in both, leaving them with a very low percentage of body fat. With little stored-up energy to power their systems, the Chinese start to wilt by midday and the hour's rest is needed to get them through the rest of the day.

Just before five o'clock, I walked into Building #8. The exterior of the building held no clues as to what was inside, but the interior of the building had changed drastically in the ten days since my first visit. *Dazibao* lined the walls in the hallway and ran up the staircase to the first landing. A large portrait of Hu Yaobang hung in the foyer. Skillfully drawn in pencil, the portrait was a powerful piece of art. Having produced an excellent likeness of Hu, the artist had also managed to capture his energy and the qualities that had set him apart from other Chinese leaders: gentleness and compassion. It was those qualities which had caused him great difficulty within the upper echelon of the Chinese Communist Party, while winning him the affection and respect of many students and older intellectuals.

A large sheet of white paper with the single character *dian* written on it hung next to Hu's portrait. The character, which means to pay respect or make offerings to the dead, was written with incredible sadness. The thick black strokes appeared to have been drawn by an unsteady hand, as if the calligrapher had been overcome with grief as he wrote. Dramatically, a few drops of ink had splattered below the character, making it appear as if the character itself had wept black tears.

Since white is the color of mourning in China, several white paper flowers had been pinned along the borders of the portrait and the poster. A large wreath of white paper flowers stood against the opposite wall. The display was quite moving, and I stood looking at the portrait for several minutes before I realized the *shiwuyuan* was standing by the door to her office watching me. Not wanting to attract any more attention than I already had, I walked up the stairs at a normal gait, trying desperately to read the *dazibao* out of the corner of my eye. However, I could only manage a glimpse at the posters. Most were too long for me to read anything more than a phrase. Only a couple were short enough for me to read in their entirety. One, along the side of the stairs, said, "Students weep for Hu Yaobang. Students weep for China." Another, hung at the top of the landing said, "Why does history have to repeat itself?"

The poster which really piqued my curiosity was the first poster at the base of the stairs. I only had time to read "Mao Zedong said . . ." as I walked past it. Hong Xin would have to tell me which of Mao's quotes the students had used. She could also tell me if I was correct in assuming the students had used one of Mao's quotations because it would make it difficult for those in authority to criticize the students for posting *dazibao*.

I walked up two more flights of stairs, to the end of the hallway to Hong Xin's room. The building seemed quieter than usual, so I tapped softly on the door. When no one answered, I knocked again, a little bit harder, causing the unlocked door to open a few inches. Sticking my head inside the room, I called out to Hong Xin, but the room was empty. Quickly shutting the door, I jotted a note to Hong Xin, telling her I had stopped by and again inviting her to visit me at *San Lou*. As an afterthought, I wrote my room number under my signature, then folded the note several times and scooted it under the door.

Since the halls were empty and it appeared no one was coming up the stairs, I planned to stop above the first floor landing where I could read Mao's quotation without being observed by the *shiwuyuan*. However, when I looked down over the banister, I saw a young woman was standing in front of the poster reading into a tape recorder. Immediately, paranoia set in. While she might be a student recording what was written on the *dazibao* for her own information, my first thought was of the *Gonganju* (the Public Security Bureau). While I had never had personal contact with the secret police, I had heard both foreigners and Chinese talk about the infamous Division Thirteen. According to the stories, these undercover cops were everywhere, watching everyone and everything. The very mention of Division Thirteen always made me think about a story my father had read to me when I was a child. It was called "A Little Bird Told Me," and the intent of the story was to terrorize children into perpetual obedience. I detested the story and despised the Little Birds who were always watching, waiting for you to slip up so they could tattle on you. For all I knew, the woman with the recorder was either attached to Division Thirteen or the "Little Birds." If I stopped to read the poster, Hong Xin might be nailed for befriending an overly curious American. Since I had left a note that not only provided my name, but my room number as well, I thought it best to practice some discretion and walk casually past the posters as if they were Greek to me.

My disappointment at not being able to read the posters vanished as soon as I stepped onto the first landing. A *dazibao* was posted directly in front of me on the small patch of wall between the first floor ceiling and the second floor stair railing. Since it was facing those coming down the stairs, I hadn't noticed it on my way up. It was so brief that I didn't even have to slow my stride in order to read it, and although the *dazibao* contained only one word, it was a more powerful political statement of the times than anything that Mao Zedong had ever said. The word, formed with two characters and written three times with a trail of exclamation marks following it, was "*MINZHU MINZHU MINZHU!!!*—in English, DEMOCRACY, DEMOCRACY, DEMOCRACY.

CHAPTER SEVEN

OLD ONE HUNDRED NAMES

I dashed across *Xianghualu* (Fragrant Flower Road), weaving through the throng of bicycles, trucks, and cars coming toward me from all directions. A gust of wind blew through the tops of the poplars that lined the narrow street, then swept down to the drainage ditch creating miniature tornadoes in the dust. The long line of poplars on either side of Fragrant Flower Road had been planted in regimental fashion. Each stood tall and straight, like a wooden sentry guarding the street to prevent the sun's warmth from seeping through. Shivering as I waited at the bus stop, I pulled my cotton jacket tighter around me in a feeble attempt to shut out the crisp spring wind.

Having traveled up and down its entire length several times without seeing even a single fragrant flower, I had often wondered why the street had been named *Xianghualu*. But then, I had never seen a nightingale at *Yeyinglu*. Naming it Poplar Street would have been just as foolish since so many streets in Beijing are lined with poplars. Perhaps whoever named it merely yearned to see fragrant flowers along the road.

Bus #305 made its way slowly past *Yeyinglu*. Strange clanking and sputtering sounds could be heard coming from the engine as it drew closer, leaving a trail of putrid carbon smoke floating in its wake. The brakes squealed and ground, then the entire bus shimmied as it came to a gradual halt several yards past the bus stop. The waiting crowd paused for an instant, as if contemplating the sanity of boarding a vehicle that neither ran nor stopped with any certainty, then moved in a surge to the back door of the bus, jostling and pushing each other as they all attempted to board at the same time. A few of us ran past them to the front door where we boarded with ease.

Having made the trip several times, it was no longer necessary for me to look out the window for landmarks or count the stops until we reached Double Well Village where I had to transfer to bus #18. Instead I used my time in the same manner as the other commuters, drifting off into the privacy of my thoughts, going over my visit to Hong Xin's dormitory the day before and my conversation with Lu Minghua later that evening.

Although eager to tell Lu Minghua about the *dazibao* and find out if there had been a similar reaction to Hu's death on her campus, I had waited until after seven to leave for her apartment, knowing she would insist on feeding me if I arrived earlier. Gathering my jacket and purse, I opened the door to find Lu Minghua standing there, her fist poised in midair ready to knock on my door. We stood face to face, frozen by surprise until we burst out in laughter when another foreign student walked straight into a wall, mesmerized by the extraordinary sight of a tiny Chinese woman about to strike a foreign woman twice her size.

After inviting Lu Minghua inside and pouring a cup of tea for her, I turned to see that she was still standing by the door. She looked at me with lips pursed, eyebrows raised, and hands on her hips. The expression on her face was that look of disapproval, which seems to come automatically with motherhood or a teaching certificate. Patting the chair by my desk, I insisted that she sit down.

She eased into the chair with a dramatic sigh, then said, "Little Sister, where have you been? I have not seen you for four days. Twice I came to your room and no one was here. I was starting to worry that something might have happened to you!"

Jinjin looked up from her desk and said something in Japanese. I was certain the Chinese translation would follow. She did that frequently. If she wasn't sure how to say something in Chinese or English, she would say it in Japanese before she gave it a go in the other language. I sensed she was trying to tell Lu Minghua about my bicycle wreck, so I whispered to her in English not to mention the wreck. Lu Minghua would be upset and the entire evening would be wasted talking about who, when, how, and where. I hoped Jinjin had understood me, but just to be safe, I started jabbering away about how difficult my classes had been and explaining that I was leaving to go to her apartment when she arrived at my door.

As I spoke, Lu Minghua reached for my tape recorder and switched it on. The first time she had come alone to my room, I had asked permission to tape our conversations for language practice when I returned to the States. She was delighted with the idea and soon took over working the recorder. A regular demon with the pause button, she pushed it frequently when she thought we were wasting tape, particularly when one of us took too long looking up a word in the dictionary or when our laughter was prolonged. Usually, I wouldn't say anything, but there were times when I insisted on letting the recorder run, knowing that listening to her comments on the tapes months or even years later would bring back treasured memories.

I had only waited minutes to rerun one tape, which we recorded during an impromptu tap dancing lesson I gave to Lu Minghua and Jinjin. Granted, we were not exactly the Rockettes and made a rather bizarre chorus line, but nevertheless, we had finally mastered the steps in unison: shuffle-ball-change, step-shuffle, step-shuffle, shuffalo from Buffalo. After our performance, the three of us collapsed on my bed in laughter. Lamenting the lack of an audience to appreciate such rare talent, Jinjin rushed off and rounded up two of her Japanese friends who watched with hand-covered giggles as we did a repeat performance. After our somewhat astonished audience had left, I rewound the tape and the three of us laughed again at Lu Minghua's commentary in the background.

After my idle chitchat about classes, I told Lu Minghua about the *dazibao* I had seen that afternoon in Building #8. Sipping her tea, she listened attentively as I spoke.

When I had finished my story, she put her cup down and said, "Today the students on our campus were very agitated. There are also posters on our campus, as there are on many campuses in Beijing." She paused, then said, "I understand that students have held meetings at Beijing University. . . ."

The recorder clicked off as the tape came to an end, interrupting her sentence. She opened it, flipped the tape over, then closed the machine, and started it again. Thinking she might feel awkward recording a conversation that involved politics, I pointed to the recorder and said, "You can leave it off if you prefer."

"No problem," she responded with a flick of her hand, as the recorder continued to run.

I told her I was aware that students had great respect for Hu since he had supported their demands for political reform in the student demonstrations of 1986-87.

"Yes," she said, "But it wasn't only students who admired and respected Hu Yaobang. Many intellectuals appreciated Hu's support of reform, and people were saddened and discouraged when he was forced to resign." Shaking her head, she added, "In China, one step forward is often followed by two steps backward." She was silent for a few seconds, then added, "You know, Little Sister, Hu Yaobang made two mistakes. He was outspoken and he was compassionate. There were those in the Party who saw him as a threat because he was outspoken, and those who saw his compassion as a sign of weakness."

She leaned forward in her chair and said, "I heard many, many students, maybe thousands, have gone to demonstrate at the front gate of *Zhongnanhai** and at Tiananmen Square."

I was surprised and asked, "You mean today, tonight?" That was probably why Building #8 had been so quiet and the halls empty of people. Perhaps Hong Xin and her roommates had also gone to *Zhongnanhai* or the square.

Lu Minghua nodded and said, "Yes, I know students from Beijing University have gone, and perhaps students from other universities have joined in."

It was poetic justice that students were protesting as a result of Hu's death, as it was his tolerance of the earlier demonstrations which had forced him from power. Yet, the possibility existed that heads might fall again if the demonstrations continued. It was not a reassuring thought, especially since I had worried about the future direction of China when Li Peng was elevated to the position of Prime Minister in the shakeup that followed

---

*Located west of Tiananmen Square, *Zhongnanhai* is the compound that includes the residences and offices of some of China's highest officials.

Hu's resignation. If Li Peng, a darling of the hard-liners, gained control after Deng died or his health declined to the point where he could be set aside, China's future direction just might be a U-turn.

I asked Lu Minghua if she thought there would be more demonstrations. She shrugged her shoulders and said, "I don't know, Little Sister, but I am worried because . . ." Before she could finish her sentence, there was a knock at my door. It startled us both, and Lu Minghua quickly pressed the stop button on the recorder, then shoved it into the desk drawer as I got up to answer the door.

It was only one of my classmates, an Australian named Joan, who had come to ask for help with the next day's lesson. I was pleased when Lu Minghua volunteered to answer her questions, thinking it would speed up the process so Lu Minghua could finish her statement. However, she didn't get the chance since Joan stayed on to chat until Lu Minghua rose to leave a little after ten o'clock. Lu Minghua didn't object to my formality when I proceeded to go through the "Chinese goodby." I thought it would give us a chance to complete our conversation while I walked with her to the main road, but Joan was so taken with Lu Minghua that she insisted on walking with us.

Waving goodby to Lu Minghua at the main road, I thought of all the questions that had been left unanswered. Primarily, I had wanted to know if she had seen a similarity in the present leadership's reaction to Hu's death and that of the Gang of Four to the death of Zhou Enlai.* During our conversation, I had been reminded of Zhou's death on January 8, 1976, and the events that followed it. The Gang of Four had met with disastrous results when they attempted to prevent the people from mourning Zhou properly, and the present leadership appeared to be following the same path by down-playing the loss of Hu and ignoring the grief the students were expressing. Of course, there were differences. While respected and admired, Hu was not revered by the people as Zhou had been, and although there was dissatisfaction with the present leadership due to corruption, inflation, and a lack of personal freedoms, they were not loathed by the people as the the Gang of Four had been. However, one of the *dazibao* in Building #8 had brought to mind the similarity. It asked, "Why does history

---

*Chou Enlai, the Wade-Giles spelling is more familiar to Americans.

have to repeat itself?" If the question was prophetic, things could get pretty nasty in Beijing.

While the people of China had been grief-stricken at the loss of Zhou, Jiang Qing, Mao's wife, and the other members of the Gang of Four were elated at their good fortune. His death had eliminated their most powerful adversary, the one man who had stood between them and complete control of China as Mao became more infirm. Eager to see Zhou's corpse go up in smoke at *Babaoshan,* they had allowed only six days of official mourning before Zhou's body was carted off to be cremated without the usual pomp and ceremony of a funeral for a statesman. Even during the official mourning period people were instructed not to wear black armbands or white flowers, and memorials or commemorative meetings in Zhou's honor were banned by the government. In an effort to prevent crowds from gathering, the people were not told when Zhou's body would be taken to *Babaoshan* for cremation; however, one and a half million people, alerted by small lane news, assembled on January 11th to pay tribute to Zhou as the hearse carrying his body, followed by a skimpy official procession, proceeded down Eternal Peace Avenue.

While the people mourned inwardly, the Gang of Four used the press to lash out at Zhou Enlai. By March, the people's grief and anger could no longer be contained when the Shanghai newspaper, *Wen Hui Bao,* printed articles written by supporters of Jiang Qing, inferring that Zhou had been a "capitalist roader." On the 19th of March, people brought wreaths in memory of Zhou to the Monument of the People's Heroes at Tiananmen Square despite the government's ban on memorials. On the 30th a eulogy to Zhou was posted on the monument and a flood of poems followed.

The wreaths and poetry infuriated the Gang of Four, especially since many of the poems were direct attacks on Jiang Qing. The police were ordered to remove the wreaths and poems, but as fast as they came down others were put up to replace them. The war of wills escalated in April when steelworkers from the Beijing Heavy Duty Electrical Machinery Plant constructed an enormous steel wreath, too heavy to be easily removed, and carried it to the square on Qingming.

Qingming, which fell on April 4th that year, was the traditional day for remembering ancestors in old China. After the founding of the People's Republic of China, the day became a holiday for honoring the fallen heroes of the revolution. The Gang of Four, knowing massive crowds would come to the square on Qingming to publicly mourn Zhou, started a campaign to debase the holiday, ridiculing Qingming, and labeling it a "ghost festival." Still, people filled the square. Two million came and piled their wreaths high, their stirring eulogies expressing the people's affection and regard for Zhou, while their poems leveled even more venomous attacks against Jiang Qing.

Darkness concealed the police who were brought to the Square to clear away the wreaths and poems and arrest the people who had remained on the square into the evening. However, dawn and small lane news brought an even larger crowd to the square on April 5th. Outraged at finding their tokens of grief again destroyed by the police and the monument ringed by guards, the angry crowd demanded the release of those who had been arrested the night before. When their demands were refused, the crowd turned over the vehicles that had brought the police and militia into the square, then burned the vehicles and a command post that soldiers had set up on the square. At nightfall, police and militia surrounded the mourners, beating them savagely with clubs, arresting over two hundred, injuring hundreds, and "disappearing" an unknown number of people. The Gang of Four was not overthrown until October of 1976, after the death of Mao Zedong, but the seeds of their downfall were planted that April 5th on the cold stone slabs of Tiananmen Square.

The voice of the *shoupiaoyuan* announcing Double Well Village interrupted my thoughts. I joined in with the other voices calling out *"Xia che ba!"* (Getting off the bus) and stepped down from the bus, crossing over to the row of street stalls that sell cheap clothing, drab material, spools of dusty thread, out-of-date parts to out-of-date machinery, ugly plastic sandals, and such. After I caught bus #18 around the corner, I would transfer to the trolley that stopped on Wangfujing about a block from the Beijing Hotel.

Although I arrived a few minutes early, Li Yuanli was waiting for me in the bar, sitting alone at the last table against the wall. The bar was usually so crowded that empty chairs at any table were quickly filled by strangers, causing people to become cautious, conversations stilted, and the choice of topics mundane. Yuanli and I were in luck since several tables had empty chairs, and someone looking for a place to sit would probably approach one of the front tables first.

He waved to me as I crossed the lobby, flashing me one of his dazzling smiles. His truly is a smile that dazzles, filled with even white teeth and dimpled on each side. He looked very westernized and handsome in the pale blue polo shirt I had brought for him from the States. Seeing him from that distance, it struck me how much his son Leilei resembled him. I had arrived just in time for Leilei's second birthday, and as his honorary aunt, had celebrated the occasion with Yuanli, his beautiful wife Suyu, and the rest of the family several days before.

Yuanli was my very first friend in China. We had met in 1982, just before he and Suyu were married. A few months later he was sent to America in connection with his job, and having a friend in America with whom he could talk frequently on the telephone had made his separation from Suyu a little easier to bear. Before returning to China he was able to come to my home for a brief visit, and his fluency in English had allowed him to develop quite a rapport with my family. Through the years we had kept up with each other by mail, telephone, photographs of our families, and spending time together whenever I was in Beijing.

We made small talk until our drinks had been served, then immediately switched to politics. Yuanli had also heard that students had marched in the streets near Beijing University and the People's University, then assembled at *Zhongnanhai* and Tiananmen Square. When he had passed the square at mid-morning, a large crowd of students were still gathered at the Square where wreaths had been placed at the base of the Monument to the Peoples Heroes along with a banner calling Hu Yaobang the "Soul of China."

We talked about the Pro-Democracy Movement which had lain dormant through Deng's earlier years in power, then erupted in spurts over the last few years. Although the failure of the student demonstrations in 1986 and 1987 had caused the students to retreat from their demands and become more cautious, it was obvious to the government that the movement still existed.

Over the past several months, students and other members of the intellectual community had gradually become more outspoken regarding their frustrations with the system. Philosophizing in coffee houses, holding democracy salons on the campus of Beijing University, and gathering for political discussions over beer in each other's homes had recently become a favorite pastime. However, it was even more significant that the *laobaixing*, or "old one hundred names" as the common people are called in China, were also expressing their discontent.

While intellectuals were distressed about the lack of political reform and human rights under the Communist system, the unhappiness of the *laobaixing* seemed rooted in more practical, economic problems. Vast numbers of people were unemployed and each year brought a fresh crop of youths who were, as the government so delicately stated, "waiting for work." Those who were employed found themselves stuck in mindless, low-paying jobs that fed their boredom and resentment while their wages were rapidly devoured by an ever-rising rate of inflation.

Of course, intellectuals also struggled with the economic problems. Many were not assigned jobs on completion of their studies, and those who did were often placed in jobs beneath their capabilities. Intellectuals who had gone off to study abroad returned home to find that antiquated technology made it impossible for them to fully utilize their knowledge, and even those who were not in technological fields were unable to get jobs that challenged or fulfilled them. Considered tainted by the West, and therefore untrustworthy, they found themselves stymied in their careers by superiors who were not only suspicious of their Western education but envious and resentful of their expertise. Furthermore, both intellectuals and *laobaixing* were incensed by the corruption and nepotism that had reached epidemic proportions in officialdom and clogged the massive bureaucracy, which controlled every aspect of their lives.

When I told Yuanli how the present situation reminded me of the Tiananmen Incident of 1976, he nodded in agreement and said, "There always has to be that one thing that makes people decide they won't take anymore. Back then it was when the Gang of Four began to attack Zhou. That was the last straw." He shook his head and said, "I don't know if the loss of Hu is the last straw, but I do know that people's anger has been festering for a long time. The students have just been waiting for the next opportunity, the next reason to take to the streets."

Describing my visit to Building #8, I told Yuanli about the sign that had referred to history repeating itself. He laughed softly and said, "It's ironic. I remember the day the Gang of Four was arrested. Everyone went around buying four bottles of Beijing Beer to celebrate.* People were so happy to get rid of Jiang Qing, and we knew it was only a matter of time before Deng would be in control."

The bar became more crowded, so we switched to less sensitive conversation. Yuanli told me he had seen our mutual friend Sun Shanli and given him my phone number. Having grown up in the same neighborhood, Sun Shanli and Yuanli had been close friends since early childhood, and Yuanli had introduced him to me on my second trip to China. While I sometimes teasingly complained to Sun Shanli that he was a rascal, I did so with affection, and I looked forward to hearing from him.

Having promised Lao Pang I would stop by after dinner, I rushed back to the campus after leaving Yuanli. The Professor had already retired for the night, so Lao Pang served me tea, which she claimed aided digestion, then entertained me with stories about her childhood. Little Ma sat near the lamp in a corner of the room, mending clothes and giggling merrily each time I uttered a word.

As I lay in bed that night, thoughts danced around in my head, floating in and out as I tried first to sleep, then when sleep would not come, to concentrate on all that Yuanli had said. The day's wind had calmed to a gentle breeze throughout the evening, but later it returned with new strength. The wind whistled past the building, banging a screen that someone had neglected to latch, then plucked at the electrical wires strung from the buildings to connecting poles causing them to hum a long, low note. As it swirled around the laundry someone had left on the clothes line, towels and shirts and slacks cracked and snapped like a chorus of bullwhips. Something, somewhere, clattered and clanged as it fell to the ground, startling a dog who barked out in surprise.

Listening to the wind, I recalled a sentence from one of my Chinese language textbooks. When I first read it, the translation had sounded like a line from a poem:

---

*The number four represented the Gang of Four and since Deng's given name, Xiaoping, can also mean "little bottle" in spoken Chinese, they had bought four bottles of beer. It is a typical example of the way Chinese use their strong sense of satire and the complexities of their language to express subtle humor through puns.

"Spring is lovely in Beijing, but all too brief and the winds are great."

Now those words seemed more than poetic, and I wondered what the spring winds might bring; how long they would last. Most of all, I wondered what harm they might do.

CHAPTER EIGHT

THE CURSER

Saying *"Wei,"* I answered the phone in the Chinese manner. There was a chuckle from the person on the other end of the line, then he said, "Lao Ban, I'm glad I caught you. This is Jack."

He didn't have to say who was calling, since only one person in the world calls me Lao Ban. It means "the boss" in Chinese, and it's the nickname Sun Shanli gave me as a joke when we first met. We have both long since forgotten what the joke was about, but the name stuck.

Jack is the English name Shanli uses. He chose it because he thought it sounded so American: direct but friendly. It is odd that while Shanli signs his letters "Jack," and identifies himself as "Jack" whenever he telephones, I can't remember ever once having called him that. Instead, I've always called him Shanli, just as I call Yuanli by his given name. Although it's not traditional to use the given name in China, knowing that Americans enjoy this formality, Yuanli had insisted that I address him by his given name. Perhaps because Yuanli introduced us, I did the same with Shanli, preferring that to "Jack."

I told Shanli he almost didn't "catch" me since I had only stopped by *San Lou* after class to get my meal tickets before heading to the *shitang* for lunch.

Chuckling again, Shanli said, "Good, you haven't eaten yet. I've been sitting here at the Golden Peacock Hotel hoping some rich American would buy me lunch."

"Listen, how many times do I have to tell you, I am not a rich American. Haven't you heard? I'm a poor scholarship student!"

"Okay, Okay," he laughed, "I'll buy you lunch, but do you think you could part with a couple of bucks to take a cab? I'm starving! If I wait for you to come by bus, I'll be weak with hunger."

Although I promised Shanli I would get there as fast as possible, finding a taxi driver on campus willing to take a fare to the Golden Peacock—Mafia or not—was always difficult. Since it's only about a ten minute trip, and the hotel has its own fleet of cabs to handle the return trip, most drivers feel it's hardly worth the effort. Additionally, during lunch or *xiuxi*, paying in RMB was out of the question. If one didn't agree to pay in FEC, all available drivers immediately went off-duty. I decided not to let the added expense bother me since I had not seen Shanli in two years.

The first driver I approached reluctantly agreed to take me after we had settled on a fare that was twice what it should have been—payable in FEC, of course. Immediately, the driver shoved a cassette in the tape player, then turned the volume up loud enough to discourage any conversation, making it apparent that he was not in the mood to throw in a little language practice to justify his inflated price. That was fine with me since it meant I wouldn't have to answer the standard queries regarding my nationality, occupation, age, marital status, number of children, and gross annual income.

Shanli was waiting in the lobby bar, and after a warm hello, we headed for the coffee shop to eat. Normally, I would not allow a Chinese to pay for my lunch at the Golden Peacock, which is as expensive as it is plush. But with Shanli, I was not so concerned about the prices since I knew he could afford it, and we always took turns paying the check anyway.

Shanli works in the Chinese film industry. Although the salary he receives from the government-owned film company is only equivalent to about US$40.00 a month, he is in great demand with foreigners making films in China, and they always manage to supplement his low salary with more than a little something on the side.

If you ask Shanli to describe his job, he is likely to tell you he is a "crap cutter." He is usually assigned as one of the assistants to the director, but his actual duties are numerous and varied. He frequently ends up doing the bulk of the interpreting even though official interpreters are assigned to a foreign film crew. However, Shanli is not only fluent in the technical language of the film industry and American slang, but foreigners trust him since they know he will translate accurately. Many interpreters either lack the language skills or are hesitant to translate exactly what one or the other party has said when the exchange gets a little heated. They have also been known to suddenly go mum and forget how to speak English if their bosses in the Chinese film company or other officials do not wish to give a reason for denying a request. Not Shanli! Additionally, he makes it a rule to discreetly inform an unsuspecting foreigner when the Chinese he is dealing with understands English.

Surely Shanli's most valuable asset is that he manages to get things done. He can persuade or dissuade recalcitrant officials, and is adept at using his *guanxi,* humor, charm, and instinct to get around provincial officials who are either terrified by or take delight in the bureaucratic mountains they can build. Shanli is indeed a "crap cutter."

The back section of the Golden Peacock Coffee Shop is closed at lunch, so Shanli gave the hostess one of his most seductive, sleepy-eyed smiles. Explaining that we had important business to discuss, he asked if we might have a table in the back. The hostess hesitated a moment, giving Shanli the opportunity to increase the intensity of his smile. Another victim of Shanli's charm, she giggled as she returned his smile, then led us to the most secluded table in the back.

We sipped Qingdao beer and chatted as we waited for our food. I delayed asking Shanli what he thought about the demonstrations until we had relaxed for a few minutes. Anyway, I knew what he would say. Shanli always had the same comment for any political situation in China. "F------ Communists!" he would say.

Actually, Shanli has a rather odd attitude about cursing. Among friends, he will toss out expletives in English with little concern, although he usually saves the "Big F Word" for use in conjunction with the Communist Party or its leaders. Yet, when it comes to cursing in Chinese, he displays uncharacteristic reserve.

I once asked him to teach me all the Chinese curse words, but he refused at first, saying that it wouldn't be proper. After pointing out that it is necessary to know the curse words in a language to really understand it, I reasoned with him that I certainly couldn't find the words in a Chinese language textbook, and everyone else I knew would probably be shocked by my request. Finally agreeing to teach me, Shanli spoke the words in such low whispers that they were barely audible and shielded the paper with his free hand as he wrote the characters. He only wrote the last set of characters after issuing a stern warning that I must never, ever, under any circumstances say them to anyone. They are the nuclear weapon of Chinese expletives. You can possess them in your arsenal, but to use them would be unthinkable. When he had finished writing out the characters, he folded the sheet of paper several times before handing it to me surreptitiously, as if he were turning over state secrets.

After our food was served, I brought up the subject of Hu's death and the demonstration. Just as I thought he would, he rolled his eyes and through a mouthful of noodles said, "F------ Communists! They talk about the people, the masses, The PEOPLE'S Republic of China!" After swallowing the noodles, he added, "They don't care about the people. To them the people, their precious masses, are just ignorant peasants with a few troublesome intellectuals mixed in. The f------ Communist Party cares about the f------ Communist Party and that's all!" Waving his chopsticks in the air, he said, "the students in Beijing . . . no, all the students in China can march on the streets, but it won't make a difference. It will take more than students. Until the *laobaixing* decide to join in, it won't make a difference. Every couple of years, students demonstrate for a few days, then the f------ Communists throw a few of them in jail and scare off the rest. Afterwards, things are just the same as they were before, or worse."

While I agreed with Shanli to a certain extent, the demonstrations of 1986 and 1987 had made a difference. The forced resignation of Hu and the resulting "Campaign Against Bourgeois Liberalization" were setbacks for those in favor of political reform, but people had become more open in airing their discontent with the political and economic status quo. While the demonstrations had only lasted a brief time, they had signaled that the voice of Democracy Wall had not been silenced and, in fact, was growing stronger and stronger. The demonstrations started in Hefei on December 5,

1986, then spread to Wuhan on December 10th, then to Shanghai, and finally on to Beijing. Hefei, a nondescript industrial city of about half a million people, is the capital of Anhui Province, which is better known as the site of Huang Shan (Yellow Mountain), than as a site of political reform.

However, Wuhan, a municipal area that combines the cities of Hankou, Hanyang, and Wuchang, has played a part in political reform since the Self-Strengthening Movement, which began in the early 1860s and supported the theory of Wei Yuan, a nineteenth century scholar who stated that China should "learn the superior barbarian techniques to control the barbarians." The issue of just how much foreign expertise and technology can be allowed into China without contaminating the culture and ideology of the Chinese is a problem that the leaders of China, be they Confucians or Communists, have struggled with throughout modern Chinese history up to the present time.

In Wuhan, on December 10, 1986, seven thousand students demanding democracy marched in the streets to a Hubei Province government building. In Hefei up to two thousand students hung *dazibao,* which quoted Abraham Lincoln and Patrick Henry, then marched through the city calling for democracy.

The demonstrations began as a result of an argument between Wan Li, then a vice premier and Fang Lizhi, an astrophysicist who was Vice President of Hefei's Science and Technology Institute, during which Fang had called for democratic reform and referred to socialism as "the scourge of humanity in this century." While the students also protested against inferior living conditions and food, as well as demanding student representation in the local legislature, the emphasis of the demonstrations was on democracy, or as one poster declared, "We had freedom, we had democracy, but it has been lost in the darkness."

By December 19, 1986, the protests had spread to Shanghai. Students gathered in People's Square, then went to City Hall to meet with Jiang Zimen, the Mayor of Shanghai, where they issued four demands: greater democracy, freedom of the press, that their protests be declared legal, and the guaranteed safety of the protesters. By December 20th, the number of protesters in Shanghai had grown to thirty-five thousand.

Students in Beijing had only hung *dazibao* in support of the movement until December 24th when four thousand students marched from campus to campus. As the protests spread through the four cities, students became more pointed in their criticism of the Communist Party and its leaders, demanding that Deng and the Central Committee reverse themselves on the "Four Bigs": writing big character posters, speaking out freely, airing views fully, and holding great debates. These were the rights that Deng had had stricken from the constitution in 1980 as a result of Democracy Wall. However, the most bitter attacks came on December 27th. One poster stated, "The Chinese Communist Party is in every respect identical to the most tyrannical feudal despotic governments we have had!" Another *dazibao* quoted a damning statement made by Vice Premier Wan Li: "Democracy can only be something which we bestow on someone as a favor."

Party leaders were furious with the students, but it was not their fury alone which defeated the movement. Despite the passion of the protesters and that students had demonstrated in at least eight other cities, the movement was doomed from the beginning by its lack of leadership, failure to suggest methods of implementation in achieving its goals, and lack of support from the *laobaixing*. While the students were interested in ideas and political theory, the workers wanted the government to curb inflation and raise their wages and standard of living. Although some workers in Nanjing and Shanghai did demonstrate, they did so as a means of expressing their sympathy for the students rather than their support.

Hu Yaobang urged that the students be dealt with patiently since examinations were scheduled to begin, and he felt that those demonstrating would soon return to the business of the classrooms. Furthermore, Hu was not unsympathetic to the students demands, as he favored a reduction of government control over the economy, supported a rise in subsidized prices of basic consumer goods, supported the Household Responsibility System and other programs of privatization, as well as increased investments by foreign businesses. Hu's downfall was not his support of economic reform; it was his support of political reform. He wanted a freer atmosphere for intellectuals and felt it was time for the "old men" to step aside, urging that new blood was needed in the leadership of China. By doing so, Hu got snared in the political trap of the hard-liners versus the moderates, and even alienated his mentor, Deng Xiaoping.

The tug of war for power between the moderates and hard-liners has been a consistent feature of political disputes since the founding of the Peoples Republic of China. It was evident in the great debate of whether "Red or Expert" was the essential ingredient necessary to bring China out of the Third World and to the top of the heap. It was the question of whether to take a "Great Leap Forward" or dawdle on the path to collectivization. It was the essence of the Cultural Revolution, and it was behind the argument of just how much "Spiritual Pollution" and "Bourgeois Liberalization" would be tolerated in order for China to achieve the Four Modernizations.

The hard-liners could point to the disorder that the demonstrations had created, the threat they posed to the Party, and, in particular, to the Old Guard. This threat loomed even greater since there had been some participation by workers, and the Old Guard thought it was time for the moderates to get their leashes jerked. Furthermore, while Deng had led China in a more liberal direction economically, he sided with the hard-liners on political reform. Economically, he might (as his famous quotation infers) tolerate "a black cat or a white cat so long as it catches the mouse," but politically, Deng lacked that flexibility.

In a meeting of the Central Committee held at Deng's home in January 1987, the same old men whom Deng had encouraged to retire "requested" the resignation of Hu Yaobang as General Secretary of the Chinese Communist Party and successor to Deng Xiaoping. Deng capitulated, but Hu was allowed to remain on as a member of the Politburo.

Hu was not the only victim of the 1986-1987 demonstrations and the Party's campaign against bourgeois liberalization and intellectual dissent. The astrophysicist Fang Lizhi was stripped of his party membership and fired from his position. Wang Ruowang, a former Deputy Editor of the *People's Daily* and a member of the Chinese Writers' Association, was also expelled from the party. Wang, who had been a victim of the Campaign Against Spiritual Pollution three years before, was criticized for several statements he had made. His most heinous crime was to refer to himself as the "founder of bourgeois liberalization." Additionally, Liu

Binyan, Vice Chairman of the Chinese Writers' Association and a very popular reporter for the *People's Daily* who specialized in exposing corruption in the government, was also expelled from the party. Not only had he trod squarely on the toes of Party officials, Liu had described the Four Cardinal Principles of Socialism as "outdated, rigid, and dogmatic concepts and worn-out phrases that have led China to calamities several times." While all were expelled from the party and lost their positions, the Politburo did stop short of declaring them "counterrevolutionaries."

For those of us watching from the outside, one of the main concerns was that China's programs for economic reform might also fall victim to the campaign against bourgeois liberalization. If nothing else, they could become bogged down in the continuing struggle between the two factions of the Communist Party. With the promotion of Li Peng from Vice Premier to Premier, there was just reason for concern. Li, a technocrat educated in Moscow and a darling of the Old Guard, is the protegé of Chen Yun who was the chief economic planner for Mao, a major critic of economic reform and sometime rival of Deng Xiaoping. Li, like his mentor, is a proponent of central planning, and although he is known for not being exceptionally bright, he is shrewd.

The moderates, however, still had Zhao Ziyang. Zhao, who had been Premier, was removed from that position and named to replace Hu as General Secretary of the Party and successor to Deng Xiaoping. Known as an innovative economic reformer who had been quite successful as a provincial leader, Zhao had promoted privatization while First Secretary of the Party for Sichuan Province from 1975 to 1979 and implemented programs there that led the nation in agricultural reforms. The economy in Sichuan greatly improved under Zhao's leadership, and his successes there won him the affection, respect, and appreciation of the people in Sichuan. In praise of Zhao and his programs, people said, "If you want grain to eat, go to Zhao Ziyang."

A less certain factor in the lineup was Yang Shangkun who became President in the 1987 shuffle. Yang had been a senior officer of the People's Liberation Army (PLA) since the 1930s, and in addition to the office of president, Yang was one of two vice chairmen of the Central

Military Commission. An eighty-year-old veteran of the Long March, Yang usually sided with Deng, but his strong military connections guaranteed that if he could manage to outlive Deng, his power would be a factor in China's future.

Hu's forced resignation had dealt the moderates a serious blow, but China was midstream in economic reform, and to turn away from reform would cause economic disaster. Yet, the argument could be made that the reforms should be slowed down to cool off the overheated economy. The question was just how these reforms might be slowed down and to what degree. With Li holding the top governmental position and Zhao holding the top party position, the tug of war was guaranteed to continue if not intensify.

However, it was the people's reaction to the aftermath of the 1986-1987 student demonstrations that was most interesting. Regardless of the skirmishes in the top leadership of the Party, after the demonstrations had died down and the political dust had settled, the *laobaixing* just continued on about their lives. The government's campaign against bourgeois liberalization was given a rather ho-hum response by the public, giving credence to the old Chinese saying, "The sky is high and the Emperor is far away."

Privatization continued to spread with the number of individual and private enterprises growing to 14.549 million in 1989. Increasing emphasis on materialism appeared to be more of a motivation than an ideology. Where the *laobaixing* had once longed for ballpoint pens and bicycles, then refrigerators and black and white TVs, they now filled their dreams with color TVs and VCRs. More and more people were actually making these purchases, and entrepreneurs even jetted about on motorbikes. The most desirable jobs were no longer those in the government's never-ending bureaucracy, but in foreign joint venture enterprises.

However, under the veneer of materialism, there was a growing display of self-expression, which was visible in the clothes people wore, the music they listened to, and the books they read. Books on Marxism and Mao Zedong "Thought" gathered dust on shelves in bookstores while translations of foreign authors and Chinese novels, which addressed the problems of corruption and injustice, were best sellers. As self-expression evolved, people became less fearful and respectful of officials, complaining openly and bitterly about nepotism and corrupt, inefficient officials.

While students returned to concentrating on their studies, they did stage some small-scale demonstrations in 1988. Furthermore, students and other intellectuals were no longer alone in their calls for changes in the system and more personal freedoms. Private businessmen (vendors, bar owners, restaurateurs, etc.) had found the best way to ensure the longevity of their investments was to finance the intellectuals' meetings and discussions on political reform.

Other voices were added to the calls for political reform as members of the Communist Party started to speak out. While in March of 1987 Zhao Ziyang had stressed the importance of eliminating the "pernicious influence" of the West, in January of 1989 he stated, "We need not only a new economic order, but also a new political order."

As we talked, I told Shanli I had noticed a gradual change over the years I had been coming to China. On my first visit, it had been difficult to get someone to hold a conversation with a foreigner, much less state his opinion. However, with each passing year, people had become more willing to state their disagreement with government policies and their dissatisfaction with the system.

Signaling for the waitress to bring the check, Shanli said, "Sure, people are willing to complain, but I don't know if that means they are willing to come out and support the students."

When Shanli and I left the coffee shop, we went outside to meet one of the drivers for the film crew to which he was assigned. Shanli wanted to take me to see a location he thought would be perfect for a business investment I was considering. The property was across the city, just past Wangfujing, on Dongdan, and with rush hour traffic, the drive would take us twice the normal time.

Lighting a cigarette, Shanli sat quietly looking out the window as we drove away from the hotel. After a couple of minutes, he turned to me and asked, "Lao Ban, did I ever tell you how I discovered Mao was a liar?"

Actually, he had told me the story before, but it was a moving story and

I wanted to hear him tell it again. I shook my head and sat back, listening as attentively as a child being told a favorite bedtime story.

"When I was young, the Cultural Revolution was going on. At first it seemed so exciting to me because Mao talked about all the great things it would accomplish. I remember thinking smugly how lucky I was to live in Beijing. Mao lived in Beijing and students from all over China were making pilgrimages to Beijing just to get a glimpse of the Great Helmsman. We had been taught that Mao was great, above all other men. Mao was a god to us, and we raised our Little Red Books in the air, praising Mao Zedong.

"My father was a good man, a kind man; but he wasn't a very clever man. He always thought if he just did his job and minded his own business, everything would be okay. He never liked to get involved in politics, and it was fine with him that he was never invited to join the Party. I remember him saying, 'Leave politics to more capable men.'

"Father believed if you went around stating your opinions, you would anger those who didn't agree with you. One day those who agreed with you might be in charge, but the next day it might be those who disagreed with you. In China, you never know. He had a very simple strategy for survival: the best thing to do is never state an opinion on anything, even on the most inconsequential matters.

"His strategy worked for awhile. At the political meetings, he listened attentively, nodding politely at whatever was said, but staying in the background and never actually stating an opinion. Eventually, people in his department began to pressure him to criticize this person or that person. The more people pressured him, the more silent he became, just nodding as he listened to them. However, when the pressure in his department became too great for him, he developed a plan. He started going in to work later, coming home earlier, and sitting farther to the back at political meetings. He thought that way he could avoid being forced to make any statements.

"Then, people from his office began dropping by our apartment to have discussions with Father, to evaluate his revolutionary attitude. We knew, of course, that these were not mere social visits. The visits affected my mother more than anyone else in the family. She had always been a nervous type of person, and she soon became very agitated. As the visits increased and the pressure on my father mounted, she began to break. I suppose she had what is called a nervous breakdown. She would scream and wail about the least little thing; screaming at my sister and me, screaming at the neighbors, screaming at people in the market. But she screamed at my father more than anyone else. Every night at dinner she would start in on him. Wailing away, she would tell him, 'You think you are so clever at playing this game. You fool, you are going to ruin this family!' I hated my mother for that, but I never said anything.

"One day, my father didn't get out of bed, saying he was too ill to go to work. I don't know if he was really ill, or if it was just another plan. Regardless, it worked better than the last plan, or maybe the people in his department just forgot about him for a time. Then one morning some people from his department came to get him. Naturally, my mother screamed and wailed, but in the end, he went with them.

"We were all terrified that he had been arrested. Late that night, my father returned and went straight to bed without saying a word. We all wanted to know what had happened, but we were afraid to ask him. The next morning he went back to work.

"It wasn't the end of Father's troubles. Until the Cultural Revolution was over, he had to write self-criticisms over and over, and he lived in constant fear of being arrested. For years, he never knew from day to day what his fate might be, and he was called in for questioning off and on. Father's suffering seems minor in comparison to those who had their lives and families destroyed. However, living for years in a constant state of uncertainty took its toll on him and our family.

"It was a dangerous time, and people had to avoid contact with those who were suspect. Although some of my friends kept their distance, most still treated me pretty well. I suppose it was because my father was never arrested or actually charged with being a counterrevolutionary. There was one boy who treated me badly. His father had the most important job of all the men in our neighborhood. That kid thought he was such a big shot. One day he told me that Mao said people like my father were not politically correct and were undermining the revolution. When he said that, I felt like someone had hit me in the gut. As much as I loved my father, I knew Mao never lied. Mao was never wrong, so that meant my father must be wrong.

"My Mother has never really recovered. Sometimes I think she's still a little crazy. She still yells and screams a lot. My father just ignores her rages. He retired recently because of his health, but he seems to be content. The saddest thing for me is that I ever doubted my father. I never told him I doubted him, that I believed in Mao more than my own father. But, I am certain he knew. He knew I had been taught that Mao was perfect. Our teachers told us that Mao was the greatest leader the world had ever known, and that he would make China the strongest country in the world. Of course, we didn't know any better. In all fairness, neither did they. All anyone knew about the outside world was what the government told us. They told us how much smarter Mao was than the Western leaders. They said we should be very grateful to be Communists, and not capitalists like the Americans. According to Mao, the capitalist system had made America a country where the people were miserable because they were destitute and starving to death.

"I remember the first time I saw a group of Americans after China opened up. They were laughing and joking, obviously very happy people. A lot of them were pretty fat and those who weren't actually fat certainly were not starving. Just looking at them I could tell they were rich. That was when I first knew Mao was a liar."

Turning back toward the window, Shanli lighted another cigarette. After a long drag, he spoke. His voice was low, almost a whisper, and I realized that he was talking to himself, not me. "F------ Communists!" he said.

CHAPTER NINE

A SINGLE SPARK CAN START
A PRAIRIE FIRE

"Snap to, mate!" said Joan, my Australian classmate, gently nudging me with her elbow. I looked up from my textbook to find the class was looking at me and laughing. Teacher Wu was staring at me with that teacher's expression on his face. I realized he must have called on me, but I had not heard him. Actually, I had heard very little of what had been said in class all morning. Blushing, I said, "Excuse me, Teacher Wu, were you talking to me?"

Teacher Wu's humor and gentle nature prevented him from holding a stern expression for very long. Breaking into a smile, he repeated what he had just told the entire class. I said, "This morning Kong Kailing is not here."

Everyone in the class laughed again, including Teacher Wu and myself. I said, "Please forgive me, Teacher Wu, I'm tired because the students who live above my room make a lot of noise late at night, so I haven't been able to get much sleep."

It was a statement which proved that two half-truths do not make a whole truth. While the students had been noisy, it was my thoughts that had kept me awake. I was also tired from biking, busing, and in general running around town trying to meet with friends in an attempt to keep up with the small lane news and to see for myself what was happening. In a country where there is neither a free nor an accurate press, I had learned that being there was the only way to really know what was going on.

After Shanli showed me the property on Dongdan Wednesday evening, I walked down Eternal Peace Avenue to the Gate of Heavenly Peace. Looking across at the heart of the square, I watched the large crowd of students who had gathered at the Monument to the People's Heroes. One student stood atop the first tier of the monument, shouting slogans that were echoed by the crowd: "Down with corruption! Long Live Freedom! Long live democracy!" Fighting back the urge to join the crowd, I reminded myself that, as a foreigner, I was only an observer. Small groups of unarmed police also watched the students from various points around the square. However, it was apparent that their intent was to contain the crowd, not disburse it. A long line of police blocked Eternal Peace Avenue, diverting traffic to the lanes east of the monument. Yet, they were unable or unwilling to stop the bicyclists approaching the square from the west.

They came by the thousands. Most were not riding their bicycles but walking beside them, continually ringing their bicycle bells as they came. The shrill brrring, brrring, brrring of the bells grew louder as they neared the square, overpowering the sounds of traffic and drowning out the cheers of the crowd.

After what seemed like only minutes I glanced at my watch to find that over an hour had passed. With the traffic tied up, it was unlikely I would be able to reach Double Well Village in time to catch the last bus of the evening, so I walked back to the Beijing Hotel to get a taxi.

The driver muttered under his breath when I told him my destination, then said he would have to detour around Eternal Peace Avenue. As I knew the meter charged by mileage and any delay would cost him money, I offered to pay extra if he would drive me past the square. Giving me the once-over in the rearview mirror, he asked my nationality. I wondered if he thought the answer might explain my irrational behavior, but when I said "American," his face broke into a wide grin, and he gave me the same warm response that answer usually receives in China. Holding his thumb in the air, he said, *"Hao jile* (Terrific)!"

As we turned toward the square, the crowds' cheers blended in with the sounds of engines idling, impatient drivers honking their horns, and traffic police blowing on their whistles. With a nod toward the square, the driver said, "You should take photographs," then clucked his tongue in disappointment when I told him I hadn't brought my camera.

"You're a teacher?" he said, using the Chinese grammatical form that made it more of an assumption than a question. It was the most logical assumption because of my age and destination, but I had to disappoint him once again by admitting that I was merely a student. Hoping to regain some face, I quickly added that I studied Chinese language and history. He nodded as if he finally understood my interest in what was happening on the square, then braked and moved the car forward even more slowly than the traffic would allow. The policeman standing just ahead of us was less understanding. Blowing a long, shrill blast on his whistle, he motioned us forward with an exaggerated gesture, then snapped at the driver, *"Kuai, kuai, kuai* (Hurry, hurry, hurry)!"

The driver picked up even more speed as we rounded the corner. As we drove down Front Gate Avenue, he pointed back toward the square and said, "That is Chinese history!"

I waited for him to say more, but he turned his attention to the traffic. He didn't speak again until we reached Great Knowledge Boulevard. As we neared the campus, he looked at me again in the rearview mirror and told me that the students had gone to *Zhongnanhai*, the leaders' compound, Tuesday night despite the government's broadcast warning the students not to demonstrate again. "The students were reminded that they should consider their parents and their future," he said. Nevertheless, they had marched to *Zhongnanhai* and stayed in front of the compound until almost dawn.

He slowed the cab and turned onto Fragrant Flower Road, then drove toward the back gate of the campus. "They shouted slogans," he said. "They even shouted 'Li Peng come out!' Then they demanded that the leaders reveal how much money they have." Shaking his head in amazement, he repeated "Li Peng, come out," as he pulled the cab to a halt just a few feet from the gate.

As I paid the driver, I asked what he thought about the students making demands. He shrugged and answered, "I would also like to know how much money the leaders have." He chuckled softly, probably at the absurdity of such a thought.

When I returned to *San Lou,* Jinjin told me Hong Xin had come to our room that afternoon. She had left a message telling me that she had plans for the evening, but would try to come to visit me again on Thursday afternoon. I couldn't help wondering if her plans for the evening had included going to Tiananmen Square.

Thursday was a cold, gloomy day, and it started to drizzle shortly after noon. It was a perfect afternoon to take advantage of *xiuxi,* but I stayed awake waiting for Hong Xin to stop by. However, she didn't appear and at three o'clock, I went down to call Mr. Liu at the association.

As a scholarship student, I was entitled to a white card, and since the Association had given me only Renminbi for spending money, I really needed the card. Earlier in the week, I had gone to the administrative office in my classroom building to request a white card from the university. Jin Caihong, the teacher who had processed my registration when I arrived at the university, listened to my request sympathetically, but explained that the university could not approve the card since I was a "special case." As my scholarship had not been granted through the university but through a government agency, it was up to the agency to provide me with a white card. Teacher Jin did offer to assist me by contacting Mr. Liu to request the card, and Thursday during break she looked me up to ask if he had called with any news about the card. Actually, I had not heard from either Mr. Liu or Mr. Jiang since our luncheon at the Beijing Hotel. However, they had encouraged me to contact them if I had a problem, so I dialed the Association's number, mentally preparing myself to contend with the switchboard operator.

In general, switchboard operators in China do little for one's sanity and are a contributing factor to high blood pressure. The first few calls to any Chinese institution usually result in a busy signal. Persistent dialing will eventually result in the line ringing through, but that does not ensure that the switchboard operator will answer it. If she does answer and agrees to put your call through, you say a silent prayer that the person you are calling will answer his extension immediately. Otherwise, after two or three rings, you get the old "click-buzz" routine, and find that the operator has discon-nected the line unceremoniously, without giving you a chance to ask for another extension or leave a message.

That day the gods were with me. The line rang through on the first try, the switchboard operator understood my Chinese, and Mr. Liu answered on the first ring. After a polite exchange of greetings, I inquired as to the status of my white card. Mr. Liu replied that things were progressing smoothly, and reported that after speaking with Teacher Jin, he and Mr. Jiang and other members of his department staff had held meetings to discuss the matter. In a cheerful voice he assured me that a decision would probably be made "any day now," and suggested that I check back with him "in a couple of weeks."

Thanking Mr. Liu graciously, I hung up the phone knowing full well that I had been assigned to bureaucratic purgatory. Just as the school hadn't wanted to take responsibility for the decision, it appeared Mr. Liu's department was also unwilling to take on the burden. The cause of the problem was clear. Although I was not a self-financed student, I was also not the standard scholarship student. In short, as a "special case," I was a bureaucrat's nightmare, and therefore an untouchable. I had become a victim of the "NFNF Syndrome." As "neither fish nor fowl," any decisions regarding me should best be avoided. Decision making can be especially perilous in China, and to make a decision without a long list of precedents only increases the risk. The most logical way for those at the Association to deal with this situation was to DISCUSS. If they could continue to DISCUSS the matter until I left China, so much the better, as there would no longer be a need for a decision. As Mr. Liu had requested, I would call back in a couple of weeks, aware that it would be an exercise in *deja vu* with our conversation repeated word for word.

Depressed by the telephone call and the drizzle that soon turned into a steady downpour, I went back to my room to drown my sorrows in a cup of jasmine tea. I had given up on Hong Xin coming to visit, and since Jinjin had gone to study with friends, I expected to spend a miserable evening alone. However, a few minutes after eight o'clock, a rather damp Lu Minghua arrived. Worried that I might not have an umbrella, she had trudged through the rain to bring me the small black umbrella that I had sent her as a Christmas gift.

Lu Minghua was just the medicine I needed to cheer me up, and she had come full of small lane news about the demonstrations. She turned on the recorder while I poured her a cup of hot tea to take away the chill, and gave her a bowl of nuts to munch on. My hostess duties completed, I sat back on my bed and told her what I had seen on Wednesday at Tiananmen Square.

"You left too soon!" she told me. "The students marched from Tiananmen to *Zhongnanhai*. I heard there were as many as six thousand students. After midnight the police moved in, pushing and shoving the students, cursing them and hitting them with their belts. They arrested over one hundred, and I heard several students were injured."

I was surprised that the situation had escalated to violence since the police at Tiananmen Square had appeared to pay more attention to the traffic than the students. However, Lu Minghua was better educated than I in tactics of suppression.

"Little Sister, they waited until after midnight so fewer people would see what was happening. *Xinhua* News Agency* claimed that the police thought the students were going to try to storm the gate at *Zhongnanhai*. They accused the students of throwing shoes, bottles, and bricks at the guards, injuring four or five guards, but my students say that's a lie. My students said that everything was orderly until the police began to beat the students and make arrests. Then, students in the crowd yelled at the police, calling them Fascists and Nazis."

Lu Minghua went on to tell me she had heard that those who were arrested had already been released, and the students at *Beida* (Beijing University) had held a rally at noon to protest the violence. "They planned to march to the square, but with this rain, I don't know how many made it. The government announced there will be an official funeral for Hu Yaobang on Saturday, but they said the square would be closed off. I think the leaders are concerned because they didn't expect the students to react to Hu's death so strongly. They should realize that people are angry that Hu was sacrificed, and more and more people believe that political reform is long overdue."

Since it was almost time for the evening news, Lu Minghua suggested we go downstairs to the TV room. The door was locked as usual, but Lu Minghua got the key from the *shiwuyuan* in time for us to watch most of the news. The reception on the television set ranged from multi-colored

---

*Xinhua (New China) News Agency is the largest of China's two news agencies. It releases news reports, feature articles, and news photos to newspapers, radio stations, and television stations in China and abroad.

snow to pictures that had multiple ghost images. However, even that poor reception was a miracle considering that the antenna was a piece of wire that ran from the TV to the window where it dangled outside about a foot from the ground.

The announcer stated that any further demonstrations would be dealt with "severely according to the law," then added that "further protests will not be allowed." In a stern voice, the announcer stated, "Comrade Hu should be honored with a dignified funeral and those who mourn should not disrupt public order."

Lu Minghua rolled her eyes at me as the announcer ended his report by saying, "A small minority of demonstrators desire to overthrow the government and the Party. It is their aim to have a China dominated by chaos."

Despite the weather and Lu Minghua's protests, I walked with her to the front gate, insisting that I was glad for the opportunity to get outside. When we reached the gate, I asked Lu Minghua what would happen if the students demonstrated at Hu's funeral. With a sigh she said, *"Zenme ban, zenme ban* (what's to be done)," but in this case, it meant she was worried what the outcome might be.

The rain had stopped by Friday morning, and it was a beautiful, cloudless day. I had planned to ride over to *Beida* to check out the *Sanjiaodi* (Triangular Area), the traditional place for posting *dazibao* at *Beida,* but Hong Xin arrived full of apologies for not having come the day before.

As she inquired about my classes and what news I had from my family, she was as animated and friendly as she had been the first day I met her. When she asked what I had been doing, it gave me the opening to discuss Hu's death and the student demonstrations. I told Hong Xin about the demonstration I had seen at Tiananmen Square, and mentioned the *dazibao* in her dormitory. Although she wasn't actually reticent about discussing the demonstrations, she did appear to become more cautious, choosing her words very carefully. While part of the reason could have been that we were speaking in English, I felt there was more to it than that. Of course, Hong Xin and I barely knew each other, so I certainly did not expect her to bare her political soul to me. Nor was I about to tell her exactly what I thought until I had a clearer idea of where her sympathies lay.

I switched the topic of conversation away from the demonstrations, but Hong Xin only stayed for a few minutes longer, announcing abruptly that she had to be leaving since she was "keeping me from my busy schedule." As I walked her to the front door of the dormitory, she mentioned again that she wanted to bring her friend, Mr. Liang, to meet me.

It was too late to ride to *Beida* and get back before the *shitang* closed. Instead, I rode up Fragrant Flower Road, then cut off on one of the small lanes tucked back behind the main streets. There is another world back there; a world filled with a maze of alleys connecting small neighborhoods that look like something out of rural China, alien to the surrounding city. Belonging to another century, tiny, box-like clay brick houses are jammed together in tight little clusters. Without room for a blade of grass to grow, much less a tree, they are set in a world of monochrome. The houses, the narrow dirt paths that wind past them, and even the slivers of sky that peak through between the roofs are all cast in pale shades of sienna.

The paths twisted and turned so sharply that, at times, I feared I might ride straight into one of the houses, bringing terror to some unsuspecting family as they sat down to eat their evening meal. As it was, I startled more than one hapless soul who rounded a corner only to find himself face to face with a *yang guizi* (foreign devil) on a bike. Older children met my sudden appearance with expressions of amusement, if not outright laughter. Younger children looked at me with trepidation, and a toddler, squatting bare-bottomed in his doorway, stared up at me in frozen horror. Too frightened to move, he screamed for his mother who peered out to see what was causing the commotion. Stopping my bike briefly, I apologized for having scared her son. She smiled and said, "No problem," then grabbed her terrified child by the hand, scolding him as she pulled him inside.

As I rode through the alleys, I thought about Hong Xin's visit. I remembered how candid she had been in discussing the problems of Chinese students when we first met. However, discussing those problems was not the same as stating any personal support for or involvement in the demonstrations. The more I thought about it, the more convinced I was that Hong Xin did support the demonstrations, and perhaps had even participated in them. Yet, it had been foolish of me to initiate the discussion. I should have waited until she brought up the topic herself. Although Chinese usually spoke more openly with foreigners than with other Chinese, as Mr. Gao had pointed out, Chinese are taught by their culture and history to guard their words. The very structure of the Chinese language not only lends itself easily to poetry and puns, but is also filled with euphemisms and idioms so that something distasteful or sensitive can be said in a more delicate or obscure manner.

The Chinese know the danger of criticizing those in power and frequently avoid doing so directly by reaching back into history for a parallel. Even that could not always guarantee protection as Wu Han, a former vice-mayor of Beijing had found out. The first attack of the Cultural Revolution was launched against Wu Han in 1965 for his play, "The Dismissal of Hai Jui." Although the play was set in the Ming Dynasty, Wu Han was attacked for using this historical reference to criticize Mao's demotion of Defense Minister Peng Dehuai in 1959 when Peng dared to expose the failures of the Great Leap Forward.

Others had learned another harsh lesson on communication during the Cultural Revolution. They had become distrustful of everyone after many people had been reported, not only by friends but also by spouses and children, for making counterrevolutionary statements. After living through the Cultural Revolution, people had learned the value of prudence the hard way by being persecuted or imprisoned for something they had said in the past. More often than not, their remarks had seemed harmless at the time.

Although she had spoken only in general terms, Hong Xin had discussed the demonstrations briefly. She had told me that a thousand students at *Beida* had decided to boycott classes, and since Beida usually takes the lead in political action among the students of Beijing, it would be reasonable to conclude that students from other universities would join the boycott. She had also mentioned that students from several Beijing universities planned to stage a sit-in at Tiananmen Square that very night.

It was a logical plan. Since the government had declared the square would be closed off to the public on Saturday for the funeral, the students would defeat the government's purpose in closing off the square by going Friday night, thus avoiding conflict with the police.

As I rode back to the dormitory, I decided I would not go to the square the next day for the funeral. Although I wanted to go, if for no other reason than the chance to witness a historical event, after my discussion with Hong

Xin, I felt that the funeral and the sit-in were a "family matter." Despite my deep affection and admiration for the Chinese people, I am not family.

Saturday I dealt with my frustration at not being on the square by busying myself with housekeeping chores. I did take a break from my chores to watch the official memorial for Hu Yaobang, which was carried live on television. However, the reception on the dorm television was at its lowest point. On Sunday I went with Yuanli and his family for an outing to Grand View Garden. The garden was built as the set for the televised adaptation of the classic Chinese novel, *A Dream of Red Mansions,* and after the filming was completed, it was turned into a public park. Yuanli had arranged for a driver and car from his *danwei* to take us, and he, Suyu, and Leilei arrived around nine to pick me up.

As we rode across town to the garden, Yuanli told me that more than one hundred thousand students had gone to the square on Friday evening and stayed there through the night. There had been numerous speeches honoring Hu and calling for political reform. In addition to students, Ren Wanding, a veteran of Democracy Wall, had addressed the crowd. During the time of Democracy Wall, Ren had been the leader of a group known as the Chinese Human Rights Alliance. After Wei Jingsheng had been arrested, Ren had put up a *dazibao* protesting Wei's arrest although they were not members of the same group and did not always agree politically. As a result of his support for Wei and his poster criticizing Wei's arrest, Ren was also imprisoned. In his speech at Tiananmen Square, Ren had told the students that their demonstrations and their demands for political reform were necessary, declaring "Democracy Wall lives again!"

Growing more excited as he described the scene on the square during Hu's memorial service, Yuanli said, "There was a police line in front of the Great Hall of the People that was three people deep. At one point, two or three thousand students tried to walk through the police line to enter the Hall, but the guards refused to let them pass. The students outnumbered the police, but since they didn't want a violent confrontation, they obeyed the police. When the broadcast of the services started, all the students sat in the square in silence, listening. After the service, three students were allowed to cross the police line. They climbed the steps of the Great Hall of the People to present a petition stating the students' demands."

The students had knelt on the steps of the Great Hall of the People to present their petition demanding a dialogue with the leaders, freedom of the press and speech, more money allotted for education, a re-evaluation of Hu and the reforms which he had supported, and an end to official profiteering and nepotism. As he knelt with arms stretched, one student held the petition high over his head. It was the manner in which petitions had been presented to emperors in the past, to show the petitioner's respect for authority. While the students had asked that Li Peng accept the petition, and there had been rumors on the square that Li had agreed to do so, no one came forward to accept the Petition. The three were finally allowed to enter the hall as a delegation representing all the students on the square. Once they were inside, the petition was accepted; however, it was received by a minor official.

"The leaders wanted to humiliate the students," Yuanli said bitterly. "The students treated the leaders respectfully, but the leaders just ignored them."

The students in the square had been angered by the government's treatment of their classmates. Many had cried in frustration, seeing the government's slight as further proof that nothing would change in China as long as the present leadership was in control. I told Yuanli that I felt the government had made a grave tactical error by showing contempt for the students and ignoring their demands. Had someone come out to accept the petition, even the minor official who had received it inside the hall, it would have indicated to the students that their demands would be addressed. By refusing to accept the petition on the steps of the hall, the leaders were sending a message to the students, and the people as well, that Party leaders were above criticism. The image of the three students kneeling on the steps was a symbol of the leaders' disregard for the will of the people, and that symbol would linger in people's minds for a long time to come.

Yuanli nodded in agreement. "It was foolish. To slight the students just stirs up more anger. Now the students will boycott classes until the leaders agree to meet with them and hear their demands."

Having grown impatient with the long ride, Leilei started to whine.

Yuanli reached over and took him from Suyu. Speaking softly to his son, Yuanli calmed him with the promise of a popsicle as soon as we arrived at the garden. I felt guilty for having spoken in English for such a long time. It had excluded Suyu from the conversation, and probably contributed to Leilei's restlessness.

Suyu took my hand as we walked through the compound, explaining which character had lived in each house, retelling the stories of the novel that seemed so real to her. Listening to her talk, one could believe the characters had actually existed, and had lived at Grand View. By the time we reached the small pavilion where the main characters, Baoyu and Daiyu, had frequently met, I half expected to see the ill-fated lovers standing there in the flesh.

As Suyu tended Leilei while he fed the fish in the large pool at the center of the garden, Yuanli and I sat on a rock near the water, talking and watching Leilei as he played. Yuanli asked why I had not gone to Hu's funeral. When I explained that I felt I didn't belong, he shrugged and said, "I understand your reasoning, but I think you should have gone. Have you heard about the demonstration planned for May 4th?"

Even before I had left for China, there had been articles in the press predicting that students would demonstrate on May 4th because of the historical significance of the date. As the seventieth anniversary of the May 4th Movement of 1919 approached, a movement that had also been started in Beijing by university students, it now seemed a certainty that a major demonstration would be held. Over the past few days the small lane news had carried the rumor that a grand-scale demonstration was in the works.

Yuanli said, "You should go. It's important for foreigners to see what is happening here." As further enticement, he added, "It will be much larger than the other demonstrations."

As we talked, I realized that I had already decided to go to the May 4th demonstration. I told Yuanli I would not only go, but photograph it as well.

"Good. I am also glad that you are taking notes. You must continue to write everything down, but keep your notes in a safe place."

Laughing, I told Yuanli that I was not only taking notes, but my letters to my family had become my journal. Since Hu's death, the letters were each at least twenty pages long. It had seemed safer to mail my journal home than to leave it lying around my room where someone else could read it. I had made that decision after Teacher Jin stopped by my room for a visit. As we chatted, she made a thorough inspection of every item on my desk, opening each container and examining the contents, picking up my notebooks and flipping through the pages, and reading every scrap of paper on my desk. Had she opened the desk drawers and rummaged through them as well, it would not have surprised me. However, knowing the Chinese attitude toward privacy, my Western sensibilities had been neither offended nor shocked. In fact, I had learned long before to keep anything that wasn't meant for public consumption locked away in my suitcase.

We sat quietly for awhile, then Yuanli asked, "Do you know the idiom, *'xingxing zhi huo, keyi liao yuan'*? It means, a single spark can start a prairie fire."

"You really think this is going to escalate, don't you?"

"Yes. People are tired of living lives filled with nothing but bitterness. There is no real freedom in China, and unless things change drastically, there is no future in China. People are fed up with the corruption. We are tired of the same old promises and the same old lies."

Although wide-spread corruption had been a popular topic for Western business and political journals as well as newspapers both inside and outside of China, it seemed that very little was actually being done to correct the situation. There were periodic investigations and even some arrests, but the arrests usually involved only lower level officials or their relatives. As China became more open to Western investors and expanded the programs of privatization, officials and their relatives had taken advantage of the economic reforms, using their power and *guanxi* for personal gain. Many foreign individuals and corporations doing business with China had found that one business tradition of old China, paying "squeeze" to those officials who could assist them, was once again in fashion. "Squeeze" could be anything from imported electrical appliances to sponsorship of an official's child who wished to attend college in the West.

Officials who managed factories would help themselves to products their company produced without bothering to pay for them and order items for their own personal use while billing the factory for their purchases. Officials and their relatives also used their *guanxi* to obtain licenses for private enterprises, which were limited in number and, therefore, difficult to obtain. They would use the licenses to establish trading companies, then turn a hefty profit by speculating in the black market on products that were rationed or otherwise in short supply.

One case of *guandao* (official profiteering) which received considerable attention in the Western press involved the questionable business practices of Deng Pufang, the disabled son of Deng Xiaoping. During the Cultural Revolution, Deng Pufang, a student at *Beida*, had been thrown from a building and denied medical treatment for his injuries when his father came under attack by the Gang of Four. The incident left Deng Pufang paralyzed, and after Deng Xiaoping came to power, he appointed his son head of the China Welfare Fund for the Handicapped.

In October, 1988 the Kang Hua Development Corporation, a company run by Deng Pufang, and which benefited from his tax-free status, was ordered to cut its ties with the China Welfare Fund for the Handicapped. Additionally, the company was ordered to stop dealing in foreign goods and scarce products.

As a result of the investigation, which involved Kang Hua Development Corporation and other companies with connections to relatives of high-ranking officials, hundreds of companies were ordered to suspend business activities. However, rather than being a serious crackdown on corruption, the investigation and subsequent penalties were a tactic used by Deng Xiaoping to protect his program of economic reforms from further attacks by Chen Yun and other hard-liners, who criticized the reforms for providing opportunities for profiteering. Additionally, by slapping the hand of his own son, Deng could stonewall the push for political reform, which might have led to a genuine investigation of corruption in the government. With corruption extending from the local and provincial levels all the way up to the central level of government, such an investigation would certainly have had profound consequences and could have struck at the very core of China's leadership. As Yuanli had said, "the same old promises and the same old lies" had left people disillusioned with their leadership and angered by its corruption.

The campus appeared to be as serene as usual when Yuanli brought me home Sunday evening. However, by Monday morning, *dazibao* were posted along the front wall of Building #8, out in the open for all to read. It was apparent that the "*dazibao* fairy" had spent a busy night on our campus, for there was even a *dazibao* hanging in the glass-covered, wooden stand in front of Building #12 where my classroom was located.

The *dazibao* on Building #8 gave a full account of all that had transpired at Tiananmen Square on Friday and Saturday, and listed the demands the students had made. While the crowd gathered around the *dazibao* in front of Building #12 made it difficult for those of us in the back to see, I could read enough to determine that it announced the student boycott, called on professors to join the students in the boycott, and stated that students would not return to their classes until the leaders had agreed to a dialogue to address the students' demands.

Thinking I would be able to read the *dazibao* without having to peer over someone's shoulder, I rode back to Building #12 just before dinner. However, I was astonished when I pulled up to Building #12. The *dazibao* and the glass-covered, wooden stand in which it had been posted had vanished. All that remained were a few splinters of wood, and the two holes in the ground where the stand had been anchored.

CHAPTER TEN

CHINA'S HOPE

Lu Minghua paced back and forth across my small room, her voice rising with anger as she spoke about the editorial in the *Renminbao* (*People's Daily*). Although the editorial had appeared in the Wednesday, April 26th edition of the paper, it had been read word for word over national television on Tuesday. It had also been read over campus broadcast systems throughout Beijing, along with an admonishment to students stating that the boycott of classes was in violation of the law and in opposition to the Communist Party. Once again, the students were warned to think of the consequences to themselves and to their families, and cautioned that they must not respond to peer pressure or allow a small group of troublemakers to mislead them.

Clearly, the leadership of China had growing concern that a massive social movement was on the verge of developing throughout China. In addition to the sit-in at Tiananmen Square on Saturday, Xinhua News Agency had reported incidents in Xian and Changsha.* Although students had not been involved in either incident, these events were perhaps more troublesome to the leaders as they indicated that other segments of society were taking to the streets.

The support the students were receiving from workers and the general population of Beijing surely heightened the concern of Party leaders. There had been visible support from the crowds who had gathered around

---

*Xian, the capital of Shaanxi Province is approximately 1200 kilometers west of Beijing, and Changsha, the capital of Hunan Province is approximately 1600 kilometers south of Beijing.

Tiananmen Square during the funeral proceedings for Hu, and although police had prevented people from entering the square during the service, afterward the crowd moved in to join the students. Crowds had also lined the streets and applauded the students when they marched back to the campuses Saturday evening.

Although the government had intended to humiliate the students with the incident on the steps of the Great Hall of the People, it was the government who had actually lost face. The students had achieved a victory. They had not been cowed by the government's warnings to stay away from the square, and by arriving on Friday night, they had outwitted the government's attempt to prevent protesters from congregating in the square during Hu's Memorial. The visible support the students had received from the *laobaixing* made that victory even sweeter.

The obvious success of the students' boycott of classes alarmed Party leaders and further encouraged the students. Xinhua News Agency had estimated that 60,000 of the 160,000 college students in Beijing had joined the boycott. However, it was more likely that the students were correct in claiming that the government's estimate was too low since students from forty universities were participating.

Students had gone to the *laobaixing* to collect donations, distributed leaflets explaining their demands, and staged rallies on their campuses. In less than two weeks, the student demonstrations for democracy had surpassed those of past years. They were better organized, had more financial support, and most important, had support from the *laobaixing*.

It was apparent that the students were developing a true political movement. Under the umbrella of the Autonomous Students Associations of Beijing (ASAB), students on campuses throughout the city had established independent student organizations. These organizations, unlike the government sanctioned student organizations, had been formed by the students themselves. The founding of ASAB was a critical step in organizing the student movement and a bold move, as it was the first time any organizations independent of government control had been established in the People's Republic of China.

Several student leaders had emerged on the various campuses, and they worked together to coordinate the efforts of the student movement.

Wang Dan, a twenty-two year old native of Jilin Province and a history major at *Beida,* along with Wuer Kaixi, a twenty-one year old education management major at Beijing Normal University, were the most visible student leaders and spokesmen for the movement. Wang Dan, a brilliant student, a natural leader, and a friend of both Fang Lizhi and his wife Li Zhuxian, had been active in organizing democracy salons at *Beida.* Wuer Kaixi, an Uighur (one of China's minority nationalities), had been raised in Beijing even though his parents were from Xinjiang Province. His boyish good looks, his flamboyant style, and his bold and eloquent speeches had vaulted him into a position of leadership.

The students' boycott of classes had left Party leaders in the position of having to make the next move. There were several ways the leaders could respond to the students. The most benign approach would be to capitulate to at least some of the student demands. They could agree to a dialogue with representatives from ASAB; intensify campaigns to expose corruption within the government; remove, or at least loosen, government control of the press; and rescind the 1980 restrictions on freedom of speech. It was unlikely, however, that the leaders would consider this option. The hard-liners would not accept any of these concessions, and Deng had already demonstrated repeatedly that he queued up with the hard-liners on political reform.

Deng, a veteran of the Long March, and the other Old Revolutionaries of the Party had survived the war against the Japanese, civil war with the *Guomindang* (Nationalists), and the turbulence of the Mao years, most significantly, the Cultural Revolution. In their minds, only they knew what was best for China and only they or their appointed successors had the right to rule. Moreover, the success of Deng's economic reforms had already been placed in jeopardy, and the continuing game of political musical chairs within the upper echelon of the Party between moderates and hard-liners had weakened the Party. To allow political reform at such a vulnerable time would certainly diminish the power of the Old Revolutionaries and might bring down the Communist Dynasty. While Deng had announced his intention to resign his only remaining official posts as Chairman of the Party Central Military Committee and the State Central Military Committee, he would continue to be the supreme leader of China even after his planned retirement. Deng and the other Old Revolutionaries would not voluntarily relinquish their power; nor would they allow students, other intellectuals, or the *laobaixing* to have a voice in determining government policy.

The more drastic response to the boycott—to immediately arrest all of the student leaders, and perhaps even declare them to be counterrevolutionaries—was also highly unlikely. With May Fourth just days away, the arrests of students would only serve to exacerbate the dissension within the Party and the discontent within the populace. Indeed, arrest or other overt political harassment of students might mobilize the *laobaixing* to "storm the Bastille."

Another option would be to de-emphasize the movement, with the hope that it would lose momentum and die a natural death. The students did have to consider their futures, and as the end of the term drew nearer, examinations might take precedence over politics. However, when Hu had used that tactic during the 1986-1987 demonstrations, it had resulted in his forced resignation.

A factor the leadership would certainly consider in deciding how best to deal with the students was the upcoming Sino-Soviet Summit. As the first meeting between Chinese and Soviet leaders in thirty years, and the first visit to China by a Soviet head of state, the summit would be Deng's most dramatic accomplishment as a world leader. Gorbachev had made concessions to Deng in order to get him to agree to the summit, making the summit all the more prestigious for Deng. In addition to agreeing to meet in China, Gorbachev had withdrawn troops from Afghanistan, pressed the Vietnamese to leave Cambodia, and reduced the number of troops stationed along the Chinese border. Unquestionably, the success of the summit was a top priority for Deng, as it was a splendid finale to his career as the leader of China.

After the Politburo meeting on Monday, April 24th, the immediate strategy of the leaders was to fire a "warning shot" by launching a verbal assault on the students that would signal the government's intention to take a hard line in dealing with the student movement. The leaders used the April 26th editorial in the *People's Daily* for this purpose, lashing out in a fierce attack against the student movement in terms that sounded like something left over from the Cultural Revolution.* The intent of the editorial was to make clear the hard-line attitude of the leadership, and to send the students scurrying back to their classrooms while intimidating those who might support the students into a silence of fear. It was the same tactic the government had used successfully to abort student movements in the past.

However, people were shocked by the use of exceptionally harsh language and the general tone of the editorial, which attacked the patriotism of the students and labeled the movement counterrevolutionary. Moreover, the use of certain "code words" from the Cultural Revolution gave the editorial added psychological impact. One such phrase was "*da-za-qiang*" (beating, smashing, and looting), but the most malicious and offensive word was "*dongluan.*" While the English translation is turmoil or chaos, in Chinese *dongluan* is a word which brings forth images of plundering and rioting in the streets, and the use of *dongluan* was especially contemptuous since the Cultural Revolution is known as "*Shi NianDongluan Shi Qi*" (The Decade of Turmoil).

The Cultural Revolution was the most disastrous period in the history of the People's Republic of China. Having scarred every Chinese either directly or indirectly, it had left China a nation of victims. Although it had been instigated and directed by the government, no one could forget the part the Red Guards had played in the horrors of the Cultural Revolution. By using *dongluan* repeatedly, the editorial implied a similarity between the students of 1989 and the Red Guards of the Cultural Revolution; a less than subtle reminder of what could happen when students were allowed to go on a rampage.

However, the leaders had overplayed their hand and factored in the wrong reaction to the editorial. It was a miscalculation that underscored just how out-of-touch with the populace the leaders of the Party had become. People were not intimidated by the editorial, but infuriated by it. Mistrust of the Party, Party officials, and the leaders of China had deepened over the past few years. But the people did trust the students and did know

---

*The organ of the Central Committee of the Chinese Communist Party, the *People's Daily* has a daily circulation in excess of five million copies.

them to be patriotic. Furthermore, they felt the students' demands were reasonable and represented the will of the people. Therefore, the Party's attack on the students' patriotism for voicing these demands only intensified the frustration and ire felt by the *laobaixing*.

The editorial was the chief topic of conversation throughout the city. Both Yuanli and Shanli called to ask if I knew about the editorial, and when I saw Hong Xin on my way to breakfast, she stopped to ask if I had heard the broadcast of the editorial. While she had been reserved in speaking about the student movement before, now her eyes flashed with anger and she spat out her words as she labeled the editorial a vicious attack that had twisted and distorted what the movement was trying to accomplish.

After *xiuxi,* I stopped by to check on Lao Pang and The Professor. The Professor was still resting, so I only stuck my head into his room to say hello, but Lao Pang and Little Ma sat down with me over a cup of tea. Although Lao Pang had little to say about the editorial, I could tell she was concerned about The Professor's reaction. She worked hard at keeping their lives as serene and uncomplicated as possible. To her, the editorial was an unnecessary agitation that had angered The Professor, put him in a foul mood, and caused him to only nibble at his food.

Little Ma, on the other hand, was excited by the controversy. With enthusiasm, she repeated the comments she had overheard while doing her daily shopping at Yeyinglu. I expressed my dismay that people had been discussing the editorial in such a public place, and asked, "Isn't it dangerous for people to speak so openly?"

Little Ma shrugged her shoulders and said, "But everyone has the same opinion. No one agreed with the editorial." She giggled and added, "It certainly made shopping more interesting."

Lao Pang lent me her copy of the paper so I could take it to my room and read the editorial in full. Although I had heard the radio broadcast, I only understood enough to get the general gist of what was being said. With the assistance of my dictionaries and a large cup of tea to fortify me, I went to work on the translation in the solitude of my room.

The editorial opened by stating that during the Memorial for Hu, "a number of abnormal situations had occurred," and "a very small number of people took advantage of the opportunity to fabricate baseless rumors and attack leaders." It accused this "small number of people" of attempting "to seduce the masses to attack Xinhuamen* at *Zhongnanhai.*"

According to the editorial, the authorities had asked for "discipline and order so that the funeral ceremony for Comrade Hu Yaobang could be carried out with dignity in a solemn manner. However, after the ceremony a small number of people with ulterior motives took advantage of the grief felt by the young students at the passing of Comrade Hu Yaobang to fabricate rumors, corrupt the hearts and minds of the masses, and use big and small character posters to defame and vilify the leaders of the party."

The editorial accused the "small number of people" of "openly violating the constitution by inciting opposition to the leaders, the Party, and socialism," as well as using the "banner of democracy" to destroy both democracy and the legal system. It further claimed that their purpose was "to poison the hearts and minds of the people, create turmoil throughout the country, and sabotage the political stability and unity of the country."

The editorial claimed that if the situation were tolerated, it would result in absolute chaos. "Programs such as reform, opening to the outside, rectification, and regularization of prices, raising the living standard, opposing corruption, and the development of democracy and legality would vanish into thin air. A China filled with hope would be transformed into a land of turmoil without peace or hope, and the great reforms of the past ten years would have been for naught."

It declared the independent student organizations illegal, and stated that, "those who are deliberate rumormongers, who circulate false accusations, should be thoroughly investigated. We must stop illegal marches and demonstrations." According to the editorial, the only way that democracy could be implemented or corruption could be abolished would be under the leadership of the Party. It ended by declaring, "We must resolutely struggle to swiftly end this incitement to turmoil."

After reading the editorial, I could understand even more clearly why the people were so distraught. There had been no attempt to list or explain the demands of the students. Although China had been saturated with the

---

*Xinhuamen, the front gate of the leaders' compound is located on Eternal Peace Avenue.

editorial, there had not been any articles in the press outlining the problems and issues that the students wanted the leaders to address. While the people of Beijing knew the truth about the student movement, the rest of the country had not been given a fair and accurate account of what the students were trying to achieve. By referring to the incidents, which had happened in Xian and Changsha, the editorial had associated the student movement with those who had rioted, looted, and burned property, leaving the impression that the movement was composed of a small band of ruffians out to demolish the government and destroy China in the process.

Although Lu Minghua had not told me she would stop by, I felt certain that she would come over to discuss the editorial. Just as I finished translating the editorial, she arrived. As she entered the room, I noticed the dark circles under her eyes. She sat down at the desk and turned on the recorder while I poured her tea and set out a bowl of nuts. She shook her head when I set the bowl in front of her, and told me that she had not been able to eat all day. I urged her to at least drink the tea, telling her how exhausted she looked.

"Little Sister, I hardly slept last night. I couldn't stop worrying about the students. I was so angry about the editorial that my heart raced as I lay in bed thinking about it."

Pointing to the newspaper and my notes on the table, I told her that I had been working on the editorial. Lu Minghua picked up the paper and went over the editorial with me, grimacing each time we came to the characters *dongluan*. When we had finished reading it, Lu Minghua told me that according to the small lane news, Deng Xiaoping had personally supervised the writing of the editorial.

Rising from the chair, she started to pace back and forth as she talked. "Deng Xiaoping is not the hope of China. The Communist Party is not the hope of China. It is the students who are the hope of China. They are our best minds, our future. They are not a bunch of hooligans. They are patriotic Chinese who care deeply about our country. This country is the People's Republic of China, not the private property of a few old men." Shaking her head sadly, she said, "why won't they listen to the people? If they would just sit down and meet with the leaders of the student movement, and show serious intent to deal with the problems that the students have addressed, the students would go back to their classrooms."

I asked Lu Minghua if a dialogue would really accomplish more than a moral victory for the students. Tyrants are always superb at excusing their actions. The Party leaders would just say they were already addressing the problems of China, and as proof, point to the economic reforms and improvements that had been made in living standards over the years. As to political reforms, the Chinese constitution already guarantees freedom of speech. Of course, freedom of speech "Chinese style" means that it is illegal to say or print anything that runs counter to the Four Cardinal Principles of Socialism. However, the Four Cardinal Principles (to keep to the socialist road, uphold the dictatorship of the proletariat, uphold the leadership of the Communist Party, and uphold Marxism-Leninism-Mao Zedong Thought), are so vague that almost any statement can be interpreted as being in opposition to them.

"That is the same old argument we have been given for years. They tell us to look at how much better things are today than they were in the past. For years we did compare the China of today with old China. We applauded the advancements our country had made. We were proud of our accomplishments. We knew people were still poor, but we were told to just be patient. After all, Chinese are experts at being patient.

"We were told to believe in the Party and the leadership. But after China opened up to the outside world, we no longer compared new China to old China. Instead, we began to compare China to the rest of the world, and we didn't like what we saw. Look at the Four Little Dragons of Asia: Singapore, South Korea, Hong Kong, and Taiwan. Look how much better the people live in those countries. We see how our cousins in Taiwan, Hong Kong, and Singapore live, and we are furious. It only proves that the Chinese are a hardworking, diligent, and ambitious people.

"Look at Japan, the giant dragon of Asia. Japan is not a better country than China. The Japanese based their written language on Chinese, and took so much of their culture from our culture. The Japanese people are no better than the Chinese people. We could also achieve a strong country if we were given the freedom to do so. We just want the opportunity to determine our own future. If one does not want to work to achieve a better life, then he should be willing to accept a life of bitterness. But, if he is diligent, if he is willing to work hard, he should be rewarded for his sacrifices. Only Party officials and their relatives live well in China. For the rest of us, it does not matter how much a person struggles, his life is still mostly bitterness.

"The editorial talks about turmoil. What has brought more turmoil to China than the Communist Party and its leadership? In the beginning, the Party improved our lives, but mostly, the Party leaders have given us empty promises. People cannot eat empty promises or live on empty promises. The old men have had forty years to live up to those promises. After forty years, if something has not been successful, it would be foolish to believe it will ever be successful."

A tiny vein running across Lu Minghua's forehead throbbed as she spoke, and her cheeks and throat were flushed with anger. I poured more water into her cup, insisting that she sit down before she had a stroke. She sat down with a sigh, took a sip of tea, then asked, "Little Sister, did you hear about the list of official's relatives that was posted at Beida last Sunday?"

"No, what list?"

"So many names, everyone in power takes care of their own. The Director General of the Political Department of the People's Liberation Army is Yang Baibing. He is the younger brother of Yang Shangkun, the President of China. The Chief of Staff of the PLA is Chi Haotian, a son-in-law of Yang.

"The Mayor of Shanghai is Jiang Zimen, the son-in-law of Li Xiannian. Li used to be President of China, now he is a member of the Politburo and the chairman of an organization that supervises state policies.

"The General Manager of the Hua Mei Company in Hainan is Zhao Dajun. He is the son of Zhao Ziyang, the General Secretary of the Party and Deng's successor.

"The original head of Hua Kang Company was Deng Pufang, the son of Deng Xiaoping. The Head of the Office of the National Science Committee is Deng Nan, the daughter of Deng Xiaoping.

"The Premier of China, Li Peng is the adopted son of Zhou Enlai. There are over twenty-five names on the list, and these are just the people at the very top! These are the people who benefit from the misery of the Chinese people. They live in palaces, drive the most expensive foreign cars, and eat the best food. They live like emperors! But, it is not just the officials at the top. It's the same from the bottom to the top."

There was little I could say other than to tell Lu Minghua that I understood her frustration. Anyway, she didn't want or expect answers from me. She just wanted me to listen. We sat in silence for a moment, then Lu Minghua told me about a foreign student she had befriended. The student had spent a great deal of time traveling through China and had shown Lu Minghua the photographs she had taken during her travels.

"You know, Little Sister, China has not only opened up to the outside, it has opened up to the inside. When Westerners started coming to China, we learned a great deal about the West, but we also learned more about our own country. The restrictions on travel have been eased, and many ordinary Chinese take business trips or travel to see relatives in other parts of China. I have only traveled to and from my native village, but I saw a great deal of China through those photographs. When I saw the photographs, I was shocked. I knew people still had hard lives in China, but I didn't know how bad it was for so many people. I saw photographs of people living in dirt hovels, children who are hungry, dirty, and ill-clothed, and I wept for China. I asked myself how long must China wait? How long must China be patient? We have waited for forty years and still we only have promises."

As Lu Minghua spoke, her voice cracked with emotion and her eyes glistened with tears. I was so moved by the depth of her feelings that I also had to fight back tears. Lu Minghua squeezed my hand and said, "Oh, now I have upset you, and both of us will go without sleep tonight."

Jinjin came charging into the room, as nineteen-year olds have a tendency to do. She stopped short when she saw our faces, certain something terrible must have happened. Lu Minghua assured her there had not been a disaster, explaining that she had told me a story that was so sad it had made us both cry.

When Lu Minghua left, I walked with her toward the front gate of the campus. When we reached the main road, she told me I had come far enough. Waving goodby, she quickened her pace toward the front gate, and I called out to her, *"Man man zou!"*

Turning down the main road in the opposite direction, I walked back toward the Chinese student dormitories. I was tired, but I knew anxiety would keep me awake. The students had planned another demonstration to protest the editorial, and I was worried about what might happen to them the next day as they marched through the city. The editorial and the warnings that were being broadcast had given everyone reason to fear for their safety. Just as Lu Minghua looked at the students and thought of Little Heping, I felt a mother's concern as well. Had I been born in China, my children would be preparing for the march. I thought of the question I had heard so many people ask since Hu's death. "Why did the wrong man die?"

The buildings were dark except for #8. Lights glowed from the open windows, and I could see that the top hallway was packed with students. A lone, hoarse voice shouted out slogans, and a chorus of exuberant voices responded. Stopping for a moment, I watched and listened, stirred by the calls for freedom. I walked on, past Building #8, then cut through the park along the narrow path that leads to *San Lou*. As the students' voices faded in the background, my heart called out to them, *"Man man zou!"*

8. May 15, 1989—Students had prepared for Gorbachev's visit by writing banners in Chinese and Russian. This banner stated, "Democracy—Our Common Goal."

9. May 20, 1989—This painting of Mao Zedong, Zhou Enlai, and Zhu De was a reminder to the leaders of today that they were not respected as much as the leaders of the past.

10. May 20, 1989—In this painting, the artist placed the head of Deng Xiaoping on the body of Cixi, the Empress Dowager. The painting implies that despite Deng's retirement, he was still the supreme ruler of China, and therefore, when Li Peng spoke, Deng "ruled from behind a screen."

11. May 20, 1989—Although martial law had been declared, the students showed their intent to carry on with the Democratic Student Movement. The literal translation for the two large characters on the sign, *"Mei Wan"* is "It's not over." In Beijing dialect, the words have a much stronger meaning, and the sign is a declaration that the students would never give in.

12. May 20, 1989—Medical students and doctors who treated the hunger strikers at Tiananmen Square.

13. May 19, 1989—Deng's given name, Xiaoping, can also mean "little bottle" in spoken Chinese. The characters on this sign state, "Jing Shan, one scene, transported." This is a historical reference to the last Ming Emperor who hanged himself at Jing Shan when he lost the Mandate of Heaven. The message this sign conveys is that Deng Xiaoping has also lost the Mandate of Heaven and should hang himself. The chain reminds Deng that he is not an emperor, but an ordinary criminal.

14. May 4, 1989—A sign held up by a student on Tiananmen Square wishes "Long Life to True Democracy."

CHAPTER ELEVEN

AN INCREDIBLE DAY

The strap on my backpack had slipped from my shoulder and was binding my arm like a tourniquet, cutting off the circulation. Pain turned to numbness, and the numbness crept down my arm into my hand. Out of the corner of my eye, I checked to see if my hand was still gripping the steel bar above me. I was afraid as the numbness increased, I might lose my grip and my hand would fall, lifeless as a bird shot from the sky, onto the bald head of the old man standing under it.

A little girl stood in front of me, her head just beneath my chin. A man who was probably her father stood next to her, with the side of his head only inches from my face. If I looked straight ahead, I had a perfect view of the inside of his ear. A young man stood with his back pressed against my right shoulder. The man behind me to my left breathed garlic over my shoulder, while the head scarf worn by the woman behind me to my right tickled the back of my neck. But it was the woman jammed in between them who caused me the most discomfort. I knew it was a woman because I heard her tell the man with garlic breath not to push. It was cheeky of her to complain about pushing since she was leaning heavily against my backpack. With the child in front of me only a hair's distance away, I worried that the bus would lurch forward when it started up, and the weight of the woman would propel me onto the child. All I could do was lean back against the woman in order to maintain my balance. However, when I leaned against her, she pushed back even harder against me. As I fought to keep my balance with her weight against me, the muscles in my lower back began to throb in little spasms of pain.

I had boarded the bus at Fragrant Flower Road, and even then, it was especially crowded. When we came to the first stop on Great Knowledge Boulevard, I had hoped that at least a few people would get off. However, when the doors opened, only one old lady stepped down while a dozen or so new passengers squeezed their way onto the bus. The doors wouldn't close, but some helpful soul on the outside shoved against the crush of bodies until the doors finally snapped shut.

The driver cut off the engine to wait until the traffic moved more than a couple of feet at a time. In the fifteen minutes it would have taken us to reach Double Well Village under normal traffic conditions, we had only managed to move a few yards. The weather was pleasantly cool outside, but even with all the windows open, the air couldn't circulate through the clump of bodies. My light cotton jacket felt as heavy as a fur-lined coat. Beads of perspiration formed on my upper lip and my stomach quivered as a wave of nausea went through me. Just when I was certain that I was either going to retch or faint, the driver started up the engine, and we began to roll forward. Those around me rode in silence, except for the old man standing under my hand. Every so often, he sucked in air through his teeth and muttered in classic understatement, "Too many people, too many people!"

The *shoupiaoyuan* announced the next stop, asking if anyone wanted to get off, but when no one responded, the driver passed it by. Pointing to the roof of the bus, the *shoupiaoyuan* turned, and shouted something to the man in front of me. He strained to release the latch above him, then pushed against a panel on the roof. A large vent popped open, letting in a gust of fresh air. When the air swirled over us, there was a collective sigh of relief. More cool air rushed in through the windows as the bus picked up speed, and the passengers began to converse with each other as usual. The *shoupiaoyuan* announced another stop and then another, without any takers. At the next stop, we cheered when a man answered that he wanted to get off, then laughed when someone shouted out *"Xie xie* (Thank you)!" to him as he stepped from the bus.

The traffic grew more congested as we neared the final stop, and the bus crept along inch by inch until the driver shut off the engine again before we reached the intersection. A passenger in the front of the bus called out in excitement, "They're coming! I can hear them, the students are coming!" A young man behind me shouted, "Open the doors, we'll miss the students!" Several passengers joined in, chanting over and over, "Open the doors!" After a few seconds delay, the doors snapped open. The *shoupiaoyuan* made a futile attempt to collect money for the tickets, then threw up her hands in frustration as people swarmed past her onto the street. Once I was outside, I reached up through the window next to her, handing her my fifteen fen. With a smile of gratitude, she thanked me, then handed me a tattered ticket in return.

The avenue was a hornet's nest of cars, trucks, and buses, that were jammed so close together it was impossible to walk between them. Several people climbed over bumpers and wormed their way through the four lanes of traffic to the bicycle lanes on the south side of the avenue where the students were marching. Two trucks blocked most of my view, but I could see the red and white banners held high above the students' heads.

I waited until one truck moved a couple of inches, leaving me just enough room to squeeze between it and the car behind it. I crossed to the opposite lane, but in the process, I was nearly mowed down by a shiny, black sedan as it cut across traffic to a side street. The driver of the sedan shook his fist at me, cursing me as the car brushed up against me. It was a close call, but the only injury I received was the loss of my lens cap. The car's side mirror knocked the cap off when it bumped against my camera, and the rear tire of the sedan shattered the cap when it rolled over it.

It was impossible to see who was riding inside the sedan because the back windows were covered by curtains. However, I was certain it was an official's car since officials and their relatives have a preference for shiny, black sedans with curtained back windows. Besides, only an official would have the audacity to order his driver to cut across that snarl of traffic.

The anxiety of the previous day had been replaced by elation. Spectators, both sympathetic and curious, had come out in the hundreds of thousands to line the streets all along the route of the march. Moved by the courage and commitment of the students and angered by the editorial, the citizens of Beijing were sending a clear message to the leadership that their frustration could no longer be contained.

Throngs of people were everywhere. They flooded the sidewalks and medians, leaned out of office windows, stood on rooftops, and even perched in trees. Despite the government's order that workers were to stay at their posts, office workers and factory workers had come out to show support for the students. Shopkeepers had locked up their shops, and vendors had left their stalls empty to join the crowds who cheered, applauded and shouted their encouragement to row after row of students carrying banners and chanting slogans. It was like Mardi Gras, and I felt as if I were back home in New Orleans on Carnival Day. There was that same festive atmosphere, that same spirit of enthusiasm and gaiety, when spectators and participants are joined together to create something sensational.

I looked back toward the west and saw row after row of students. They had started their march at *Beida* around nine o'clock and had already marched for three hours by the time they reached Double Well Village. Following a route that wound through the northwest section of the city, they went from campus to campus, their number growing larger as they headed toward Tiananmen Square. The lines of students stretched down the avenue as far as I could see. Students from each university marched in groups, ten abreast, the first row of each group carrying a banner announcing the name of the students' school. To each side of the marchers, student guards walked with their bodies turned in toward the marchers and their arms linked together, forming a human chain of protection.

My heart pounded with excitement as I rushed to the corner of Double Well Village where the students were turning south. I climbed atop the iron railing around the little island of concrete where passengers line up to board buses. It was the perfect spot to photograph the students as they rounded the corner. Scanning the crowd, I saw that I was the only foreigner around. Several students spotted me as they turned the corner, waving as they shouted, "Welcome, honorable foreigner." I returned their wave, then raised my camera to photograph them. Smiling broadly for my camera, they posed with their hands held high, two fingers extended in the "V" for victory sign. Automatically, I responded with a "V" sign, and the crowd cheered as the students shouted *"Shengli* (Victory)!"

A group of vendors greeted the students, the flatbeds on their three wheeled bicycles piled high with boxes of popsicles for the students. The procession stopped while the students took a brief rest, and quenched their thirst with the popsicles. The popsicle break gave me a chance to move closer to the front of the procession and to photograph some of the banners I had missed. Jogging along, I zig-zagged between people, bicycles, and vehicles, doing my best not to trample small children.

At the next major intersection three young workers stood atop the large wooden traffic stand in the middle of the avenue. They motioned for me to come up and join them, but when I reached the stand, it looked much higher close up than it had from a distance. I thanked them, but told them I didn't think there was enough room for four people. "Besides," I added, "I don't think I can step up that high!" They laughed, and one of the workers shrugged off my concern with a "No problem!" then jumped down from the stand to make room for me. The other two reached down and took me by the arms, pulling me up to the stand. Once I was situated more or less securely atop the traffic stand, people around us laughed and applauded our accomplishment.

While we waited for the procession to start up again, I took photos of the crowd and chatted with the workers. The worker who had given me his place asked, "Honorable foreigner, do you think the students' demands are correct?"

I was uncertain how I should answer his question, but I decided the best thing to do was to tell him my true feelings. "As a foreigner it really isn't any of my business, but as an American, I believe wholeheartedly in democracy, freedom of the press, and freedom of speech."

The workers smiled and nodded, while several people nearby applauded my response, making me think of my husband's warning during our telephone conversation the day before. Just as I was about to hang up he had said, "Remember, keep a low profile!" I doubted if standing on a traffic stand in the middle of a major intersection making statements about democracy would conform to his idea of keeping a low profile.

The march resumed, and the crowd cheered the slogans on the passing banners: "Down with official profiteering!" "Carry on the spirit of May Fourth to promote democracy!" "It is not a crime to love your country!" They applauded as the students chanted "Long live democracy! Long live freedom of speech! Long live freedom of the press!" When the students chanted "Long live the Communist Party!" everyone around me laughed.

One of the workers explained, "The people are laughing because the students are so clever. If the students wish the Party long life, how can the leaders accuse them of plotting against the Party?"

The traffic stand gave me a perfect view of the students, their banners, and the people gathered at the intersection. The faces of the students were flushed with excitement. Their pride was visible as they marched with heads held high and backs straight, showing no signs of fatigue. They were putting on a spectacular show for the crowd, chanting their slogans with vigor and waving their banners high in the air. In return, the people gave the students great face and honor by their enthusiastic reception. At times, they would shout out spontaneously, "The people love the patriotic students!" and the students would respond, "The students love the people!"

It was a spirited crowd, but no one was boisterous. Both the demonstrators and spectators were orderly and disciplined, aware that any disturbances would be used by the government as evidence that the editorial was justified. Granted, the traffic was incredibly congested, and at least one official in a shiny, black sedan had been inconvenienced, but there were no signs of the turmoil the editorial had accused the demonstrators of creating.

After the last group of students had marched past, the workers jumped down from the stand, then helped me to the ground. Shaking hands with each of them, I thanked them, and trotted off to follow the procession. A man a few yards ahead of me was standing off to the side of the street reading one of the leaflets the demonstrators had handed out. I jogged over to him to ask if I might look at the leaflet after he had read it, but he said that he had finished, and insisted that I take it immediately. After the routine of polite refusals and insistences, I accepted the leaflet and began to read it.

Sometimes I forget and do one of those amazing things that foreigners do that is guaranteed to attract a crowd. Clearly, reading Chinese is one of the most amazing. In no time, a group of people had surrounded me, and there was general speculation among my audience as to whether or not I was actually reading the leaflet. Unable to contain her curiosity any longer, one young woman asked if I could "read and understand" the leaflet. When I replied that I could "read and understand" most of it, there were murmurs of approval from the crowd.

Although I attempted to return the leaflet, the man insisted that I keep it. "It is important for foreigners to know what is going on in China, to understand why the students are demonstrating. Take this back to your country so others will know the truth."

The leaflet, which was called "Our Point of View" and signed "Beijing University Students," disputed the editorial, and began with two questions. The first asked, "If the student movement represents only a small number of people who had long plotted opposition to the Party, why had the one hundred thousand students who participated in the April 22nd demonstration received warm support from the masses? Just imagine, could it be that one hundred thousand students are all so simple-minded that they could be manipulated by a small group of people?"

Secondly, the leaflet declared that all the proposals the students had brought forth would actually "push China forward on the road to democracy, speed up political reform, guard the constitution, and guarantee the power of the people." The leaflet pointed out that none of the proposals opposed either socialism or the Party and stated that it would be unreasonable to "negate the just demands of the vast majority of students just because a small number (if any) shouted counterrevolutionary slogans." Contrary to the accusations of the editorial, the leaflet stated that the students were well-disciplined, nonviolent, and did not desire national turmoil, which was ". . . obvious to all and had moved those present." In closing, it explained, "We demonstrate and we boycott classes, not for ourselves, nor as tools of a small number of people, but for the sole purpose of opening a dialogue with the government to legally express our concern for society. We go to the streets to demonstrate for the purpose of publicity, not to confuse and poison the minds and hearts of the people. We only hope that what we do can be recognized by people from all walks of life and that we can gain your sympathy and support, not, as the editorial said, 'to agitate workers, peasants, and the masses.' " The last line of the leaflet issued an appeal to the Chinese people not to be swayed by others, but "to use their own minds and eyes to judge the truth."

In the distance, I saw that the procession of demonstrators was turning west, away from the square. Since I had only glanced at the map of the protest route that students had posted on our campus, I did not know if the turn was planned, or if the marchers had been diverted. However, when I reached the intersection, I saw that lines of riot police had formed a semicircle blocking access to the lanes heading east and south, the most direct routes to the square. Since I was uncertain how far the students would have to march before they could loop back toward the square, I decided to try to get past the riot police and go directly to the square.

My "stupid tourist" routine seemed the best approach to use on the riot police. Walking up to the first row of policemen on the cross street, I pointed to the southeast, and asked, "Is this the way to the Beijing Hotel?" The hotel was in the same general direction as the square, and a logical destination for a foreigner. The policeman nodded, but told me it was much too far for me to walk. When I shrugged and said, "No Problem!" they moved aside and let me pass.

It was a long walk, but I hoped that buses might be running on some of the side streets away from the demonstration. After walking a couple of blocks without seeing any buses, I caught up with a man walking ahead of me, and asked him the shortest route to Tiananmen Square. As luck would have it, he was a cab driver who had parked his taxi nearby, then walked to the avenue to watch the demonstration. Although the police had set up barricades blocking off Eternal Peace Avenue, he offered to take me as close to the square as he could get. He attempted to go down the side streets that would take us directly to Eternal Peace Avenue, but each time we got within a block of the avenue, we were turned away by police.

As we drove around in circles, the driver talked about the demonstrations, telling me that the students were right to demand a retraction to the April 26th editorial. "The students are patriotic. If they didn't love China, they would stay in their classrooms and ignore China's problems. They are only trying to help the people. That is the reason so many people came out today to support them." As he spoke, we were turned away from Eternal Peace Avenue once more. Laughing, he added, "However, the demonstrations make my work very difficult."

To my surprise, the driver reached over and shut off the meter when it registered twelve yuan. Then he headed west and we crossed the avenue a couple of miles above the square. About a mile above the square, he pulled off on a side street, and apologized telling me I would have to walk the rest of the way. I didn't mind walking, and assured him the ride had been well worth the twelve yuan since it had provided me with a comfortable place to rest and the opportunity to hear his opinions.

It was strange to walk down Eternal Peace Avenue without seeing so much as a solitary bicycle on the main street of the city. The dozen or so guards in front of *Zhongnanhai* eyed me suspiciously as I walked past, but they were less intimidating than the massive line of police that stretched across Eternal Peace Avenue to the side of the Great Hall of the People. The steps of the Hall overflowed with guards, and dozens of policemen stood in small clusters on the street in front of the Hall. The center section of the square was surrounded by police who stood about five feet apart. Approximately one hundred policemen were sitting inside the square on each side of the Monument to the People's Heroes. The monument had been cleared of wreaths and a scaffold had been erected around the photograph of Hu Yaobang, so that it could be replaced with one of Sun Yatsen. It was the leadership's way of stating that mourning for Hu had ended.

The pedestrian underpasses that crossed Eternal Peace Avenue were still open. However, the underpass entrances to the center section of the square had been barricaded, and signs forbidding entrance to the center of the square were posted on the barricades. Four policemen stood guard in front of the barricades at both entrances.

While the whole of Tiananmen Square had once been a vast open area, in 1987 the pedestrian underpasses had been constructed to allow passage to all sides of the square, which had been partitioned off with iron fences installed around the center section of the square and lining the streets along each side of the square. Yuanli had told me the iron fences and underpasses had been constructed after the 1986-1987 demonstrations in an effort to prevent massive numbers of protesters from assembling at Tiananmen Square.

I crossed to the east side of the square where thousands of spectators had gathered between the Gate of Heavenly Peace and the Beijing Hotel. Looking down toward the hotel, I saw another line of police stretched across East Eternal Peace Avenue near the corner of *Nanheyan* Street.

Several minutes before the first group of students arrived at *Nanheyan*, the riot police advanced in a sweep toward the crowd. With their arms locked together, the police lines moved down the avenue from the west and up the avenue from the east, forming a dragnet that spanned Eternal Peace, crossing the sidewalks up to the walls along both sides of the avenue. There was no way out, and as the two lines advanced toward each other, the crowd was compressed between them. The only exit from the avenue, *Nanchizi* Street, was blocked by a row of police. The police were unarmed; still it seemed their intent was not to disburse the spectators, but to apprehend them.

I wanted to cross Eternal Peace Avenue to *Nanheyan* where the students planned to turn onto the avenue. Since my "stupid tourist" routine had worked once, I thought perhaps it might work again. I walked up to the police line coming from the east and approached the last three men nearest the wall. Pointing toward the Beijing Hotel, I asked if I could return to my hotel. They were extremely polite, and even apologized for my inconvenience, but they adamantly refused to let me pass. One policeman told me to head back toward the square, but I pointed toward the police line behind me, and told him they had already refused to let me pass. The logic of my argument did not impress him. I was trapped! A few young men in the crowd tried a more subtle approach, attempting to escape the dragnet by scaling the walls. However, the police pulled them down, then pushed them back into the crowd.

I was certain that getting arrested was definitely not in keeping with maintaining "a low profile," but there was nothing I could do. However, the lines of policemen were moving at a fairly slow pace, and since getting past them was out of the question, comfort was my next priority. There was a low retaining wall at the midpoint between the two lines of soldiers, and while the building behind the wall just happened to be the Public Security Ministry, I sat down on the wall, lit up a cigarette, and waited to see what would happen next.

A man who appeared to be in his late thirties came over to sit down beside me. In crisp and formal English, he turned to me and said, "It is unfortunate that your day of visiting historical sites has been disrupted." At first I was confused by his comment, but it dawned on me that he must have been standing nearby when I had spoken to the three policemen. Hearing my conversation with them, he had assumed that I was a tourist.

Professor Fang, a teacher at Qinghua University, introduced himself and told me he had come to the square since several of his students were taking part in the demonstration. When I explained to Professor Fang that I was not a tourist, but had also come to Tiananmen to see the demonstration, he nodded and said, "Oh, you are more interested in today's history than in yesterday's history."

There was a commotion from the other side of the avenue as the students arrived at *Nanheyan*. We heard them before we saw them, so I climbed on top of the retaining wall to get a better view. The police were holding the students back at *Nanheyan* in a last ditch attempt to prevent the marchers from reaching the avenue. However, the police were vastly outnumbered. By the time the students reached the center of the city, their number had swelled to over 100,000, making it impossible for the police to hold them back.

At the same time, the police lines were pressing harder against the crowd, and moving faster than they had before. When the line moving from the east was only a couple of feet from us, Professor Fang said, "I think we should evacuate!" Under the circumstances, the formality of his statement struck me as amusing, and I started to laugh. Obviously, Professor Fang found the situation less than amusing. Grabbing my arm, he pulled me down from the retaining wall, through the crowd toward *Nanchizi* Street. There were still police lining the entrance to the street, but they were letting a few people at a time go by.

I wanted to stay on Eternal Peace Avenue, but Professor Fang was afraid there would be violence. The students in the lead broke through the police line and poured onto the avenue just as we reached *Nanchizi* Street. Police surrounded the lead students, then people in the crowd surrounded the police, chanting "Police, don't hurt the students!" Looking back over my shoulder, I saw the first banners moving down the avenue, and knew tens of thousands would follow.

Once we had passed the police on *Nanchizi*, Professor Fang steered me down a series of winding alleys to a small cafe on a side street near *Wangfujing*. He suggested that we stay there to let things cool down a little before we returned to Tiananmen Square. While we sipped beer, which Professor Fang had ordered "to calm our nervousness," I asked him if he approved of the demonstrations. Although I expected him to answer my questions, I was surprised at how frankly he spoke.

"You must understand that in China this is the only way in which students can express themselves. The street is the only political forum available to the students. Marching in the streets is the only way they can express their dissatisfaction.

"Many people like to complain that the students of today are materialistic and self-centered. I don't agree. If the students have a shortcoming, it is that they are too idealistic. They are deeply committed and set high standards for themselves. They feel that as intellectuals, they have a responsibility to participate in government and to find the solutions for the problems China faces. They also set high standards for the leaders, and they are frustrated by the leaders' refusal to respond to their ideas and opinions. When the leaders ignore them, and accuse them of plotting to create turmoil, it angers the students, and leaves them with a deep sense of hopelessness and contempt for the leaders."

I told Professor Fang it reminded me of the American college students who had protested the war in Vietnam, telling him there had been the same "crisis of confidence."

Professor Fang nodded enthusiastically, and said, "Yes, that is it precisely, 'a crisis of confidence.' The students have no confidence in China's leaders, China's government, and China's future.

"In the West, students are considered intellectuals in training, but in China, students represent such a small, exclusive minority. Membership in that minority means that they have already achieved the status of intellectual. However, the universities do not provide a forum for their intellectual expression. A university should be a place for open discussion, a place where theories and ideas can be discussed, studied, explored. A university should be the place where independent ideas are encouraged. The students feel frustration because they are bound by oppressive institutions that stifle their curiosity and restrict their intellectual pursuits. Their intellect is China's greatest natural resource, and the leadership should encourage the students to participate in the advancement of our country."

As we talked, I told Professor Fang that the leadership had painted themselves into a corner each step of the way, beginning with their reaction to Hu Yaobang's death. Hu had been a veteran of the Long March and a revolutionary hero. On that basis alone, the government should have responded immediately to his death in a manner befitting a national hero. The leaders had continued to misjudge the response of the students and the populace, and set the stage for a massive outpouring of support and sympathy for the demonstrators by ignoring the petition presented by the students at Hu's Memorial and issuing the April 26th editorial. At each juncture, the leaders' miscalculations had cost them a severe loss of face.

When we left the cafe, Professor Fang and I walked up *Wangfujing* to Eternal Peace Avenue. Hearing "Lao Ban!" called out behind me, I turned to see Shanli trotting up to me. After introductions were made, Shanli told us the students had broken though all the police lines, and had reached Tiananmen Square. Excited to hear the news, Professor Fang quickly exchanged cards with me, then rushed off to find his students.

Shanli asked me to walk with him to the International Hotel where he had a meeting with a European crew who were preparing to film a documentary on China. As we entered the hotel, Shanli reached into his pocket, pulled out a ticket, and handed it to me. The film crew to which he had been assigned when we last met would be leaving the next day, and Shanli had arranged to take them to a performance of Chinese music after their farewell banquet. He suggested that I meet him at the performance, then return with him to the hotel afterward for a late supper.

Although I had intended to go back to the square, I decided to take Shanli up on his invitation. With Shanli, it was always a case of catch as catch can, and not knowing how long it might be before I would see him again, I didn't want to pass up the opportunity to spend some time with him.

Traffic was still being detoured away from Eternal Peace Avenue when I came out of the hotel after five o'clock. Since the buses were not running, I looked for a pedicab to take me to the Friendship Store where I could pick up a few things that I needed, then get a taxi to the theater. As I looked around for an empty pedicab, I saw an old woman come out of the crowd and approach the black sedan that was blocking Eternal Peace Avenue. The sedan was probably from the Public Security Bureau, and people watched in amazement as the old woman attempted to climb up on the hood. When she was unable to manage that feat, she began beating the hood of the car with her purse. The driver honked the horn repeatedly, in an attempt to frighten her away, but the old woman continued to attack the car. Finally, she flung herself against the hood, refusing to move even when the driver got out of the car and jumped up and down, screaming at her in absolute rage. People on both sides of the avenue were watching the scene, laughing at the driver's antics and cheering the old woman's courage. When the driver's temper tantrum failed to budge her, he grabbed the woman's arm, and tried to pull her from the car. Dozens of men rushed from the crowd to intervene. Several of them surrounded the driver while others coaxed the old woman down from the car, then hurried her safely across the street. The driver was infuriated that the old woman had gotten away. Stomping back to the car, he raised his fist at the crowd, then shouted a few choice words before he got into the car and slammed the door. As the crowd jeered at him, he started up the engine, gunned the motor, then sped off leaving a trail of rubber and the laughter of the people behind him.

Unable to find a pedicab, I walked to the Friendship store and hailed a cab. As he drove down Eternal Peace Avenue, the taxi driver tapped his fingers on the steering wheel in frustration, cursing the other drivers for their stupidity as he switched from the left lane to the right lane, then back to the left again. With the traffic being diverted away from the center of town, the ride had already taken twice as long as it should have. He tried one side street and then another, but there was no escaping the long lines of vehicles.

The performance had already begun by the time I reached the theater, but when I looked inside, Shanli and his group were not there. Although it had become quite chilly when the sun set, I decided to wait outside. Ten minutes passed, then twenty, then thirty. Still there was no sign of Shanli. I grew more anxious with each passing minute, as did the man collecting tickets in the lobby of the theater. Twice he had stuck his head outside the door to tell me I was missing the performance. The third time, I went inside just to pacify him.

I couldn't concentrate on the performance. If Shanli didn't show up, I had no way of getting back to my campus. When an hour had passed, I gave up on Shanli, realizing the traffic had probably prevented him from reaching the theater. Although the man in the lobby obviously disapproved, I went back outside to ask the gatekeeper where I could catch a bus or hail a cab. When the gatekeeper asked my destination, I told him Great Knowledge Boulevard. He grimaced, then shook his head in sympathy, saying what amounted to, you can't get there from here. There were no buses, and it was not a neighborhood that was frequented by taxis since people from outside the neighborhood came to the theater in hired cars or tourist buses. For an instant, I considered grabbing his rickety old bicycle, which was leaning against the gatehouse, then fleeing on it into the night. Perhaps he noticed me eyeing his bicycle longingly, for he immediately offered to go inside the gatehouse to telephone for a taxi.

A few minutes later, he came out of the gatehouse shaking his head as he delivered the bad news. There were no taxis available. In frustration, I plopped down on the wooden bench near the gate house. I was at least twenty kilometers from my campus, and I was cold, thirsty, tired, and hungry. I wished I had worn something heavier than my cotton jacket. I wished I had eaten breakfast, or lunch, or taken a popsicle break with the students. I wished I had eaten something at the cafe when I had been with Professor Fang. More than anything, I wished I could strangle Shanli.

The gatekeeper told me to wait on the bench, then walked outside the compound to the street. After a few minutes, he returned with an old man, a friend of his who had come to discuss my problem. After several minutes of discussion, the old man thought of a solution. He knew someone who worked as a truck driver in a *danwei* nearby, and thought the driver might be willing to take me back to the campus.

Several minutes later, the old man returned full of smiles, telling me to hurry because the driver was waiting. The truck was actually a tiny mini-van with two seats in the front, one seat in the back, and a minute storage area in the rear. Thanking the old man profusely, I climbed into the van.

In addition to the driver, a woman, who I assumed to be his wife or girlfriend, and a young man had come along for the ride. As soon as I was in the van, there was a discussion between the three of them as to how much they thought I would be willing to pay. Little did they know that, at that point, I would have been willing to hand over my entire life's savings and my first born just to get back to the university.

The young man sat in the back next to me. Since he could speak a dozen or so words of English, he started a conversation speaking in sentences that were Chinese except for a single word. No matter how hard he tried, the one English word was always incorrect. He asked me "why" my name was, "who" country I was from, and "when" was my profession. By the time we had gone only a couple of blocks, the four of us were convulsed with laughter as I explained in Chinese what he had actually said.

The students had begun their march back to the campuses a couple of hours earlier, and streets were still clogged with traffic. The driver didn't mind the traffic. In fact, he seemed glad to have the opportunity to get out in the middle of things. He and his two companions spoke admiringly of the students and praised both their bravery and patriotism, while they had less kind words for the leaders and Party officials. The driver described them as "small men who only worried about filling their own stomachs and pockets." His companions agreed enthusiastically, telling him he had spoken the truth.

Many spectators had been stranded along the route, unable to take buses or taxis back to their homes. It was a good opportunity for the driver to make a few extra dollars, so he stopped to pick up two men who flagged us down. When the price was settled, the "English speaker" climbed into the storage area, and the two men sat next to me on the back seat.

The two men were teachers at People's University. Since my campus was nearer, the driver told them that he would take them there after he had dropped me off. Regardless of whether or not they were interested, the "English Speaker" filled the two professors in on all that he had learned about me. However, he had forgotten to ask my age. When he managed to use the correct English word, asking me "<u>How</u> old are you," I rewarded him by answering in English. Obviously, his knowledge of English numbers was lacking. In Chinese, he told the others that I was thirty-two. They all nodded, accepting the information as accurate, and I was not about to correct him on that mistake.

When we reached my campus, the driver, the woman, the two teachers, and the "English Speaker" all got out of the van and shook hands with me. After warm goodbys, they climbed back in the van and waved to me as they drove off. Laughing to myself as I watched them drive away, I could no longer be cross with Shanli for leaving me stranded.

Jinjin let out a squeal of delight when I walked into the room. She had been apprehensive when I told her I was going to the demonstration, and since it was after eleven o'clock when I returned, she was certain something had happened to me. Giving her a brief description of my day, I undressed and put on my pajamas, then collapsed on the bed with a moan. I was hungry but too tired to eat, and exhausted but too keyed up to sleep.

Jinjin turned off the light and climbed into her bed. As I closed my eyes to sleep, I could hear a faint noise. Jumping out of bed, I groped for my jeans in the dark, and finding them, put them on over my pajamas. Startled, Jinjin sat up and asked what was happening. Shushing her, I told her to listen. In the distance, I could hear students singing as they marched down Great Knowledge Boulevard. They were the last demonstrators returning to their campus.

Jinjin hopped into her jeans and came running after me, out of *San Lou* toward the side gate of the campus. As the students marched past, their faces were still flushed with excitement, and their chants were still spirited, just as they had been that morning. They had marched over twenty miles and spent hours in the square, yet their energy still flowed. Now they were returning to their campus; triumphant heroes, savoring their victory.

We stayed at the gate watching until the students had disappeared from view, listening until their distant chants were too faint to be understood. In every way, from beginning to end, it had truly been an incredible day.

CHAPTER TWELVE

A TASTE OF HOPE

Friday morning brought bright, cloudless skies to Beijing. The anxiety, which had hovered over the city like a fog on Wednesday, had evaporated with the success of Thursday's march. Beijing had the feel of a city that had just won the Pennant. Pockets of people stood here and there, discussing "yesterday's game." Vendors and their customers, workers and their colleagues, students and their classmates, and neighbors throughout the city spread the story through the small lane news. The students had told the Emperor that he and his Gang of Old Men from *Zhongnanhai* wore no clothes.

Those who had participated, either as demonstrators or as spectators, shared in the victory. Those who had been too cautious to take part for fear of reprisals and those who had been too pessimistic to defend their beliefs—doubting that the protests would have any impact—had to be content with the role of audience to those who had been there.

As many as a million people had lined the route of the march. They and the hundreds of thousands of demonstrating students made it painfully clear to Party leaders that their hard-line strategy had failed. With each step the marchers took, the Party and the leaders lost face.

The overwhelming success of the march forced the leadership to back down from their heavy-handed threats. Appearing on television Thursday evening, Yuan Mu, the spokesman for the State Council, announced that government officials had agreed to meet with students at the All-China Youth Federation offices on April 29th.

By Friday afternoon, *dazibao* spanned the entire length of Building #8, and ran all the way across the long wall connecting it to Building #9. As if to reflect their high spirits, the students used red, yellow, pink, and blue paper for the *dazibao,* which praised the police for their restraint, expressed appreciation to the citizens of Beijing for their support, and quoted slogans from the banners which had been carried during the march. On vivid red paper, a six foot long *dazibao* proclaimed joyously, "Victory to the Patriotic Student Democratic Movement!"

Friday evening, gentle breezes carried the sounds of celebration across the campus. Students laughed and chatted as they strolled around the grounds, exploding strings of firecrackers in celebration, and hurling bottles to the ground. Each time a *xiao ping* (little bottle) shattered, it was further evidence of Deng Xiaoping's loss of face.

Saturday's issue of the *People's Daily* reflected the Party's change in tactics from outright threats to a cautionary tone. However, the government continued to emphasize unity and stability, stating, "If we permit the spread of slander, cursing, and attacks on the Party and its leaders, the widespread use of big character posters, and the boycott of classes everywhere, China will fall into overall chaos."

The meeting between the government's representatives, Yuan Mu and He Dongchan, Vice Chairman of the National Education Committee, and forty-five students from sixteen Beijing universities began Saturday at 3:10 p.m. and lasted for three hours. The entire procedure was broadcast live on national television and radio.

Before the meeting had even begun, student leaders realized it would not be the open dialogue they had requested. The majority of the student participants had been selected from university organizations that were sanctioned by the government, and representatives of the ASAB were denied the right to participate. As the Party maintained that the ASAB was not only illegal, but also subversive, Wuer Kaixi was informed that he could only take part in the dialogue as an individual. Protesting that the dialogue was "a sham" and declaring that the government was "just buying time" and refusing to negotiate with the "student representatives of choice," Wuer Kaixi declined.

Yuan Mu chaired the meeting. With puffy eyes lined by dark, heavy bags; drooping, hound-dog jowls; slicked-back, black lacquered hair; and long thick sideburns, he looked like someone who had been chosen by central casting to play the role of an aging Chinese gangster. Yuan opened the meeting by restating the government's position that there would be no negotiations with students. The selection of He Dongchan as one of the government's representative instead of his superior, Li Tieying, emphasized that point. While Li, a moderate and a supporter of Zhao Ziyang, was more popular with the students than He, a rigid Marxist, Li Tieying's position as a Minister placed him too high on the scale of leadership for participation in the meeting.

I watched the broadcast with Lu Minghua at her apartment. Her television set was more reliable than the dormitory set, and her commentary was invaluable. As Yuan Mu orchestrated the meeting, turning it into a Party-propaganda, double-speak farce, Lu Minghua talked back to his televised image.

When Yuan Mu opened the meeting by assuring the students that all participants would have an opportunity to express their opinions, Lu Minghua asked him, "Then why do you and He Dongchan have a dozen microphones while the students have only one?"

In a patronizing tone, Yuan Mu assured the students that the Party and the government had deep, sincere feelings for the well-being of the students. Lu Minghua asked him, "Then why did the government order thousands of troops from the 38th Army* into the city to stop the march?"

Yuan Mu informed the students that Li Peng wanted the students to understand that the editorial of April 26th was not aimed at them, but at a small group of instigators who were attempting to bring down the Communist Party. Lu Minghua asked, "Does Li Peng think that Chinese students are not bright enough to form their own opinions or express their own ideas?"

To one student's question on corruption, Yuan Mu responded that the purchase of foreign-made luxury cars would be banned, and announced that the traditional summer relocation of the seat of government from Beijing to Bedaihe, a resort on the coast of Hebei Province, would be

---

*The 38th Army is attached to the Beijing Military Command and is stationed southwest of Beijing in Baoding.

canceled for all but the top leaders. Lu Minghua exclaimed, "I hope they choke on the sea air!"

Another question on corruption caused Lu Minghua to gasp. When a student asked about the extravagance of one top official who played golf every week, Yuan Mu told the student that his inquiry would be directed to the appropriate officials. Lu Minghua shook her head and said, "They are talking about Zhao Ziyang. Everyone knows Zhao is the only leader who plays golf. Old Xiaoping is trying to make him the next Hu Yaobang. They want to blame him for the student demonstrations."

However, one statement from Yuan Mu left Lu Minghua speechless. A student stated that the most important demand that the students had issued was freedom of the press. Yuan Mu replied that the Chinese press did not have censorship, and therefore, China already had freedom of the press. Then Yuan stated that because of its responsibility to the people, the press was obligated to work under "certain restrictions." This convoluted reasoning was more than Lu Minghua could bear. She threw up her hands in disgust, then picked up her sewing basket and went to work mending, as if to announce that the meeting was no longer deserving of her full attention.

Saturday evening Hong Xin finally brought her friend Liang Zhenjiang to meet me. When Hong Xin had first told me about Mr. Liang, I had assumed he was more than just a friend. Seeing them together, I was certain my assumption was correct.

Hong Xin looked especially lovely. Although she wore only a simple cotton blouse and skirt, it was obvious she had taken great pains with her appearance. Her hair had been brushed carefully, pulled back on each side, and clipped neatly with barrettes that were the same soft shade of blue as her blouse. She had even used a dab of lipstick, something I had never seen her wear before.

Smiling proudly, Hong Xin introduced Mr. Liang to me in such a formal manner that I had to restrain myself to keep from bowing. I wasn't quite sure whether she was displaying Mr. Liang for my benefit or me for his benefit, but she was clearly pleased with her accomplishment in bringing us together. After the introduction, I insisted that we dispense with formal titles, and asked both Hong Xin and Liang Zhenjiang to call me Lao Kong, telling them in turn, I would call them Little Hong and Little Liang. Hong Xin was delighted with my suggestion, as it put us on closer terms.

At Hong Xin's encouragement, Little Liang spoke in English. He spoke haltingly at first, laughing in embarrassment each time he stumbled on a word or made a mistake, but after a few minutes, he relaxed and spoke more easily. At twenty-six, Little Liang appeared to be at least five years younger. His full, round face and boyish grin would guarantee him a lifetime of looking younger than his years.

We talked for more than an hour before Hong Xin brought up the student movement, telling me that she had not expected any concrete results from the meeting between government officials and students.

"It's clear that the leaders were only interested in making a show of cooperation. Some students will pull back from the movement. They will say the movement has been victorious because the officials agreed to hold the meeting. Truthfully, it accomplished nothing."

I asked if the students would still demonstrate on May 4th.

"Oh yes, there will be demonstrations. There was a great deal of discussion in the meeting about spending more money for education, but the more serious demands were not discussed freely. I would be more optimistic if someone other than He Dongchan had been selected to meet with the students. He is not going to listen to our demands for political reform. He has used his position to press for more courses on Marxist theory and political study in the universities."

When I mentioned the reference made to the golf-playing official, Hong Xin's response was much the same as Lu Minghua's. Pointing out that Zhao had returned that very day from an official visit to North Korea, she said, "There are rumors that he did not agree with the editorial. Many students believe that the government planted that question since the student who asked it was from the student organization supported by the government." Frowning, she added, "It is not a good sign for Zhao or for the student movement."

I wanted to ask Hong Xin how many students from our university had participated in the demonstration on Thursday, but she checked her watch and announced to Little Liang that it was time for them to leave. No amount of coaxing would convince Hong Xin to stay any longer, so I walked with them to the front door.

Sunday I rode over to the Yellow Mountain Hotel to study and visit with Susan. On my way back to the campus, I rode to Qinghua University to read the *dazibao* that were posted there. Tucked between two larger posters was a copy of an open letter to Deng Xiaoping from Wang Ruowang, the famous writer who had been purged from the party along with Fang Lizhi and Liu Binyan after the 1986-1987 demonstrations. The letter, signed "A Citizen Writer from Shanghai," was a protest against censorship. To underscore the problem of censorship, Wang explained that he had been forced to send the letter out of China in order to get it published. He wrote that "censorship of matters in the media stems from a desire to protect evil people and sanction evil practices." In regard to the censorship of history in China, Wang stated, "In order to conceal the true history of the Cultural Revolution, the government has prevented the establishment of a Museum of the Cultural Revolution or criticism of Mao Zedong." Further criticizing the restrictions against writers and journalists in China, Wang stated, "the leaders in power cannot be criticized or opposing points of view expressed," and he argued that the government should "allow private periodicals and publish students' viewpoints."

Defending the student protesters, Wang wrote, "A true Marxist should not view the massive number of youths struggling for democracy as wild beasts gone berserk or flood waters out of control, but should view them as a moving force pushing forward the historical process." He called attention to the similarity of articles following the Tiananmen Incident in 1976 and the April 26, 1989, editorial, charging that while the dates and names were different, the content was identical.

Wang ended his letter by issuing a warning to Deng Xiaoping. "You are approaching a crossroads in history. Will you be remembered as a great statesman or as a cruel tyrant?"

It was unlikely that a letter as bold and honest as Wang Ruowang's would go unnoticed or ignored. Furthermore, the letter and the posters around it, which called on the students to stay united and to demonstrate until there was a sincere dialogue and true political reform, made me wonder just how hard the students would push, and just how long the leadership would allow the demonstrations to continue. In the past, the leaders of China had not exhibited traditional Chinese patience when it came to tolerating criticism.

Well rested from Monday's May Day holiday, I returned to *San Lou* after classes on Tuesday to drop off my books before taking the bus to the Beijing Hotel so that I could stock up on foreign newspapers and magazines. As I walked down the hallway toward the staircase, someone behind me called out my name. Turning, I saw a rumpled Wei Wenfu, standing by the *shiwuyuan's* office. I could not believe my eyes—Wei Wenfu belonged in Luoyang, not Beijing.

I had first met Wei Wenfu in 1985 in Hangzhou when I was looking for an antique shop which was listed in a guide book. I had managed to find the street where the shop was supposed to be, but not the shop. Crossing over to a nearby street market, I asked a group of people to give me directions to the shop. When they looked at each other in confusion, then answered me with a shrug, I was certain we had a communication problem. Just as I was about to give up, a man in a Western style suit approached me, offering his assistance since he could speak English. Turning to the same group of people, he repeated word for word the question that I had just asked. I burst out laughing when again, they looked at each other in confusion and answered the question with a shrug. As it turned out, it was not my Chinese that was incorrect, but the guide book which had listed the wrong address.

Wei Wenfu introduced himself and apologized for not being more helpful, explaining that he was from Luoyang, not Hangzhou. He had come to Hangzhou for a business conference, and after the day's session was over, he had decided to spend the rest of the day sightseeing.

The conference was the reason Wei Wenfu was wearing Western style clothing since Western suits were replacing Mao suits as a result of increasing business ties with the West. However, the suit looked more like a costume on Wei Wenfu than clothing. It seemed inappropriate to his thin frame, accenting the sharp angles of his cheekbones, chin, Adam's apple, shoulder blades, and elbows. Truthfully, he would have looked just as out-of-place in a Mao suit. Indeed, a traditional Chinese gown would have better suited his character, for Wei Wenfu had the look of old China.

Abandoning his plans for the afternoon, Wei Wenfu volunteered to help me search for the "missing" antique shop. Although we never did find the shop, we did spend an enjoyable afternoon wandering through the streets of Hangzhou, snacking on different delicacies sold by street vendors, and discussing Chinese and American literature over Dragon Well tea. Although we kept in touch by letters, I had not seen Wei Wenfu since 1985.

I had written to tell him I would be studying in Beijing again, but would not be able to come to Luoyang. When he did not answer my letter, I thought perhaps he had been insulted that I would be making yet another trip to China without paying a visit to him and his family. Actually, it had never occurred to me that he might show up in Beijing.

From a distance, I though Wei Wenfu had aged considerably in the four years since I had seen him. A serious man, he had a tendency to set his face in a look of intense concentration, wrinkling his brow and pursing his mouth. The wrinkles on his face appeared to have deepened, but as I walked closer to him, I realized that his face was covered with soot and dust, making the lines appear deeper than they actually were.

Apologizing for his appearance, Wei Wenfu explained that he had come straight from the train station to the campus. I asked how he had managed to get past the guard at the gate, since it was well before visiting hours. With a slight grin, he replied, "The guard took pity on me. I told him that I had just come all the way from Guangzhou. That is thirty-six hours by train in a hard seat, and I still have the dirt on me to prove it."

As a man of very proper and formal demeanor, Wei Wenfu looked as much forlorn as disheveled. Although I didn't want to offend him, I could no longer restrain my laughter. To make amends I offered to lend him a washcloth and soap, which he gladly accepted. After he had washed up, we took a bus downtown so he could find a hotel room.

Although Wei Wenfu said he had been to Beijing before, he didn't seem very familiar with the city. I followed him around for over an hour while he looked in vain for a place to stay. Finally, with a "follow me," I led him across the square, behind Front Gate Street, where there are numerous small hostels, hotels, and guest houses that accept only Chinese guests. Wei Wenfu found it humorous that a *waiguoren* (foreigner) had to act as tour guide for a Chinese.

Wei Wenfu checked in at a small hotel, then came outside to tell me that he wanted to eat Mongolian Hot Pot. After asking around the neighborhood, we were directed to a nearby restaurant which specialized in the famous mutton dish. Only one other table in the tiny restaurant was taken. However, shortly after we sat down, the other four tables were filled, and a crowd of people stood outside, peering through the window to see the entertainment. As a foreigner in a neighborhood restaurant, I was the entertainment.

The other original customers, four peasants from Hebei Province, were celebrating some occasion by playing a drinking game. In fact, it was the men from Hebei who broke the ice, by trying to teach me the drinking game. Before long, everyone in the restaurant wanted to know where the *waiguoren* came from and why I was in Beijing. As the conversation warmed up, I pulled out photographs of my family, which were passed around to the other customers, to the cook and his assistant in the kitchen, and to the people standing outside.

One of the other customers, a young man who looked as if he might be a student, asked what I thought about the student movement. I answered that the demands the students had made seemed reasonable to me, and that they represented the rights that I valued most as an American. Everyone started talking at once, asking me questions, making it impossible for me to understand what was being said. When I asked Wei Wenfu if I had said the wrong thing, he smiled and said, "No, they just have a lot of questions about America."

The young man who had spoken to me about the student movement came to our table to ask if he could sit with us for a minute. There were four empty stools, and as soon as I invited him to sit down, the others were filled as well. The young man and his friends who were workers in a factory, stayed at our table, asking one question after the other.

How much money would a factory worker makes in America? Can a person really say what he thinks and do what he wants in America? Can an American quit one job and apply for another without getting approval from his *danwei?* Why do Americans marry and divorce so many times? When one of them asked if America was truly a freer country than China, everyone in the restaurant laughed at his question. The barrage of questions required complex answers which crossed cultural, political, and economic barriers. As I answered them, I silently chastened myself for not being the shy, retiring type.

While they gave me a chance to eat the mutton, the workers told me that earlier in the day over fifty students had bicycled to town from their universities to deliver a petition of twelve demands to the National People's Congress and other government agencies. The students were asking that ASAB representatives be allowed to participate in an open, ongoing dialogue with high-ranking government officials, with both government and student representatives having equal rights to speak. They wanted full and open coverage of the dialogue by both Chinese and foreign press, as well as political and personal security guaranteed for all representatives. The petition declared that the students would demonstrate on May 4th if they had not received an affirmative response from the government by noon, Wednesday.

It was my turn to ask questions. In answering them, the workers and other patrons in the restaurant expressed the same frustrations and discontent with the leadership of China that I had heard others express over the past several days. They were proud of the students, certain of their patriotism, and felt that the desires expressed by the students were more representative of their own concerns than those of the leadership. However, the workers doubted the government would agree to the stipulations listed in the students' petition. Their general consensus was that the students would have to march again on Thursday, and perhaps hold later demonstrations to get the government to agree to a genuine dialogue. The peasants from Hebei were not up to a political discussion, but they did manage to drink a toast to "the patriotic students."

Wei Wenfu seemed to enjoy the lively exchange at the restaurant, although at times, I though he was a bit overwhelmed by the attention we received. However, he gladly acted as my interpreter when I ran into language difficulties, and he was even less formal than usual. When we left the restaurant, Wei Wenfu insisted on accompanying me to my bus stop. As we walked toward Eternal Peace Avenue, he commented that it had been "a most enlightening evening."

While we waited for my bus, we made plans to meet the next afternoon. As the bus pulled up, he gave me the mandatory "be careful of the pickpockets" warning, then waited until I was safely aboard before leaving for his hotel.

The Summer Palace, located in the northwest suburbs, is one of the loveliest places in Beijing, and within bicycling distance from my campus. I suggested that Wei Wenfu meet me there on Wednesday since it was not only a perfect place to spend a spring afternoon, but a walk around the grounds would provide us with ample opportunity to talk.

As we walked, Wei Wenfu brought me up to date on his family and his job. He had been in Guangzhou on business for several days, and since I had written to say I would not be coming to Luoyang, he had decided to detour by Beijing to visit me. As Luoyang is approximately twelve hours south of Beijing by train, it had been quite a detour.

Wei Wenfu had not said how long he intended to stay in Beijing, which caused something of a problem for me. He had come to Beijing specifically to see me, so I felt obligated to spend as much time as possible with him. However, I intended to go to the square the next day for the May 4th demonstration, and I worried that he might offer to go with me, against his better judgment. When I told him that I would be going to the square, I insisted that it was not necessary for him to accompany me. Assuring me that he wanted to go, he told me that he had made his decision after listening to the workers in the restaurant.

Although I expressed concern that it might cause him problems in Luoyang if someone were to find out he had attended the demonstration, he shook his head and said, "No problem." A moment later, he added, "In Guangzhou, I watched reports about the student movement on Hong Kong television. I saw demonstrations in Beijing and other cities. Now I have the opportunity to see what is happening with my own eyes."

Wei Wenfu and I agreed to meet on Front Gate Street at nine o'clock Thursday morning. That way, I could leave the campus early enough to avoid another crushing bus ride, and we could go to the train station to buy his ticket before we went to Tiananmen Square.

The purchase of train tickets in China requires time, patience, stamina, and sometimes, a few packs of famous brand cigarettes. When we arrived at the station, the queue to purchase tickets for Wei Wenfu's train was one of the longest. After we had reached the halfway point in the line, Wei Wenfu groaned, pointing to a sign that the clerk was posting at the ticket window. Only hard seat tickets were still available for the midnight train to Luoyang, and even those were limited. Hard seat is the cheapest class of travel, and the seats are as described—hard. People sit crammed into the booth-like, straight-backed, wooden seats, and since standing room tickets are also sold, they jam into every available inch of space, even stretching out under the seats and in the aisles. Having just traveled from Guangzhou to Beijing by hard seat, the thought of spending another twelve hours traveling that way was more than Wei Wenfu could bear.

However, there is always another option in China. Corruption provides alternatives. Wei Wenfu and I left the line and went outside the building to the window where platform tickets are sold. For only five fen, a ticket can be purchased allowing a person access to the platforms. With a platform ticket, Wei Wenfu could board the train, present the conductor with a couple of packs of cigarettes, and the conductor would make room for him. He might even discover that a ticket for the sleeper car was available.

In order to buy a platform ticket, a person must present a telegram or some other form of documentation to prove he is meeting an incoming passenger. As a foreigner, I had a better chance of buying a ticket without a telegram than Wei Wenfu since I could either plead ignorance of the regulation, or "not understand" what was being said. I felt rather corrupt by taking advantage of the "back door," but if I refused to help him, Wei Wenfu would probably have to wait until the next day to return home.

The platform ticket window was covered with a board which had a small rectangular slot at the bottom where the purchaser presented his telegram for inspection, and the tickets were dispensed. When my turn came, I shoved five fen through the hole. Although the clerk could not see me, it was evident the hand before him was attached to a foreigner. The Chinese in front of me had been required to show telegrams, but the clerk took the coin, then handed me a ticket in return without asking for my papers.

By the time we returned to Front Gate Avenue, hundreds of riot police lined each side of the street. Guards blocked off the west side of the square in front of the Great Hall of the People, denying entry even to pedestrians. Just as they had on April 27th, police surrounded the barricade around the center section of the square. Wei Wenfu and I walked past the museums on the east side of the square, down through the pedestrian underpass, across Eternal Peace Avenue to the Gate of Heavenly Peace. By noon, as many as one hundred thousand people had assembled along both sides of the avenue. Relaxed and confident, some strolled around eating popsicles as they waited for the students to make their appearance. Others napped under the shade of trees, or stretched out on the grounds to doze in the warm sunlight. Others nodded off as they sat on the curbs. Wei Wenfu tried to appear calm as well, but it was his first demonstration, and I doubt that he had considered how conspicuous he would be in the company of a foreigner.

A police van equipped with a public address system drove slowly down Eternal Peace Avenue, announcing its arrival with a double-toned siren. The siren wound down to a monotone growl, then a man's voice boomed out of the speakers, shouting in a harsh voice *"zou, zou, zou* (go, go, go)!" The high, shrill voice of a woman followed, ordering the crowd to clear the streets and to move away from the barricades, warning that it was illegal for them to obstruct traffic. The crowd moved back to the sidewalks momentarily, only to return as soon as the van had passed. A man standing next to me shouted out at the passing van, complaining that it was the police who had obstructed traffic in the first place by setting up the barricades. Those around him laughed and nodded in agreement, telling the man that his comment was correct.

The lack of courteous words and the rudeness in the policeman's voice as he shouted at the crowd surprised Wei Wenfu. However, the crowd's reaction surprised him even more. He marveled that people were not intimidated by the police, but had actually mocked and ignored their orders. I could tell the incident had unnerved him, so I suggested that he remain on the sidewalk while I went back to the barricade to photograph the crowd. Giving me a tight, nervous smile, Wei Wenfu nodded in agreement, then called out to me in warning, *"Xiao xin* (Be careful)!" as I trotted off to the barricade. Wei Wenfu was probably happy to be out of the spotlight for a few minutes. With my load of camera equipment and the tape recorder I was carrying, I had attracted more curious stares than were normally directed toward a foreigner.

As I worked my way through the crowd to the front of the barricade, a man who appeared to be in his late twenties noticed that a foreigner was behind him and scooted over to make room for me. Leaning out over the barricade, I looked up and down Eternal Peace Avenue through my zoom lens. The man who had made room for me commented to the people next to him that I must be able to see quite far through such a long lens. Turning to the man, I offered him the camera, and asked him in Chinese if he would like to take a look. As he accepted the camera, he thanked me and introduced himself.

Mr. Pan explained that he was an artist. He had attended the Central Academy of Art, and after completion of his studies, he had traveled around the country for a couple of years painting the gorges of the Yangste River, the jutting peaks of Guilin, cloud-capped Mount Tai, and other scenic spots in China. When I mentioned a friend in Sichuan Province who is also an artist, Mr. Pan insisted that I come to his home so that I could meet other artists in the city and view their works. Jotting down his address, he invited me to stop by on Saturday afternoon.

When I returned to the sidewalk, I reassured Wei Wenfu, pointing out that if the police had been under orders to clear the square, they surely would have done so when the crowd was smaller. Actually, it appeared the government had made little effort to prevent or discourage the demonstration. There had been broadcasts on Wednesday stating that the square would be sealed off on May 4th, and during a televised press conference, Yuan Mu had announced that the government had rejected the conditions the students had stipulated in their petition for dialogue, describing them as "unreasonable, emotionally impulsive, and menacing to the government in the form of an ultimatum." However, Yuan Mu had neither warned nor threatened the students, only stating that he "hoped" there would not be a demonstration.

While Yuan Mu had avoided criticism of the students, he had attacked outside forces. He pointed an accusing finger at Fang Lizhi and members of the Chinese Alliance for Democracy (CAD), claiming they were using the student movement to attack the Party and the leadership. Established in New York in 1983, CAD and its magazine, *China Spring*, were founded by Wang Bingzhang and three other overseas Chinese students. Wang's purpose in founding the organization was to keep alive the Pro-Democracy movement of Democracy Wall and to establish an opposition party abroad.

While it was possible the leaders had pulled in the reins on their hard-line rhetoric because it had exacerbated the situation, it was more likely that, due to the historical significance of May 4th, they had simply accepted the demonstration as a given.

The May Fourth Movement refers not only to the demonstration by Beijing students on that day in 1919, but also to the period in Chinese history from around 1917 through 1921. It was a time when intellectuals were again turning to the West to seek solutions for China's problems. While pressing for widespread reform, the movement set generation against generation by attacking Confucianism and the traditions of Chinese culture. Young intellectuals looked to the West and to the modern world to advance China out of the past by calling for "Science and Democracy as a means to achieve a position of world prominence, which the country had lost after the Industrial Revolution."

However, democracy was not the only Western political theory that appealed to Chinese intellectuals during the May Fourth Movement. For many, the theories of Marx and Lenin offered more logical solutions to the problems of governing a country as vast and complex as China. In fact, the movement is credited with giving birth to the Chinese Communist Party, which was founded in 1920.

The slogan, "Down With the Old and Up With the New," struck at the very core of China's culture. It called for the use of *bai hua* (plain language) in literature, magazines, and newspapers instead of *wen yen*, the literary language. *Bai hua* would open these works up to the *laobaixing* who were not able to read *wen yen*. The slogan also attacked feet binding and arranged marriages, practices which had immobilized and imprisoned women to the point of social nonexistence outside their family role. More significantly, it rejected Confucianism, the philosophy that dictated Chinese social and political behavior to the extent that it defined "Chineseness." Through its emphasis on subservience in relationships, Confucianism controlled the subjects within the kingdom, the citizens within the community, and the members within the family; sacrificing the individual to the unit for the sake of harmony and order.

Yet, while Chinese traditions and culture were denounced and discredited, there was still a strong nationalistic spirit to the May Fourth Movement. In 1915, Japan had issued its program of Twenty-One Demands, aimed at increasing Japan's economic and political control over China. The demonstration on May 4, 1919, was in response to the Paris Peace Conference, which had turned Germany's rights in Shandong Province over to Japan instead of returning those rights to China. This decision not only increased Japan's position of power within China, but also compounded the humiliation the Chinese felt as a result of the Twenty-One Demands. Enraged students marched to The Gate of Heavenly Peace, then burned the house of one Chinese official who had cooperated with the Japanese. Under the banner of "Save the Nation," Chinese students called for a boycott of all Japanese goods.

With May 4, 1989, being the seventieth anniversary of the movement, with students again in the spotlight as they demanded political reform, with Japan once more an economic giant in the world and having major investments in China, and with young Chinese intellectuals again looking to "Democracy and Science" to push China into a position of power in the twenty-first century—a major demonstration was unavoidable. If the leaders used force to suppress demonstrations on such a significant day, Beijing might well explode in their faces.

There was yet another factor that came into play in the government's restraint. Perhaps those within both factions of leadership were stepping back to see in which direction the political wind was blowing. The mention of Zhao Ziyang's fondness for golf in the meeting with the students indicated that the hard-liners might be positioning themselves for a run at the top spot as successor to Deng. With Hu's body barely cold in the grave, no one could forget that student demonstrations could either make or break political careers. If the wind blew in favor of the hard-liners, they could step in and point to the economic reforms as the reason for all of China's problems from "chaos" on the streets to corruption within the government. Undoubtedly, Zhao's influence and power would also be attacked. If the winds blew in favor of the reformers, Zhao could make his move to push the hard-liners and Deng Xiaoping aside.

Wei Wenfu was not as certain as I that the police would not attack the crowd. Smiling weakly, he said, "I suppose you are right. Surely it would have been easier to clear everyone out before now." As he spoke, he took out a handkerchief, and wiped away the perspiration that had formed above his lip. Although I wasn't certain if the perspiration was due to the warm sun or his nerves, I suggested we cross over to the east corner of Eternal Peace Avenue by the museums. The crowd was not as large on that side, and there were trees that would protect us from the sun. Although he agreed, he pointed to my tape recorder and said, "There are police in the pedestrian underpass. Perhaps it would be best if you put that in your bag."

Around one o'clock, a murmur went through the crowd. I looked back toward the Gate of Heavenly Peace and saw dozens, then hundreds of people swarm over the barricades, across Eternal Peace Avenue, toward the center section of the square. When the guards made no attempt to stop them, thousands followed.

Gasping as I climbed atop the barricade in front of us, Wei Wenfu stammered *"Xiao xin, xiao xin!"* warning me to be careful. With one foot on the barricade and the other on a bicycle that was leaning against the barricade, my balance was precarious at best as I snapped photographs with one hand and pulled the recorder from my bag with the other.

Holding one of my legs to steady me, Wei Wenfu shouted up at me, "Are you sure you're not a journalist?"

"Positive!"

Grabbing my other leg, Wei Wenfu shouted back, "Perhaps you should be!"

Jumping down on the other side of the barricade, I laughed and turned to Wei Wenfu, saying "I'm going!"

With a pained expression on his face, he answered, "Wait for me."

By the time we climbed the second barrier around the center section of the square, the steps to the Monument to the People's Heroes were overflowing with people, and a miraculous change had come over Wei Wenfu. My cautious friend turned into a Chinese Steven Spielberg. Shouting directions to me, one after the other, he said, "Hold your camera up higher so you can photograph the monument over the crowd! Pointing his finger to the left of me, he shouted, "Look, see the surveillance camera on that pole. Take a photograph of the people climbing the pole!" After that shot, he shouted, "Turn around and get a picture of the rest of the crowd as they come toward you!"

Following his directions, I snapped away, laughing at the metamorphosis he had undergone. When I stopped to re-load my camera, I looked over at Wei Wenfu. He was wearing such a broad smile, that I feared his normally stern face might crack.

"Do you know what this means?" I asked.

"What?"

I shook my head in astonishment. "The students haven't arrived, yet the people have already taken the monument. This is no longer just a student movement. Today, it has become a people's movement!"

"Yes", he said, "and the police have vanished!"

Looking around the square and across Eternal Peace Avenue, I saw that it was true. Only one single, solitary line of guards stood on the bottom step of the Great Hall of the People. Hundreds in the crowd had also focused their attention on the Great Hall of the People, walking toward it calmly, almost without sound. As the people moved, I walked with them, watching the scene through my lens as I photographed. Those at the front of the crowd stopped as others lined up behind them. The people stood, face-to-face, staring at the guards. Unable to meet their gaze, most of the guards averted their eyes. As the crowd and the guards stood with less than a yard of space between them, I waited to see if the crowd would shout slogans or jeer at the guards. Instead, they stood wordlessly. Their silence and their orderliness were more powerful than the shouts of an angry mob, and their presence reminded China's leaders that the Great Hall of the PEOPLE is the seat of government for the PEOPLE'S Republic of China.

Someone in the back of the crowd called out that the students were marching down Eternal Peace Avenue. In a maneuver planned to outwit the police and force them to divide their efforts, the students had decided to approach the square in two groups: one marching from the east down Eternal Peace Avenue, and the other up the Avenue from the west.

Wei Wenfu and I hurried to the north end of the square, across from the Gate of Heavenly Peace. By the time we reached the avenue, the crowd was already so dense that we had to squeeze our way through hordes of people just to get within twenty feet of the marchers. Tugging at my arm, Wei Wenfu pointed to several signs held up by people in·the crowd opposite us. One said, "We want to speak!" while another said, "We don't like to tell lies!" A cheer went up from the crowd as the students applauded the signs. Wei Wenfu leaned over toward me, shouting over the noise of the crowd.

"Those are journalists, Kong Kailing! Journalists have joined the demonstrations!"

One sign caught my eye. It was so small that there was barely room on it for the two characters which were written side by side. No matter that the sign was tiny, the two characters, *"liang xin,"* had great impact. The message on the sign was "Conscience."

The students marching from the east entered the square first with those from the west not far behind. As each group entered behind their school banner, the crowd cheered them on. The last group received the most zealous welcome. A student beating a drum preceded the group, as if he were announcing the arrival of the gods. Behind him, another student carried the blue and white flag of their organization. Next came several young men; some bare-chested with their shirts tied around their waists, most with white bands tied rakishly around their foreheads. Each walked with the swagger of a toreador, the glow of honor in his eyes. Although the government had damned them as members of an illegal, counterrevolutionary organization, the crowd now acknowledged them as Beijing's newest heroes. The representatives of the Autonomous Students Association of Beijing had arrived.

A path was cleared for the flag to be carried to the top step of the monument's base. The flag bearer stopped briefly on the step, then pulled himself up to the top of the ledge. As he rose and waved the flag high in the air, the crowd roared in response. The surge of noise passed over the square like thunder—a sound so powerful, so electric that the square seemed to vibrate beneath me.

I looked at an old man who stood near me. I had noticed him earlier because he wore a beret. He watched intently as the flag was paraded around the monument's ledge, his hands held up in a prayer-like manner, as if they had frozen in the act of applauding. A single tear rolled down the hollow of his cheek, detouring into a crevice in his wrinkled chin, then fell, striking his jacket.

Wei Wenfu looked like a little boy, his face filled with wonder as he held the recorder up to tape the noise of the crowd. The noise would be meaningless on the tape, probably sounding more like static than anything else. I didn't have the heart to tell him. Over and over, as if he had to convince himself, he kept repeating, "this is real, this is real, this is real."

We listened as Wang Dan read the New May Fourth Manifesto, inspired by the May Fourth Manifesto, which had been presented on that day seventy years earlier by Beijing college students. The new Manifesto stated, "while New China stressed the role of science, it did not place value on the spirit of "science and democracy." Demanding human rights, the Manifesto stressed the development of the individual, protection of his interest, and respect for the nature of the individual. It urged the government to hasten political reform, to grant freedom of the press, and to permit private newspapers to be printed. It further urged that the government respect the intellectual and value education so that China might achieve a true modernization.

Although there was not total agreement among the students, it was announced that the boycott of classes had ended. In doing so, the students were urged to return to their classes, and to focus their energies on strengthening the organization of the ASAB, while petitioning for a dialogue with government officials to address the demands they had raised. Although the May Fourth demonstration had been held because the government had refused to address the demands made in the petition presented earlier by the students, there was a new hope that more positive reactions might come from the government. That hope stemmed from a speech that Zhao Ziyang had made during a Commemorative of May Fourth held the day before at the Great Hall of the People.

In his speech, Zhao had stated, "the demands of the students to promote democracy, to combat corruption, and to develop education and science corresponds with the aims of the Party." The students viewed Zhao's speech as a reasonable and positive step toward a reconciliation between the students and the government.

As we listened to the speeches, Wei Wenfu and I worked our way through the crowd toward Front Gate Avenue. We had only eaten popsicles, and he complained that his head ached from hunger. Since he had to return to the hostel before leaving for the train station, we needed to find a restaurant nearby. On our way to the square, Wei Wenfu had spotted Beijing's first American fast food import. Kentucky Fried Chicken was just across from the square, and since Wei Wenfu was curious to try American-style fried chicken, we decided it was the best place to eat.

We said very little as we ate our dinner. The sterile decor and the icy air conditioning in the restaurant discouraged conversation. Besides, Wei Wenfu seemed to have returned to his normal reserved manner, and I was simply too tired to talk. When we finished our meal, Wei Wenfu insisted that I go by taxi to the campus since he was concerned that there might not be a bus available when I had to transfer from the subway.

With the traffic so congested, it was impossible to catch a cab near the square. Wei Wenfu suggested we walk a few blocks away from the square, as he was confident we could find one farther down Front Gate Avenue. When I had all but given up, Wei Wenfu spotted a pedicab across the street from us. He first went over to bargain with the driver alone, then signaled for me to come across after the price had been settled. As I climbed into the pedicab, Wei Wenfu continued talking to the driver. With a stern expression on his face, he went through a litany of instructions. The driver, who appeared to be around eighteen, grinned good-naturedly as he listened to Wei Wenfu's lecture, nodding when it was appropriate.

"This foreigner is a valued friend of the Chinese people. You agreed to a fare of twenty-five Renminbi. You are not to charge her a single fen more or to insist on payment in FEC."

Wei Wenfu paused to catch his breath and to allow the driver to nod his head in response.

"In the past, my foreign friend has had problems with her back. You must ride very carefully so you will not cause her pain. Be certain that you avoid bumps, and cross the railroad tracks with caution. Riding over railroad tracks is very jarring, so you must cross them as slowly as possible."

Wei Wenfu paused for another breath, and the driver took his cue, nodding his head again.

"Do not ride too fast, because that is dangerous. However, do not ride too slowly, because my foreign friend is tired and anxious to return to her campus."

Sensing that the lecture was finally over, the driver nodded a final time and said, "No problem."

Content that he had covered all the necessary instructions, Wei Wenfu turned and shook my hand. Thanking him for his concern, I assured him the ride would be enjoyable. Wei Wenfu said goodby in the formal manner, then again invited me to come to Luoyang to meet his family, assuring me that I would be received as an honored guest in his home. After a final wave goodby, the driver pulled away from the curb and began pedaling in the direction of the campus.

We had barely crossed the avenue when the driver looked back over his shoulder, then braked, pulling over to the curb. I worried that he wanted to renegotiate the fare, or that he had decided the distance was too far. Leaning forward, I asked why we had stopped. Motioning behind us with his head, he said, "Your friend is coming."

Surprised, I peered around the hood of the pedicab. Just as the driver had said, Wei Wenfu was running toward us, calling out for us to wait. The driver, undoubtedly dreading another lecture, was visibly relieved when Wei Wenfu spoke to me in English.

"Kong Kailing, I'm sorry to delay you, but there is something I must say. I am deeply grateful that you allowed me to accompany you to Tiananmen Square. For years I have felt that China was hopeless, and that my life was hopeless as well. Today, for the first time in my life, I tasted hope."

CHAPTER THIRTEEN

DREAM OF FREEDOM

Bai Yan Road is the main street in Mr. Pan's neighborhood. It is located in the southern section of Beijing, an area known during the Qing Dynasty as the Chinese City. The abundance of drab, dusty, run-down shops and the scarcity of trees give Bai Yan Road, and the neighborhood that surrounds it, the look of a place which has never known prosperity.

Rows of *hutong** lined by high, thick walls branch off from Bai Yan Road. Hidden behind the walls of the *hutong* are numerous residential compounds. Mr. Pan's apartment is in a compound which is typical of those in the neighborhood. A stoop, beneath an aged wooden gate that seals an arch in the wall, marks the entrance to the compound. Inside the compound, a series of clay brick, one-story buildings form a rectangle around a small, barren courtyard. The two buildings to the east and the west of the courtyard are divided into three rooms while those on the south and the north contain smaller apartments of two rooms each. Mr. Pan's two rooms are on the north side of the courtyard next to the compound entrance. One of the two faucets which provide water for all the residents in the compound is just outside Mr. Pan's doorway. The faucet drips constantly, forcing Mr. Pan to walk through a puddle each time he goes in and out of his apartment, rain or shine.

Mr. Pan greeted me at his door, then led me into the larger of his two rooms which he had turned into a studio. The furnishings were sparse, but the clutter was dense. A small chair stood near the center of the room. It

---

Hutong is a Mongolian word for alley or narrow lane, which came into use in China during the Yuan Dynasty.

looked rather out of place, making me wonder if it had been carried from the other room so that I would have a place to sit. The only other piece of furniture in the room was a huge desk which Mr. Pan used as his worktable. It was jammed up against the outside wall beneath two wide windows. The windows, along with a bare bulb that hung from the ceiling, provided less than adequate light for an artist, even on sunny days. The rest of the room was filled with crates of books, stacks of sketch pads, and several boxes that overflowed with Mr. Pan's paintings, rolls of paper, ink sticks, brushes, and other tools of his trade. The walls were covered, in a haphazard way, with dozens of Mr. Pan's ink paintings which were done in the traditional Chinese style.

As Mr. Pan poured tea, he told me that, in addition to his studies at the Central Academy of Art, he had studied for a year under the tutelage of a master painter in Hunan Province. Although he was not yet established as an artist, some of Mr. Pan's paintings had been displayed in galleries in several provinces, and a few had been published in Chinese magazines.

His job in a factory, painting art works for the tourist trade, provided Mr. Pan with the opportunity to work in his field. However, he found the work uninspiring, and the time away from his painting distracting. A further frustration to Mr. Pan was his small salary which allowed little left over after his living expenses for the purchase of art supplies.

Mr. Pan was anxious for me to see his work. While I sat in the chair, an obedient and attentive audience of one, he went from painting to painting, telling me where each had been painted and what had inspired him. Among his other paintings were copies of works done by various past masters. Although Western artists cringe at the comment that their work is derivative of another artist's style, Chinese artists have a completely different attitude toward originality. It is not at all uncommon for a Chinese artist to pay tribute to the masters by doing his own rendition of their paintings.

When he had finished his exhibition for one, Mr. Pan announced that he had arranged for me to meet some other artists. Suggesting that I look through his sketches, he went to use the neighborhood telephone to tell his friends that we were on our way. Many of his sketches were loose, or stuffed into scrapbooks. Using whatever paper was available at the time,

Mr. Pan had sketched on scraps of newspaper, pieces of stationery, and even the backs of pages torn from calendars.

It was his notebooks that interested me most. They were filled with page after page of drawings, done in ballpoint pen. The drawings traced his journey through China with such vitality and emotion that each scene came alive on the page. Each drawing celebrated the diversity of China's scenery and her people.

Fresh from a midday bath in a stream near their Yunnan Province village, three beautiful young Dai* women stood bare-breasted, as one leaned to fasten her skirt while the other two combed their hair. A peasant, feet and legs still caked with mud from the rice paddies of Guizhou Province, paused on his way home from the fields to light his pipe. A boat on the Yangtse River struggled against the rapids of Qutong Gorge as eddies swirled around it. An old woman with a cane, as gnarled and ancient as she, hobbled on tiny bound feet down a village road in Anhui Province. These were drawings of a timeless China but Mr. Pan's pen had captured modern China as well. A peasant family in Xian stood peering in a department store window, gazing longingly at a display of stereos, television, and other electronic wizardry. While his friends stood by admiring his prized acquisition, a young man in Shanghai sat astride his new motorbike trying to achieve an expression that was the perfect balance between nonchalance and pride. A young couple, both dressed in expensive, tight-fitting, Western-style clothing, walked hand in hand down a street in Guangzhou. He hid his thoughts behind dark sun glasses, she behind heavy makeup.

As I flipped through the notebooks, I hoped Mr. Pan's phone call would be delayed by the normal difficulties of the Beijing telephone system so that I could look at every drawing. However, his call was put through straight away, and he returned before I had finished the second book.

On the way to his friend's apartment, Mr. Pan filled me in on the exhibition he was taking me to see. He and a few of his friends had joined together to set up an art society. The dozen or so members met frequently

---

*One of the fifty-five ethnic minorities in China.

to critique each other's work, discuss art, and exhibit their paintings. His friend, Mr. Yu, had volunteered his apartment as the salon's meeting place and gallery since he was the only member of the group with a three room apartment. Pooling their money, labor, and creativity, the group had turned Mr. Yu's third room into an attractive little gallery.

Although I had expected to see an exhibition of traditional Chinese art, most of the paintings were oils, and a wide range of western influences could be seen in the artists' works. There was the surrealism of Dali, the constructivism of the early abstract Russian paintings, as well as photo-realism, expressionism, romanticism, and impressionism.

Mr. Yu's paintings had been heavily influenced by impressionists and postimpressionists, and I was especially drawn to his work because of the subject matter. Many of his paintings were set in Qinghai Province and the surrounding area of Northwest China. With a high grassland plateau in the east, a basin in the northwest, and a plateau that connects it to Tibet in the south, Qinghai is a sparsely populated, desolate land of deserts, marshes, and bitter cold winters. Many people had been sent to Qinghai Province during the Cultural Revolution when intellectuals were being "sent down to the countryside." Like Siberia in Russia, it has long been a place of banishment.

There was a striking similarity in both style and subject matter between Mr. Yu's work and that of many artists in the American Southwest who paint native American and other western themes. I had observed the similarity before in other paintings I had seen of that area of China, making me wonder if this style of painting was favored by both groups of artists since it tended to romanticize and soften the harshness of their lifestyles.

In addition to Mr. and Mrs. Yu and Mr. Pan, three other members of the society had come to meet me. Mr. Xu, a twenty year old student at the Central Academy of Art, was the youngest member of the group. Although he sometimes worked in other styles, his real passion was abstract art. Miss Li, a small, plump woman in her late twenties, taught art at a middle school and was the Dali of the group. Mr. Guo, like Mr. Pan, was in his early thirties. Using a blend of Western Impressionism and Traditional Chinese style, the paintings he created were filled with delicate and dreamy imagery.

Despite the differences in artistic style, background, and age, those in the group were bound together by their love of art as well as their mutual affection and respect. Their obvious comfort with each other and their humor made our conversation all the more interesting. Although no one in the group could speak English, the conversation flowed with only occasional hitches that were easily handled by the assistance of my dictionary, their ingenuity in using a quick sketch to illustrate a point, or the use of written Chinese when all else failed.

While the original topic of conversation was art, in China it is impossible to discuss art without discussing politics. Mao had seen to that when he set the Party's position on art in the Talks at Yenan Forum on Literature and Art in May, 1942. At that time, Mao stated, "Our purpose is to ensure that literature and art fit well into the whole revolutionary machine as a component part, that they operate as powerful weapons for uniting and educating the people." In Mao's China, creativity was stifled, and artists were intimidated and persecuted since both art and literature were required to be "subordinate to politics and to serve the people." There was no tolerance for those who merely painted pretty pictures.

The worst attack on art and artists came during the Cultural Revolution when the "antisocialist poisonous weeds" who believed in "art for art's sake" or did not follow the "correct political line" suffered the wrath of Madam Mao. In the attack on the "Four Olds" (old customs, old habits, old culture, and old thinking) traditional Chinese art was scorned as feudal and antisocialist. Even the works of past masters, long dead, were vilified by the Gang of Four and torched by Red Guards. All art, new and old, had to pass the scrutiny of Madam Mao and her cronies. As a result, there was a proliferation of propaganda paintings featuring a rosy-cheeked Mao surrounded by rosy-cheeked children, rosy-cheeked peasants in the fields, rosy-cheeked workers in factories, and rosy-cheeked soldiers defending the glorious revolution.

After the Cultural Revolution and the arrest of the Gang of Four, the economic reforms and the bombardment of influence from the West brought both traditional Chinese art and Western art back into the realm of respectability. Those rosy-cheeked revolutionaries who had once graced the billboards of Chinese cities were edged out by pictures of electronic gadgets and models with gleaming smiles who advertised toothpaste. Of course, propaganda art was not totally eliminated from the scene. There were still billboards throughout China that featured a rosy-cheeked family of father, mother, and one child in support of the government's efforts to control population growth with the policy of "One Child per Family."

While Mr. Pan and the others agreed that the era of reform had created a greater opportunity for experimentation and expression in the arts, as Mr. Yu pointed out, artists still felt restrained and restricted by the Party. The lack of political reform forced artists to work without the safety net of a legal system, which would guarantee them freedom of expression.

Mr. Xu was encouraged by Zhao Ziyang's May 4th address, and felt the boycott of classes and demonstrations had achieved some success in pushing the leadership in the direction of reform. He had marched with his classmates in the May 4th demonstration, and agreed with the decision to call an end to the boycott.

Mr. Xu explained. "Zhao admitted that one of China's major problems is that we lack a sound legal system. When someone as powerful as Zhao says that the government and the students share the same concerns, and calls our demands reasonable, we have to show our willingness to give the leaders a chance to prove they will listen to the viewpoints of the students. Certainly, there won't be changes overnight, but the leaders must now understand that we will not be satisfied until the government responds with a program of political reform. Otherwise, we will demonstrate again and the people will support us."

Mr. Pan was not so hopeful that the demonstrations or dialogues with the government would have any real effect.

"I agree with the students and I support their actions," he said, "but I don't think there will be any substantial changes. The government is just waiting for the excitement to die down. The Party will not change, and I doubt that the situation for artists will change substantially. Under the leadership of the Communist Party, art will always be joined to politics. As long as the two are connected, there will be political restrictions placed on artists, and artists will suffer."

Mr. Xu shook his head and asked, "Lao Pan, how can you separate the two? Art reflects society, and politics is certainly part of any society. Even without the Party, art would be connected to politics. Art should serve the same purpose in society as a free press. It should comment on the society and the government."

Mr. Xu turned to me, asking me to settle the dispute. Laughing, I told him that I was having enough trouble just understanding all they were saying. "Besides," I added, "this sounds like a discussion that the two of you have had many times before."

Mr. Pan smiled and said, "Yes, it is true. We always disagree on this subject since I am too old and I lack Mr. Xu's youthful optimism."

Everyone laughed loudly, including Mr. Pan, when Mr. Xu smiled back at his friend and replied, "Lao Pan, if you are so ancient, then why haven't you taken a wife yet?"

Turning to me, Mr. Pan said, "Ah, another discussion Little Xu and I have had before. He has been trying to introduce me to his cousin for months, but I keep telling him she will not be interested in me since I do not meet the requirements."

Asking what the requirements were, I assured Mr. Pan that he appeared to be good husband material.

Shrugging, he said, "The requirements are the three highs. If you want to attract a wife now, you must first have a high salary. Secondly, you must have a high level of education. The third requirement is that you must be at least 1.75 meters tall."*

Mr. Pan sighed dramatically and said, "I only have one high, my degree."

I told the group about an article on folk music that had been printed in the *Liberation Daily* the year before. The article noted that the folk music of rural China had reflected the changing perceptions of what criteria should be used in selecting a husband. During the Cultural Revolution, the determining factor for selecting a spouse had been class status. Those who came from families, which had been categorized as landlord, rich peasant, rightist, counterrevolutionary, or bad elements were not acceptable mates. One little ditty, which was popular at the time, had summed it up with the lyrics, "Fine girls wish to marry workers, peasants, and soldiers. We would rather be bitter for the rest of our years than marry a man of bad class

---

*Approximately 5'7".

status." However, with economic reform in the eighties, and the introduction of such slogans as "To Get Rich is Glorious," the girls in the countryside had changed their tune. Now they were singing, "We don't need details about class status, but we cannot dispense with either houses, money, or good looks." Mr. Pan replied that he would have to wait until there was a song about girls wanting a husband who had a big appetite and little else.

The word "appetite" made me realize it was well past dinner time. Thanking everyone for entertaining me with good company and good conversation, I told them that there were two paintings that I wanted to purchase before I left. One, an abstract by Mr. Xu, was called "Winter in Beijing." The other was an ink painting by Mr. Pan of a canal scene in Suzhou. Both artists objected, saying that I had been invited to the gallery as a guest, not as a customer, and insisting that I should not feel obligated to make a purchase. After a brief exchange, I convinced them that I really wanted the paintings, and was not offering to buy them out of a sense of obligation or as a gesture of courtesy.

Goodbys were said at the entrance to the Yu's residential compound, at the end of their *hutong,* and then again at the bus stop. When the bus pulled up to the curb, I said a last goodby as Mr. Pan and the others cautioned me to watch out for pickpockets on the bus.

A cloudy Saturday turned into a gloomy Sunday with overcast skies and drizzle throughout the day. A series of dreary days had begun. The dismal weather and quiet streets during the first days of the week created the illusion of political lethargy, as people masked their concern for the future by returning to their daily routines. However, dissension within both camps intensified.

The discord within the top leadership of the government took the public stage at the annual meeting of the Asian Development Bank. In his May 4th address to the group, Zhao Ziyang stated, "Student demonstrations do not indicate political instability, and the demonstrations mean in no way to oppose the fundamental system of China, but to correct the Party's and government's errors." Li Peng's May 5th speech to the same group stressed once more that "safeguarding national stability" was the top state task. He stated, "To deal with the situation the government has adopted calm, proper, and correct measures, which have helped to prevent the unrest from spreading." The government was now speaking with two voices.

Just as the China News Agency had predicted, more and more students returned to classes on Monday. However, many students disagreed with the decision announced on May 4th to end the boycott. The students who continued to boycott classes, feared the movement would lose its momentum if their protests ceased without a retraction of the April 26th editorial, recognition of the ASAB, and clear signs that the dialogues promised by Zhao would be genuine and productive exchanges.

Others within the movement felt the best plan of action was one of nonaction: to return to their campuses and declare a victory. The massive support from the *laobaixing* had been the movement's greatest success, and Zhao's supportive remarks and his agreement to a dialogue were added evidence of a victory.

Furthermore, journalists had joined in the May 4th demonstration, and the *People's Daily,* along with other newspapers, had given the students front page coverage on Friday following the May 4th demonstration. The stories had been accurate accounts of the demonstration, even quoting the banners calling for freedom of the press.

There was also reasonable concern that if the students continued with the boycott and demonstrations, it might cost the movement the support of the people, and give credence to the government's charges that their sole objective was to create turmoil. Additionally, continued protests might weaken the position of those within the Party who had shown a willingness to respond to the students' demands. With this in mind, some student leaders urged the students of Beijing to work from their campuses to legalize the individual organizations founded under the ASAB and to prepare for the dialogues Zhao had promised.

On Tuesday, May 9th, a thousand students, undaunted by the afternoon drizzle, went to the headquarters of the All China Journalists' Association in support of five hundred journalists who had come to present a petition of complaint addressed to the Secretariat of the Association. Among the 1,013 reporters and editors who signed the petition were members of the staffs of the *People's Daily* and Xinhua News Agency.

The petition called for a dialogue between journalists and officials of the Central Committee Department of Propaganda to discuss three points pertaining to censorship of the Chinese press. The first point of protest was the dismissal of Qin Benli as editor of the *World Economic Herald,* a Shanghai newspaper that had been founded by Qin.

Shortly after Hu Yaobang's death, the *World Economic Herald* had published a lengthy tribute to Hu, praising him for his support of the 1986-1987 student movement and political reform, while criticizing those within the Party who had forced Hu to resign. The government responded to the article by confiscating 300,000 copies of the newspaper and firing Qin.

Secondly, the petition addressed the restrictions placed on press coverage of the student movement, complaining that journalists had been prevented from giving fair, truthful, and comprehensive coverage of the students' demands, and the demonstrations that followed Hu's death. The third and final complaint was in response to Yuan Mu's remark regarding censorship during the April 29th meeting between students and government officials. Yuan Mu had stated that chief editors were free to decide what their newspapers would publish. The absurdity of Yuan Mu's statement was magnified by his poor timing since it came just three days after the dismissal of Qin Benli.

The petition was not only significant because it was a forceful statement in support of the students' demand for freedom of the press, but also because it marked the first time in the history of the People's Republic of China that a sizable number of journalists had banded together to attack censorship. However, without the accompanying glamour of thousands of colorful banners, crowds in the hundreds of thousands, and lines of police, the protest seemed a modest showing at best.

On Wednesday a larger number of students chose to demonstrate in a manner most suited to the Chinese lifestyle. Ten thousand students from fifteen universities rode through the streets of Beijing on bicycles adorned with flags and small banners. Their route took them to the Central People's Broadcasting Station, the Central Television Station, Xinhua News Agency, the *People's Daily,* the *Guangming Daily,* the *Beijing Daily,* and ended at the Propaganda Department of the Party Central Committee.

On that same day, Xinhua News Agency reported that thousands of students had staged a sit-in at the provincial government building in

Taiyuan, the provincial capital of Shanxi Province. Since Hu's death, demonstrations had also taken place in Shanghai, Xian, Wuhan, Changchun, Tianjin, Nanjing, Hefei, Chengdu, and Changsha. Xinhua News Agency also carried a front page report on Zhao's speech to a delegation of the Bulgarian Communist Party, in which he had stated, "Many difficulties that have cropped up in the course of the reform of the economy apparatus cannot possibly be overcome without reform of the political apparatus."

The accurate, unbiased reporting of the Taiyuan sit-in and the statement by Zhao encouraged the students. However, with Gorbachev's arrival just five days away, the students faced the reality that more drastic action would be required to keep the movement from fading away.

As I awaited the next development, the absence of sunshine and the growing suspense left me feeling listless at times and restless at other times. I filled the early days of the week with extra attention to my studies, mundane chores, late-night chats with Jinjin, and quick trips between rain showers to visit Lu Minghua, The Professor, Lao Pang, and Susan, who had called to complain that I was neglecting her.

When the sunshine reappeared on Friday, Yuanli called to ask if we could meet. I suggested that he come to my room instead of meeting me at a hotel or restaurant where we would have to compete for table space with the hordes of correspondents, anchormen, and television camera crews who had flooded into the city from around the world to cover Gorbachev's May 15th arrival in Beijing.

At seven o'clock Yuanli arrived at my door bearing treasures. I thanked him repeatedly as he handed me a bag of newspapers dating back to May 3rd and a case of Diet Coke, which he had brought as a special treat for me. While I savored a cup of room-temperature Diet Coke as if it were a glass of the finest chilled champagne, Yuanli, not yet Westernized enough to have developed a taste for the stuff, drank a beer.

As we sorted through the newspapers looking for the most important articles, one—covering the May 10th meeting of the members of the Standing Committee of the National People's Congress—caught my eye. It announced the agenda for the June 20th meeting of The Standing Committee, which included the drafting of a new law on demonstrations.

The present law, which regulated demonstrations and marches in

Beijing, had been enacted on December 26, 1986, as a result of the 1986-1987 demonstrations, and was one of the main grievances of the current student movement. Article Three of the law states that any group wishing to demonstrate must apply for a permit five days in advance of the planned demonstration. To apply, the organizer is required to go to the Public Security Bureau of the district or districts in which the march will be held where he must fill out a form stating the purpose of the march, the number of participants, as well as the time, place, and route of the demonstrations. In addition, the organizer must list his name, occupation, and address. Article Three alone all but eliminated the possibility of "legal" demonstrations, since few people in China are willing to volunteer such damning information to the Public Security Bureau. For those who are either brave or foolish enough to do so, there is always Article Four. It allows the Public Security Bureau to revise the proposed time, place, and route of the demonstration, and to impose "other appropriate conditions" on the demonstration, or to refuse to issue a permit.

Pointing to the article, I asked Yuanli, "Is this good news or bad news? Will the revised law be less restrictive or more restrictive?"

He shrugged and said, "Considering the students' decision today, I don't know if the members of the Standing Committee themselves could answer that question right now."

A knock on my door interrupted Yuanli before he could explain his remark. Since I had the pile of newspapers on my lap, he got up to answer the door. Lu Minghua was a little surprised to see a man standing at the door, but as soon as I introduced Yuanli, she smiled and told him she was happy to meet one of my old friends.

I finished looking through the newspapers while Lu Minghua focused her attention on Yuanli. In a style not unlike that of a homicide detective questioning a murder suspect with an airtight alibi, Lu Minghua grilled Yuanli about every aspect of his background, then moved on to his current activities. When she had completed the interrogation, she smiled at him and said, "We have to be very careful that someone doesn't take advantage of Kong Kailing. She is much too trusting of people. She thinks everyone is a good person." Turning to me, she pointed her chin toward Yuanli and said, "I could tell he had a good heart the minute I saw him. I can always tell what is in a person's heart by what I see in his eyes."

Lu Minghua had waved off my offer of tea earlier while she was talking with Yuanli. When I offered again, she sighed heavily and said, "I have no appetite for tea or anything else, for that matter."

Concerned, I asked, "Are you sick, Elder Sister?"

"I am sick at heart. Since I heard about the hunger strike I have not been able to eat a bite of food."

I realized that Yuanli had been referring to the hunger strike when Lu Minghua's arrival interrupted him. He was right. No one could predict how the Standing Committee would react to a hunger strike. They might be swayed by the students' willingness to sacrifice themselves for the cause of political reform, or they might view the hunger strike as emotional blackmail.

I had heard throughout the day that a few students were going to stage a hunger strike and a sit-in at Tiananmen Square the next day. However, like a lot of small lane news, I had heard several versions of the story. Since I had been unable to get any concrete information, I thought it might be a groundless rumor.

Lu Minghua shook her head sadly and said, "No, it is fact, and more than a few students are involved. Hundreds of students from Beijing University and Beijing Normal University have already volunteered to fast until their deaths if necessary."

Looking down at my cup of Diet Coke, I felt very much the spoiled American who takes everything from Diet Coke to democracy for granted. Missing meals is serious business in China. Therefore, a hunger strike was the most drastic, nonviolent means that the students could use to force the government to respond to their demands.

Throughout China's history, war, drought, vast areas of arid land, and the capricious nature of the Yellow River have made famine the most enduring and constant enemy of the Chinese people. As recently as the early 1960s, thirty million Chinese fell victim to the famine, which resulted from Mao's Great Leap Forward.

Furthermore, the role which food has played in Chinese culture intensified the drama of a hunger strike. The Ancient Book of Rites, classical poetry, and the writings of Confucius and other philosophers have instructed generation after generation of Chinese in the rituals and customs regarding food. They prescribe the proper methods for the preparation and serving of food, advise which foods to eat or to avoid for a certain ailment, and warn which foods are considered poisonous if mixed. In China, food has always been regarded as much more than something consumed merely to fill an empty belly. Although Chinese cuisine stresses the three appeals of food (sight, smell, and taste) one doesn't eat something simply because it is appealing or tasty. Food is consumed as an antidote, a prophylactic, a stimulant, and a restorative. One eats specific foods to harmonize the system by balancing the yin and yang, to heat or cool the body as needed, to build blood or bodily strength, to strengthen the brain and other organs, as an aphrodisiac, and so on.

In traditional China, food was just as essential to the dead as it was to the living. Although the Communist Party has scorned such beliefs as superstition, custom dictates that bowls filled with delicacies should be placed at the tomb of one's ancestors to prevent them from becoming hungry ghosts. It should also be remembered that even the gods need nourishment. An offering of food will encourage their intercession in some matters and discourages their interference in others.

The cultural attitude toward food is frequently reflected in the Chinese language. One greets a friend or neighbor in passing by inquiring, "have you eaten yet?" A Chinese does not "take" medicine, but "eats" it. In English, *renkou* (population) means people's mouths, and *diu fanwan* (to lose one's job), means to lose one's rice bowl.

There was yet another cultural factor that contributed to the emotionality of a hunger strike. In Chinese society, a child's first obligation is to his parents, and a filial child repays his parents for their sacrifices by caring for them in their old age. This created a moral dilemma for the students. Dying for democracy might be heroic, but purposely risking one's life by fasting could be considered an unfilial act.

Certainly a fast would not be taken lightly by either the Party leaders or the *laobaixing*. I wondered out loud how Deng Xiaoping would react to the news of a hunger strike. It would be the ultimate loss of face for Deng if hundreds of hunger strikers were at Tiananmen Square when Gorbachev arrived for the summit.

Yuanli agreed. "I think that is what the students are counting on. They are trying to force the leaders to respond immediately instead of waiting until after the summit is over. Zhao has called for talks, but nothing has happened. Perhaps his support of a dialogue was only a tactic to prevent any disturbances during the summit. After the summit, what leverage do the students have to make the leaders keep that promise?"

Turning to Yuanli, Lu Minghua said, "Why do our leaders force the students to use such extreme measures? I worry about the health of the students and I worry about the health of our country." Shaking her head in exasperation, she added, "I don't know where the future is going to take us."

Turning back to me, she said, "Little Sister, remember your friend told you he had never tasted hope. I am older than your friend. I have tasted hope. I remember how backward and poor China was before the People's Republic was founded. The Communist Party gave us hope.

"My family are *laobaixing*. When I was young, we did not have enough food to eat or enough clothes to keep us warm in the winter. My mother was illiterate and my brothers and sister had very little education. Yet, after liberation when the Communist Party came to power, I was able to go to college and become a teacher. I am grateful to the Party for that. I loved the Party and Mao Zedong for educating me, and giving me a job so that I could feed my family and buy warm clothes for them in the winter. But through the years, I have seen so much destruction and corruption at the hands of the Party and the leaders. I saw the hope that Mao had given us erased by madness and darkness. I saw the leaders becoming just as evil as those they had replaced.

When Mao died and Deng came to power, once more I saw a ray of hope. I remember when students rallied on Tiananmen Square to greet Deng Xiaoping. They cheered, 'Xiaoping, how are you?' We thought, at last, China has the upright official who will rule justly. But that hope vanished as well. We saw leaders become just as corrupt as those in the past, and for each economic reform pushed through, there was a political crisis followed by an economic crisis. When Democracy Wall fell, we knew that as far as the leaders were concerned, democracy was still a bad word and intellectuals were still bad people.

"After ten years of reform, where are we? We have islands of prosperity in the Special Economic Zones, but they are merely playgrounds for the children of officials. We still do not have a just legal system. Officials and their families are still above the law and use the law against the people to silence anyone who criticizes them."

Wearily, Lu Minghua said, "I sometimes wonder if it is not better to feel completely hopeless than to have had glimmers of hope that are so easily snatched away."

Trying to ease her anxiety, I said, "Elder Sister, surely with so much support from the *laobaixing,* the leaders cannot ignore the students and the need for political reform. Perhaps the hunger strike will speed up the process."

Yuanli nodded and added, "Teacher Lu, people are no longer blind to injustice, and they are tired of being afraid to speak out."

Smiling at our efforts to cheer her, Lu Minghua said, "I know. When I saw how everyone came out to support the students, I was so proud that I am Chinese and that I am from Beijing. I am normally a very optimistic person. It is not like me to be so anxious. I hope you are right, Little Sister. Perhaps this time the hope will turn into more than wishful dreams."

Yuanli rose to leave, explaining he had come on his bicycle, and the trip home would take him at least an hour. Lu Minghua said she must leave as well, then tapping her head with the palm of her hand, she scolded herself for her forgetfulness. "Little Sister, I almost forgot to tell you the main reason I came tonight. Your friend, The Professor, has written a *dazibao.*"

I laughed softly, telling her I was not at all surprised. Since I couldn't wait to read The Professor's *dazibao,* Lu Minghua told me that she would take me to see it. Although most of the *dazibao* were still being posted on Building #8 and the wall next to it, others were scattered here and there. The Professor's was posted on a short wall near the library. Written in his elegant calligraphy, his commemoration of the May Fourth Movement, stood out among the dozen or so that were pasted to the wall.

Dawn comes as demonstrations commemorate the 70th Anniversary. Feudalism has reached a ripe old age. The evil of bribery has existed far too long. On the streets and in the alleys, politics is the topic of casual conversation. In the hearts of one hundred thousand intellectuals and one million workers, the desire for liberty lives on.

Just as The Professor had written, politics was the topic of conversation. Over the weekend, stories of the brave hunger strikers echoed down the streets and through the alleys. The public address systems on campuses throughout the city broadcast reports from the square and tapes of speeches that had been made on the square by fasting students.

Building #8 became the information center on our campus. *Dazibao* with quotes from *Time, Newsweek,* the *International Herald Tribune,* and Hong Kong newspapers were posted on the walls. Copies of the *News Herald,* the *Hunger Strikers' News Bulletin,* and other publications produced by the students were pasted on the walls, along with copies of their mimeographed leaflets that had been distributed throughout the city. Broadcasts and recordings of broadcasts from Voice of America, BBC, Hong Kong, and Taiwan radio boomed out of a window on the top floor of the building, so that those who gathered below each evening could hear what the rest of the world had to say about the Student Democratic Movement and the hunger strikers.

People spoke of the hunger strikers with tears in their eyes and respect and solicitude in their voices. They spoke of how the students had written their wills, then said final farewells to their friends. They spoke of how the students had written the characters for "hunger striker" on white headbands, then tying them around their heads, had marched to Tiananmen Square to begin their fast on the afternoon of Saturday, May 13th.

Some said that students had written the character for death in their own blood to show their willingness to die for freedom. Others spoke of how teachers had brought bowls of steaming jiaozi to the students for a final feast, and how the students—their hearts filled with grief—were too upset to eat. Many spoke of China's new heroine, Chai Ling, a slim, twenty-three year old graduate student at Beijing Normal University, who had inspired so many of her classmates to join the hunger strike with her eloquent speeches at *Beida* and her dedication to democracy. All spoke of their anger toward leaders who would allow the brightest of China's youth to sacrifice themselves.

The number of students participating in the hunger strike grew from several hundred to three thousand. A delegation from the University of Tianjin and Nankai University in Tianjin traveled eighty miles by bicycle to join the students of Beijing in their fast. Twenty thousand of the hunger strikers' classmates gathered around them on the square, protecting them and offering them emotional support. Weeping parents went to the square to convince their sons and daughters to stop the fast. Yet, after talking with their children, they left the square convinced that their brave sons and daughters were doing the right thing. Teachers went to the square giving their students words of comfort to ease their fears, and bringing umbrellas to shade them from the hot sun in the daytime, along with coats and quilts to protect them from the evening chill. The *laobaixing* went by the tens of thousands, just to get a glimpse of the heroes of Beijing.

Banners on the square proclaimed the students' commitment to their demands, and touched the hearts of everyone who read them. Patrick Henry's words, "Give me liberty or give me death," joined the words of the hunger strikers, "We love democracy more than rice." Other banners spoke of the hunger strikers' willingness to suffer for China, stating "Mama, I am hungry, but I cannot eat," and "The hunger of China is greater than our own."

Dazibao and leaflets explained the students' action. One, written by hunger strikers from *Beida* stated:

China is our country,
her people are our people,
the government should be our government.
If we do not speak out, who will speak out?
If we do not act, who will act?

The students issued a Hunger Strike Declaration in which they explained that their decision to fast had been made to protest the "cold and uncaring attitude of the government," the delaying tactics of the government in establishing a dialogue, and the government's charges that the students and the Student Democratic Movement were unpatriotic and creating turmoil. The declaration demanded that a "concrete dialogue" begin, and in regard to the April 26th editorial, it further demanded that the unjust charges, which had damaged the reputation of the students and the Student Democratic Movement, must be retracted.

On Sunday, May 14th, a delegation of twelve intellectuals went to Tiananmen Square to persuade the students to leave before Gorbachev's arrival the following day. The delegation included Yan Jiaqi, a political scientist who had been a member of Zhao Ziyang's think tank, The Research Institute of Political Science.* When their efforts failed, the intellectuals gave their support to the hunger strikers, calling on other members of the intellectual community to support the students.

Sunday afternoon, the hunger strikers were notified that government representatives would meet with the students at four o'clock at the Ministry of the United Front. Fifty students from thirty universities went to the headquarters with Wang Dan, Wuer Kaixi, and eleven other students acting as spokesmen for the group. However, shortly after seven in the evening the students called for a recess of the talks when the government's representatives refused to retract the charges made against the students in the April 26th editorial and denied the students' request to have the talks broadcast live to the rest of the hunger strikers at the square.** By midnight, it was apparent that the talks had failed, and that the hunger strikers would remain on Tiananmen Square. Monday morning at 1:30 a.m., the talks were officially adjourned.

It was not the students' intent to prevent Gorbachev from coming to the square to lay the traditional wreath at the Monument to the People's Heroes. Having been denied their request that he be allowed to speak at Beida, they welcomed an opportunity to meet with Gorbachev. In preparation for his visit, the hunger strikers moved away from the side of the square closest to the Great Hall of the People, and students from the foreign

---

*Other members of the delegation were *Su Xiaokang,* cowriter of the controversial television documentary in China, "River Elegy"; *Dai Qing,* a *Guangming Daily* reporter; *Li Honglin,* President of the Fujian Academy of Political Social Sciences; *Yu Haocheng,* Chief Editor of *The Legal Studies Journal*; *Bao Zunxin,* a researcher at the Chinese Academy of Social Sciences Institute of History; *Wen Yuankai,* a professor at the China Science and Technology Institute; *Li Zehou,* a scholar of aesthetics and a professor at the Chinese Academy of Social Sciences Institute of Philosophy; *Su Wei,* a professor at the Chinese Academy of Social Sciences Institute of Literature; *Li Tuo,* a literary critic and member of the Chinese Writers' Association; *Mai Tianshu,* a novelist and reporter for the *China Youth Newspaper*; and *Liu Zaifu,* a literary critic.

**Li Tieying,* Vice Premier and Minister of the State Education Commission; *Yan Mingfu,* Secretary of the Central Committee Secretariat and head of the Central Committee United Front Department; and *Wei Jianxing;* Minister of Supervision under the State Council were the government's representatives.

language institutes wrote banners in Russian that welcomed Gorbachev, praising him as a political reformer.

School flags, bright banners, *dazibao,* and umbrellas dotted the square with bursts of color when I arrived at Tiananmen Square Monday morning. Groups of students sat beneath their school banners, painting slogans on signs, banners, and small red paper flags. Periodically, one of the groups paraded around the square in a mini-demonstration, then returned to their starting point where students leaders used portable speakers to address the crowd. Hundreds of thousands of Beijingers, many with children in hand, walked around the square, stopping to listen to a speaker from one group before moving on to the next.

Chanted by the students and echoed by the crowd, a barrage of slogans—written on *dazibao,* banners, leaflets, and paper flags—encouraged the hunger strikers, urged support for the movement, and criticized the leaders for their corruption and callousness.

> *"For the sake of humanism, a dialogue should begin as soon as possible!"*
>
> *"Abolish the ten regulations on demonstrations illegally enacted by the Beijing City government!"*
>
> *"Strike down official profiteering and publicize the financial holdings of officials!"*
>
> *"Uphold justice!"*
>
> *"Everyone has a share in the responsibility of the fate of his country!"*
>
> *"Acknowledge the Student Democratic Movement as Patriotic!"*
>
> *"Where is your conscience!"*
>
> *"The hunger strikers' petition is a matter of life or death!"*
>
> *"We will never give up until we reach our goal!"*
>
> *"For the sake of democracy, we cannot fear intimidation!"*

At noon a frail young woman from Nankai University in Tianjin, climbed the steps of the monument at the center of the square to address the massive crowd. Holding their recorders high in the air, people strained to capture her powerful words on tape as her thin, high voice quavered with emotion and exhaustion.

Every time we hear the cries for democracy on the square of the Republic, our heart trembles and we are moved to tears. Why? Why? Is it that the children of the Republic are weak? No, Republic, it is not that we are weak. If we were weak, the Democratic Movement would not continue at the cost of precious lives. If we were weak, we could not leave Nankai University to make a long, arduous journey of thirteen hours to express our support for our brothers and sisters in Beijing. If we were weak, we could not stay on the square, trembling in the cold night air. If we were weak, we could not fast until we collapsed on the cold cement slabs of the square. If we were weak, we could not let hunger devour our young bodies. And, if we were weak, we could not expose ourselves to the blazing, hot sun and let it dry the last drop of sweat and blood from our bodies.

What makes us shed the last drop of water from our bodies by weeping? We weep because our people still live in poverty. That is why we weep! We weep because our nation is still suffocated by tyranny. That is why we weep! We weep because so many are still numbed by apathy. We can no longer wait to see our nation take its place in the world!

Throughout the day, the three thousand hunger strikers rested on sheets of plastic, conserving their energy as friends tended them, and volunteers from the medical community monitored their vital signs. Without a sufficient reserve of body fat, and with only liquids to sustain them, most were already in a weakened state. By evening, over one hundred had collapsed to be carried from the square to waiting ambulances.

As I walked from circle to circle, photographing banners, *dazibao,* and students, I stopped to talk with each group of students. They were eager to speak to a foreigner, to explain their demands. They wanted to express their opinions, and listen to mine. Some spoke in English and others in Chinese, but their questions were always the same. They wanted to know if Americans supported their cries for democracy. They wondered if Americans could understand their pain.

Gorbachev did not come to the square. The students stood on the steps of the monument with the large banners they had written in Russian and Chinese. They faced the Great Hall of the People, hoping that Gorbachev or someone in his delegation might read them and know there were banners proclaiming "Duplicate perestroika!" and "Democracy, Our Common Goal!"

In the afternoon, the intellectuals arrived. Professors, lecturers, scientists, journalists, researchers, artists, writers, poets, and performers all answered their colleagues' call to support the hunger strikers. They flooded Eternal Peace Avenue like a human river, as thousands upon thousands poured into the square. It took hundreds of people to carry the massive banner that waved and twisted above them, stretching down the avenue like a gigantic blue and gold dragon.

When dusk came, I realized I was exhausted. My stomach churned from too much adrenaline and too little food. I had brought fruit and a steamed bun with me to the square, but I couldn't eat in front of so many who were fasting. Pedaling along slowly on my bicycle, the ten kilometers back to the campus seemed twice that distance as I tried to ignore the throbbing muscles in my legs.

Jinjin clapped her hands in excitement when I walked into the room. Jumping up to pour me a cup of tea, she asked one question after the other. The tea was tempting, but I apologized, telling her that I was too tired to talk, too tired to shower, and even too tired to drink a cup of tea. I barely had the energy to undress and climb into bed. Assuring Jinjin that the light would not bother me, I pulled the covers over my head, eager to sleep.

I closed my eyes, wanting only to see darkness, but an image from my mind filled the blackness. I saw the face of one of the hunger strikers from Beijing Normal University. I had seen thousands of faces, and talked with dozens of students; yet, his face stood out so clearly among all of the others.

An umbrella had shaded him as he lay on a sheet of plastic. When he looked up at me, I smiled and pointed to my camera, mouthing the words, *"Xing bu xing?"* to ask if it was okay for me to take his picture. Smiling back at me, he nodded weakly. Raising his hand a few inches above his head, he held up two fingers in a "V" sign. After I had taken the picture, he motioned for me to come closer. I stepped over the bottles and litter piled near him, then squatted at his side. I didn't ask his name nor did he volunteer it. He did tell me that he was eighteen. Smiling, I told him that he was the same age as my son, Michael.

"You're an American?" He asked.

"Yes."

"Can I ask you a question?" When I had answered with a nod, he asked, "What is it like to live in freedom?"

He looked up at me, patiently waiting for my answer. Tears welled in my eyes. Words raced through my mind, but I struggled to find the right words. Finally, I replied, "Glorious."

Nodding, he said, "Thank you," then closed his eyes to rest, or perhaps to dream of freedom.

CHAPTER FOURTEEN
A POLITE REVOLUTION

I looked down the tracks to see if there were any signs of a train in the distance. Not even a pinpoint of light glimmered in the darkness. It was a few minutes after three in the morning, and the crowd at the railroad crossing had grown larger with each passing hour. Small lane news had alerted students from the campuses in the area and people from the surrounding neighborhoods. They had rushed to the crossing when the word went out that troops from distant provinces were being sent to Beijing.

At half past midnight, Premier Li Peng and President Yang Shangkun had addressed the top Party and military leaders in an emergency meeting broadcast live to the nation from The Great Hall of the People. Zhao Ziyang's noticeable absence from the meeting, and Li Peng's ironhanded speech were proof that the hard-liners were in control.

Reiterating the accusations made in the April 26th editorial and citing new charges, Li Peng justified the decision to order troops to the capital to "enforce order." Waving his fists in the air, he angrily declared that the capital was "in a state of anarchy, with laws and discipline being violated." He called on all of those present to "take swift action to halt the turmoil, restore order, and maintain stability and unity in order to ensure reform, the policy of openness, and socialist modernization."

Restating that the students were being directed by a small group of people who were intent on overthrowing the socialist system, Li Peng assured the leaders assembled in the Great Hall of the People that, in taking the necessary measures to end the turmoil, the leadership would have the support of "Party members, the Communist Youth League, workers, peasants, intellectuals, and the vast majority of people from all walks of life." His speech also included a bewildering charge that the hunger strikers were being "held hostage" by a handful of people who were "attempting to coerce the government into meeting their own political demands."

Those in the crowd around me discussed the speech and Zhao's absence from the meeting, speculating on what might happen in the next few days. One old man shook his head at the irony of the situation, saying "Comrade Zhao replaced Comrade Hu as the General Secretary. Now, it looks as if he has replaced Comrade Hu as the Party's scapegoat."

Turning away from the crowd, I walked along the embankment that ran between the tracks and the wall of a residential compound. A few yards in front of me, two men were sitting on an old railroad tie next to the wall. It looked like a good place to rest for a few minutes, but I didn't want to disturb the men. Walking a few feet past them, I squatted on the damp ground, using the wall to brace my back. The younger of the two men who appeared to be in his late twenties stood up and pointed at the railroad tie, inviting me to join them. The older man who was around fifty repeated the invitation and motioned for me to come and sit down. Thanking them, I sat down on the tie, and offered the two men American cigarettes. After the three mandatory refusals, they accepted the cigarettes, each giving me a Chinese cigarette in return.

The exchange of cigarettes put us on more intimate terms, and after determining my nationality, age, and profession, the younger man asked if I agreed with the students' viewpoint. It was a question that I had been asked hundreds of times over the last few days. Both Yuanli and Lu Minghua had urged me to be cautious in stating my opinion, warning me that the secret police were out in force. When I suspected that I might be talking with a member of Division Thirteen, I gave a pat answer to the question saying, "I am worried about the students' health, but their politics isn't any of my business." However, it was apparent by their dress and their dialect that these two men were ordinary workers. In fact, I had difficulty understanding them since they spoke in the typical Beijing street dialect with their words slurred together sounding a hard "errr" at the end of most words. But I was curious to hear what they had to say, so I gave them a direct answer.

Telling them that I had talked with many students on the square and had found them to be brave, patriotic Chinese, I added that the students' demands seemed reasonable, especially since they had focused on a dialogue and a retraction of the editorial. Putting aside the issue of face, these two demands were much easier for the government to comply with than the broader and more complex demands of adopting democratic political and judicial systems. Even the most idealistic of those in the Student Democratic Movement knew that the more difficult demands could not be accomplished overnight.

Nodding enthusiastically, the younger workers said, "Yes, it is the leaders who are wrong, not the students. The students are willing to sacrifice their lives for China, but the leaders will not even sacrifice living in mansions and driving expensive cars."

The older worker grunted in disgust, then said, "The leaders send their children to study in foreign universities, then give them big titles, and help them become rich when they return to China. Comrade Mao made mistakes when he got old, but he didn't send his son off to live a soft life in a foreign country. He sent his son to die in Korea."* Pausing, he put out his cigarette in the dirt and then said, "You know what the people are saying—in China, we have had only four days of freedom." The younger worker repeated the phrase, "Four days of freedom," then counted the days off on his fingers, "May 16th, 17th, 18th, and 19th." Shaking his head in wonder, he said, "Only four days of freedom, but no one in Beijing will ever forget those four days."

How true! So many times over the past four days, I had found it hard to believe that I was actually in China. The Beijing of the "Four Days of Freedom" was an open city where people publicly challenged and ridiculed the absolute power of the leadership. All four days had been extraordinary, with each more extraordinary than the last. During that time, I had seen and heard things that I had never dreamed possible in Beijing. The previous demonstrations and the intellectuals' march to the square on Monday now seemed like dress rehearsals—a prelude to the drama, intensity, spectacle, and excitement of the "Four Days of Freedom."

*Mao Anying, Mao's eldest son, was killed in an American air raid in 1950, just weeks after he was sent to fight in Korea.

On Tuesday, one thousand intellectuals signed the May 16th Declaration, criticizing the Party and government for not "reacting sensibly" to the movement and citing as examples the leaders' refusal to recognize the ASAB as well as their characterization of the movement as one intent on creating turmoil. In an open letter to the leadership, ten university presidents urged a dialogue with the students. They encouraged "a reasonable, rational, and realistic attitude," and called on both government officials and students to "exercise restraint so that the situation would not be further aggravated and matters that would be regretted and difficult to amend could be avoided."*

Half a million people came to the square in support of the hunger strikers. The number of students participating in the fast had grown to 3,147, while the number of volunteer medical personnel had risen to 1,000. The frequent sound of ambulance sirens was a constant reminder to the people that the students' lives were in jeopardy. When twelve fasting students refused water and other liquids and rumors spread that four students had threatened to burn themselves alive, the people of Beijing wept and cursed the leaders of China for their inhumanity.

Before dawn on Wednesday, May 17th, Party and government leaders appealed to the hunger strikers to cease their fast and check into hospitals for treatment, promising that when the hunger strikers and their supporters left the square, there would be no attempt to "settle accounts." However, the promise did not ring true. The leaders still refused to retract the charges made in the editorial of April 26th, and while they promised to continue a dialogue, there was no indication that ASAB would be recognized or included in any future talks. Having already witnessed the collapse of over three hundred and forty of their classmates, the students had lost all

---

*The university officials who signed the open letter were *Fang Fukang*, President of Beijing Normal University; *Zhang Xiaowen*, President of Qinghua University; *Chen Jiaer*, Vice President of Beijing University; *Wan Mingkun*, President of Beijing University of Communications; *Wang Fuxiang*, President of Beijing Institute of Foreign Languages; *Da Huang*, Vice President of People's University; *Shen Shiyuan*, President of Beijing University of Aviation and Aerospace; *Jiang Kang*, President of Beijing University of Politics and Law; *Wang Ruan*, President of Beijing University of Technology; and *Shi Yuanchun*, President of Beijing University of Agriculture.

confidence in the leadership for allowing such suffering. The hunger strikers voted to continue the fast.

In support of the hunger strikers, a dozen of the country's top intellectuals released the May 17th Declaration. Unlike the milder declaration of the day before, it was a direct verbal assault on the leadership of China, and specifically, Deng Xiaoping. It charged that "due to the absolute power held by a dictator, the government has lost its sense of responsibility and its humanity," and went on to state that "the people of China could no longer wait for the dictator to admit his mistake."

As dawn came, the leaders of China faced their worst nightmare. In addition to deciding to continue the hunger strike, the students had called for a city-wide work strike. The students and other intellectuals represented only a small percentage of the population and were manageable. The *laobaixing* were an entirely different matter. Moreover, as one million people gathered in Tiananmen Square again, the world press was on hand to cover the story in depth and to broadcast the action.

The flat bed of the truck was filled with a few cement blocks, several large bamboo poles, a huge wooden spindle for electrical cable, six bicycles, ten Chinese students, a few small signs bearing political slogans, a large red banner with the characters for the name of the students' college written in black calligraphy, one rather reluctant Australian, and me.

Looking over at Joan, I gave her a smile of encouragement. She was sitting on one of the cement blocks with her legs wedged between the pile of bicycles and the bamboo poles. Grasping the wooden railing of the truck tightly with one hand, she held down the straw hat on her head with the other. The engine sputtered and we started to move again, the gears grinding as the driver shifted into second.

I shouted back to Joan, "You said you wanted to go with me to Tiananmen Square."

She set her face in a sardonic smile, then shouted back, "I didn't say I wanted to be in the demonstration, I said I wanted to go the demonstration. There's a difference, you know!"

Once more the truck pulled to a stop in the traffic. Joan took advantage of the opportunity to rearrange her position as best she could. Scooting over a few inches, she moved closer to the railing so she could see what was ahead. Pointing to the traffic in front of us, she said, "There's a bus up ahead. I thought you said the bus drivers were on strike."

I stood up to look out over the cab of the truck. Shouting back to Joan over my shoulder, I asked, "When was the last time you saw a public bus loaded with students on their way to demonstrate at the square, and covered with signs that say, 'Support the Patriotic Student Movement'?"

As the truck rolled forward, the two students standing on either side of me cautioned me to brace myself by leaning against the cab. Raising my camera, I photographed the lines of vehicles that stretched for miles in front of us and miles behind us. We were still several kilometers from the center of the city, yet people lined the streets and the overpasses, applauding and cheering the passing cavalcade.

Joan and I attracted special attention. People nudged each other, pointing us out and the word *waiguoren* (foreigner) ran through the crowd like a wave. Joan reacted to being in the spotlight by pulling her straw hat farther down over her face. She planned to stay in China to do research when her studies were completed, and I knew she was concerned that someone might report her to the university. But she had insisted on going with me to the square even after I had pointed out that it might be a little risky for her. Although I wasn't exactly delighted at the prospect of losing my scholarship or being "invited to leave China," I had abandoned any hope of keeping a low profile. I had decided my first priority was to witness and record what was happening.

We hadn't planned to ride to the square with students. Joan and I had left the campus on our bicycles, but after riding a couple of blocks I insisted that we pull over and park our bikes. The traffic was more congested than I had ever seen it, and there were too many starts and stops for us to bicycle safely. I was determined to get to the square, even if I had to walk the ten kilometers, but I did want to get there in one piece. As it turned out, we only had to walk from the parking lot back to Great Knowledge Boulevard. The truck was stopped in traffic just a few yards ahead of us. As soon as the students spotted us, they waved to us and called out, *"Lai, lai, lai!"* inviting us to climb aboard.

Gradually, Joan relaxed and adjusted to the spotlight. She even pulled her hat back off her face, and waved to people in the crowd. One of the students standing next to me, an eighteen-year-old boy, struck up a conversation with me. He giggled at my Chinese just like Little Ma. The other student, a nineteen-year-old girl, listened quietly as her classmate asked me the standard questions about America. When he had finished with his questions, she finally spoke. In a voice that was so soft that I had difficulty hearing her over the traffic, she asked one of the most unusual questions I had ever been asked about my country. She wanted to know if there were cucumbers in America. She asked in such a sincere manner that I suppressed a chuckle, and answered her question seriously, assuring her that cucumbers were readily available throughout the entire United States. Hearing the good news, she nodded her head decisively and stated, "Good, I think I would like to go to America!"

While the student who fancied cucumbers held my bag for me, I concentrated on photographing the crowd. I photographed soldiers in a truck, smiling as they waved "Vs" for victory to the crowd; a brigade of bicycling medical students and their professors, on their way to volunteer their aid to the hunger strikers; people gathered on the roof of a building, holding up a sign calling for support of the hunger strikers; and a worker wearing a black paper hat that mocked the traditional garb of officials in Old China. A sign on the hat labeled him a "corrupt official," inferring that modern day and ancient officials were equally corrupt.

Dozens of people lined the overpass railing ahead of us that was draped with a massive banner saying "Express Support for the Students—Long Life to Democracy!" One woman stood out among the others on the overpass. With both hands held high in the victory sign, she posed for my camera, her face beaming with a joyful, dimpled smile.

As we drove closer to the center of the city, I noticed how much more organized the traffic was than it had been the day before. Shouting back to Joan, I said, "A traffic engineer must have joined the movement!"

Workers were directing traffic at each major intersection, as thousands of bicycles, motorcycles, trucks, public buses, tourist buses, mini-vans, cars, taxis, carts, dump trucks, and even a couple of cement trucks flowed past. Those who were driving into town merely to witness the demonstrations remained in the main lanes of traffic, while the vehicles carrying demonstrators were diverted to the bicycle lane, which had been cleared of all other traffic for use as an express lane.

The driver let us off on a side street about two miles from the square. Two students carried the school banner while the other students followed behind with their protest signs. As they rushed off to join the demonstration, Joan and I jogged along beside them.

As we rounded the corner of Eternal Peace Avenue and Xidan, one-and-a-half miles from the square, I gasped at the density of the crowd. On each side of Eternal Peace Avenue, a solid wall of people stretched all the way to Tiananmen Square. Even more amazing than the multitudes was the orderliness, discipline, and organization of the scene.

Using miles of plastic twine, students and workers had divided the avenue into three lanes on each side to accommodate the traffic going to and coming from the square. The inner lanes were for ambulances, the middle lanes for the demonstrators in vehicles, and the outer lanes for the demonstrators who were marching. All the way down the avenue, students and workers stood within an arm's distance of each other, holding up the twine which formed the lanes.

Grabbing Joan's hand, I dragged her into the swarm of people. She moaned, saying "We'll never get there!"

I could only laugh, shaking my head in amazement as I answered, "Joan, I have news for you—we're THERE! THERE just covers a considerably larger area than we thought it would!"

The sidewalk was so packed with people we could only take one step at a time, stopping to wait for several seconds before the next step. The students and workers who were holding the twine repeated apologies to each passerby for the inconvenience, asking in the most courteous terms that people move on as quickly as possible. Everyone responded with equal courtesy, not only toward those directing traffic, but also toward each other. In a spirit of cooperation, no one attempted to cross the twine barriers, and with an even-tempered and patient attitude, no one pushed against others in the crowd or even complained about the delay. Although Chinese custom does not demand that one apologize to a stranger, people smiled at each other, apologizing politely when they accidentally bumped another person in the crowd. Joan kept muttering to herself, "Incredible!" while I chuckled to myself, thinking how very like the Chinese it was to stage a polite revolution.

All the while, a tidal wave of demonstrators flowed down Eternal Peace Avenue. *Laobaixing* and intellectuals, Party members and nonmembers marched together in their desire to convey to the leaders of China the message they chanted in the streets: *"Jiu jiu haizi* (Save our children)!"

Those who marched were students, teachers, doctors, ministry officials, factory workers, journalists, bankers, magistrates, celebrities, common laborers, shop clerks, postal workers, vendors, tourist guides, street sweepers, high school and elementary students, retirees, and even Buddhist monks.

The characters, *"Sheng Yuan* (express support)," were written on headbands and armbands that were worn by the people, and on signs and banners that were posted on vehicles, shop windows, trees, lampposts, and vendors' carts. *Dazibao* and leaflets hung on walls and lampposts along the way, in front of *Zhongnanhai,* the corner entrance to the Great Hall of the People, and the pedestrian underpasses that led to the square.

The messages expressed by the slogans and the banners were as diverse as the participants. Workers chanted "We support the students, and we are not afraid of being fired!" as they carried banners announcing their arrival from their factory. Staff from the Ministry of Foreign Affairs carried a banner asking "How can we discuss foreign affairs when our internal affairs are corrupt?" Magistrates, marching in uniform, called for democracy and a valid legal system. Police marched with a banner declaring, "The People's Police Love the People!" Young children chanted "Xiaoping, Xiaoping, eighty-four years old, and no longer very sharp!" Some of the slogans were clever or poetic, others bluntly expressed the people's outrage.

"Deng Xiaoping, go back to playing bridge!"

"Deng Xiaoping, where are you?"

"Can an old brain have new ideas?"

"Do something to rescue the students!"

"Angry waves of the ocean shed blood for the country!"

"Use a mother's conscience to arouse apathetic souls!"

Near the side steps to the Great Hall of the People, Joan pointed over my shoulder to a gap in the crowd. As we moved closer, we saw a small group of doctors. One was speaking through a megaphone, appealing for donations to purchase medicine for the hunger strikers. Although I had donated money on the square the day before, I couldn't resist their appeal.

Certain no one would notice me in such a large crowd, I wadded up a few bills, telling Joan that I would discreetly slip the money in their basket as we walked past. It didn't occur to me that the man with the megaphone would announce to the crowd that the "honorable foreigner" had just made a generous donation. His announcement was met with a cheer and applause from the surrounding crowd. As we dove into the nearest throng of people, Joan giggled and said, "How very discreet of you!"

With the hunger strike in its fourth day, Tiananmen Square had been transformed into a mixture of disaster area, carnival, MASH unit, circus, political convention, and festival. It had become "A Happening," unlike any other before it.

Students and workers stood guard around the perimeter of the square just as riot police had done during earlier demonstrations. On the west side of the square, another plastic twine lane formed an entrance to the center of the square, which was reserved for ambulances and the arriving demonstrators. The entrance for the general public was set up on the same side of the square, just past The Great Hall of the People.

In the heart of the square, by the Monument to the People's Heroes, the base for the hunger strikers was surrounded by student guards who formed a human chain to protect their classmates from the crush of the crowd. Tents had been set up to shield the hunger strikers from the elements. Inside the tents, bottles of glucose dangled from the support beams. Medical personnel rushed about keeping close watch over their patients and summoning ambulances for the students who collapsed.

The crowd cheered as a mailman arrived, carrying a bag filled with letters and telegrams in support of the hunger strikers. Vendors and ordinary citizens delivered baskets of boiled eggs and steamed buns along with carts piled with boxes of soda pop, popsicles, and yogurt. The snacks were generously distributed to the arriving demonstrators, and to the students and workers who manned the twine lanes. Still photographers and camera-men photographed the scene as they stood on the backs of rented bicycle carts, which carried them around the square. At the Monument to the People's Heroes, journalists scurried about interviewing student leaders, while some ventured out into the crush of people to interview spectators.

High above the square, tethered to the top of the Monument to the People's Heroes, a large, white balloon floated in the air. The single character *"Yao"* had been written on the balloon. Want, demand, essential, desire, need—any one of its multiple meanings expressed the emotion of the situation, just as the crowd's chant, *"Xian Zai* (now)!" expressed the urgency.

I wanted to find the hunger striker from Beijing Normal University, but Joan had not thought to bring her student identification. A student or teacher identity card, which is encased in a small, red plastic cover with the university's name embossed on it in gold characters, had become the passport required by the student guards for admittance to the hunger strikers' base. Although I had my identity card, we decided it was best for us to stay together. In a crowd of one million people, it was unlikely we would ever find each other again if we separated.

Squeezing our way through the crowd, Joan and I moved around the square listening to speakers, reading the signs and banners that spectators had brought with them, and stopping now and then to cheer and applaud the demonstrators as they arrived.

We had been on the square for about two hours when a man came over to talk to us. It was not at all unusual for a Chinese to start a conversation with a foreigner, and we had already talked to several people on the square. For some, it was an opportunity to practice their English. Those who couldn't speak English found it interesting to talk with foreigners who could speak Chinese. Many wanted to state their support for the students' demands, while others were curious to hear a foreigner's perspective of the student movement. However, there was something about this man that made me suspicious immediately. It could have been his arrogant manner, or maybe it was the reaction of the people standing near us. Instead of huddling around to listen, which is the normal reaction when a Chinese talks to a foreigner, they backed away from us.

Speaking English, the man asked Joan our nationality. Although it is the first question most Chinese ask a foreigner, the tone in his voice made his words sound more like a demand than an innocent inquiry. Joan complimented him on his excellent English, and with a congenial smile, answered his question. Before I could think of a signal to warn her, she replied to his next question, telling him that we were students, and even volunteering our names along with the name of our university. Interrupting Joan, I asked the man where he worked. He ignored my question, which made me even more suspicious. Normally, Chinese are not at all reluctant to tell someone their profession, or *danwei*.

I repeated my question. When he ignored it for the second time, I was convinced that he must be from Division Thirteen. Speaking to Joan again, he asked whether she supported the hunger strikers and if she thought the demonstrations were justified. Before she could open her mouth, I butted in again, telling him that since we were foreigners, we didn't feel the strike or the demonstrations were any of our business. For the third time I asked him where he worked. This time he dodged the question by saying, "It is far from your university, and you wouldn't know the place."

I was tired of the cat and mouse game, so I thanked him for taking time to chat with us, then grabbed Joan's hand, pulling her off into the crowd. As soon as we were several feet away from him, I told her of my suspicions, cautioning her to be careful about telling people her name or volunteering any other personal information. Concerned that she had probably given her name to an undercover policeman, Joan decided it was time for her to leave the square.

Since I had my ID, I headed for the hunger strikers' base so that I could look up the student from Beijing Normal and others that I had met over the past few days. When I stopped to photograph a couple of banners, my pal from Division Thirteen reappeared. Pointing to the banner I had just photographed, "Government of China, where are you?" he said, "I see you can read Chinese."

Although I didn't know if he had followed me or if it was merely a coincidence that we had run into each other again so quickly, it was apparent he was not going to be easy to shake. Deciding to use his tactic of ignoring questions, I gave him a friendly smile and said, "Excuse me, what is your name?"

That seemed to catch him off guard. It would have been exceedingly rude not to respond so he said, "Mr. Wang." Not one to give up easily, Mr. Wang said, "Your friend told me that you are studying Chinese. You are taking photographs of the signs, so you must read Chinese."

It appeared the best way to get rid of Mr. Wang would be to convince him that I was the most ignorant foreigner he had ever met. With a ditzy little smile, I said, "I've only recently begun to study Chinese, so I can barely speak it, much less read it. I like to photograph the banners because written Chinese is so pretty." Borrowing a statement that I had once overheard an American tourist make, I added, "I don't think I could ever learn to make any sense out of all those little squiggles and curvy things. I don't know how on earth you Chinese can ever learn to read."

My response seemed to assure Mr. Wang that I was an illiterate and, most likely, a complete fool. However, just to be on the safe side, he did ask me again how I felt about the student movement. Sticking to my dumb act, I replied, "Mr. Wang, I really don't know a thing about Chinese politics, and I have such a hard time with the names of the leaders. Mr. Xiaoping's name is the only one I can remember."

Mr. Wang smiled at my stupidity, correcting me politely. "That would be Mr. Deng. In Chinese, the surname comes first. Xiaoping is his given name."

I thanked Mr. Wang for the explanation, then made one more attempt at finding out his profession. He gave me a vague answer, telling me he worked for the government. The vast majority of Chinese work for the government; but his reply gave me an opening. I said, "Oh, aren't you afraid to be on the square? Since you work for the government, you might get in trouble for being here."

At last I had him. Mr. Wang thanked me for my concern, and said, "Actually, I am supposed to be here. It is my job."

"Oh, you mean police or security, or something like that?"

Mr. Wang nodded. Patting his arm, I switched to my most maternal voice and said, "Well, I am certainly relieved. I would just hate to see a nice young man like you get in trouble."

I had not only overwhelmed Mr. Wang with my stupidity, but also bored him to tears. With a polite goodby, he excused himself and left me, undoubtedly to go off in search of other more suspicious characters.

People were still coming to the square when I returned to the campus at nightfall. After I had showered and eaten, I went downstairs to watch the evening news. The coverage was refreshingly accurate and surprisingly sympathetic, featuring interviews with students, shots of the massive crowds, and coverage of marches and demonstrations in other cities.

In addition to the reports on the student movement, there was also coverage of Gorbachev's departure from Beijing, and a report of his May 16th meeting with Zhao Ziyang. During the meeting, Zhao had stated to Gorbachev that despite Deng Xiaoping's retirement from most of his official posts, he was still the helmsman of China. As it was common knowledge that Deng was the supreme leader of China, Zhao's statement was puzzling, and his timing made the remark even more curious. Judging by the expression on Gorbachev's face when he heard the translation, he too was surprised by Zhao's remark.

In making the statement, Zhao was publicly separating himself from Deng, and the hard-nosed attitude the government had taken toward the students' demand to retract the April 26th editorial. Taking into consideration the fact that Zhao had already made statements in support of political reform, and the rumors that had spread through the small lane news claiming that Zhao had repeatedly argued in favor of retracting the editorial—even offering to take responsibility for the decision to publish it— Zhao's statement was evidence that there was a rift between Zhao and Deng, in addition to the struggle for power between Zhao and Li Peng.

Zhao's statement put added pressure on the leadership to meet the demands of the students. Pressure had already intensified during the four days of the hunger strike, with open letters of appeal on behalf of the students being written by Party members, factory managers, noted intellectuals, and leaders of four of the democratic parties.[*] The letters from such varied and respected circles along with the massive participation in Wednesday's demonstration could not be easily ignored.

---

[*]The eight democratic parties in China are China Revolutionary Committee of the Kuomintang, China Democratic League, China Democratic National Construction Association, China Association for Promoting Democracy, Chinese Peasants' and Workers' Democratic Party, China Zhi Gong Dang, Jiu San Society, and Taiwan Democratic Self-Government League. These parties have limited membership and no real power since all must adhere to the Four Cardinal Principles of Socialism.

Furthermore, the student movement was gaining support throughout China. Students from other cities were traveling to Beijing by train, and demonstrations had been held across the country. In Shanghai, 100,000 had marched, 10,000 in Guangzhou, 100,000 in Wuhan, 50,000 in Hufei, 30,000 in Harbin, tens of thousands had marched in Chengsha, and hundreds of thousands more had marched in *Xian, Nanjing, Tianjin, Changchun, Shenyang, Dalian, Hohhot, Taiyuan, Yinzhou, Chengdu, Chongqing, Guiyang, Fuzhou, Hangzhou, Nanchang, Shenzhen, Zhejang,* and so on.

On Thursday, May 18th, over a million people converged on the square and the surrounding area. Although the leadership issued another appeal to the hunger strikers to abandon their fast and vacate the square, they still refused to address the students' demands. Once again, the hunger strikers voted to continue their fast. Premier Li Peng summoned the student leaders to a meeting at The Great Hall of the People. The meeting, which was broadcast live, began shortly after noon on Thursday, and as the nation looked on, twenty-one-year-old Wuer Kaixi boldly scolded the Premier for arriving late.

Li Peng opened the meeting by stating that only one topic would be addressed: "How to get the hunger strikers out of their present plight." As he began to express the leadership's concern for the students, stating, "the students are like our own children, our own flesh and blood," Wuer Kaixi interrupted the Premier. Obviously weakened by the hunger strike, but still feisty, Wuer Kaixi stated, "We don't have time for such talk. We are comfortable sitting here, but those outside are suffering from hunger."

Wang Dan then informed the Premier that although two thousand students had already collapsed, the hunger strikers had agreed they would not leave the square until their two demands were met. Wuer Kaixi added that even if only one student voted to stay in the square, the others would stay as well. In doing so, Wuer Kaixi addressed the Premier as "Teacher Li," telling him, "because of your advanced years, I feel I might call you Teacher Li." While the title, *Laoshi* (teacher) is one which is often used by a younger person to show respect for an elder, even if the elder is not a teacher, it was certainly a less formal form of address than Premier. Li Peng stiffened at the term. Judging from his reaction, he perceived the use of the more familiar term to be a further display of disrespect.

The tense atmosphere continued throughout the meeting, with the students restating their two demands, and Li Peng restating the government's position that although the leadership had not accused the majority of the students of intending to create turmoil, the movement had resulted in turmoil in Beijing, and turmoil was spreading across the country. As examples of the growing crisis, he referred to the three-hour-long blockade of a major rail bridge crossing of the Yangste River in Wuhan, as well as the influx into Beijing of "all sorts of vagrants and ne'er-do-wells." He then stated, "For the past few days, Beijing has basically been in the state of anarchy."

Li cautioned the students that they must not mistake the outpourings of sympathy toward the hunger strikers by Party members, government officials, workers, and city residents as support for the movement, and reiterated that the only solution to the crisis was for the students to leave Tiananmen Square immediately.

The meeting was little more than a spotlighted synopsis of the stalemate between the leadership and the students. Its most dramatic point came at the end, when Wuer Kaixi, who was still wearing hospital pajamas, had to be carted off by stretcher when he nearly lost consciousness.

Just as it had been since Monday, the scene at Tiananmen Square on Thursday was one of mixed emotions. With the hunger strikers' health rapidly declining, there was a somber mood around their headquarters, and the failure of the noon meeting with Li Peng deepened their despondency. However, on Eternal Peace Avenue and the rest of the square, the pageantry of the demonstrations and the energy of the crowd filled the air with festive excitement. Although the *laobaixing* were angered by the callousness of China's leaders and moved to tears by the students' patriotism and heroism, they were intoxicated by the sheer joy of expressing themselves, and the experience of voicing their frustrations, desires, and dreams in such a public forum.

Yuanli had called me early Thursday morning to tell me that he and others from his department would be demonstrating on the square, but when I arrived in the middle of the afternoon, I realized it would be a miracle if I found him. Over a million people were in the crowd, and adding to the congestion, tourist buses and public buses had been brought to the square for the students to sleep in, as well as additional tents to provide shelter for the hunger strikers who needed constant medical supervision.

Plunging into the swarm of humanity, I inched my way toward the banners and signs that I wanted to photograph, and the *dazibao* that I wanted to read. One banner had been written on a pink and white checkered tablecloth. The homey touch of the tablecloth was most appropriate considering the homey sentiment expressed in the banner. It announced to one of the hunger strikers that his elder brother had arrived.

On the edge of the square, where the crowd was not so dense, a young couple and their small son were sitting on the flatbed of a bicycle cart. The child, who was about two years old, was eating a popsicle with the look of astonished delight on his face as he watched the promenade of chanting demonstrators. Patting the empty space next to her, his mother invited me to sit on the cart, advising me to rest for a few minutes. A lovely young woman with an armful of leaflets spotted me sitting on the cart, and handing me one of the leaflets, asked in labored English, "Mrs., read, please?"

The message in the leaflet was much the same as others I had read over the past couple of days, but it was unusual in that the text had been written in English. The title of the leaflet was, "An Appeal to Chinese Citizens." It opened with the statement, "After a heavy sleep of more than seventy years, China, which has been ruled by both feudalism and dictatorship, is experiencing a renewed surge for democracy and freedom sweeping across the country. Young students once again are in the forefront of the democratic struggle, and once again they are shedding blood, sweat, and tears in order to write a new chapter in Chinese history."

The leaflet went on to urge the leaders to comply with the students' demands, declaring that this solution was the only one which "could win popular support and calm down the present situation." It ended with the warning, "However, if the government does not follow this scenario, all Chinese people will unite with the students and force the government to follow the above positive demand."*

---

*The demands stated in the leaflet were: "establish a genuine dialogue with the student representatives and both officially and judicially recognize the movement; end news censorship and allow greater freedom of the press; grant freedom and democracy constitutionally through a legal system; prosecute corrupt officials at all levels."

Stuffing the leaflet into my pocket, I looked around for a sign or a banner from Yuanli's department. Although I didn't see their banner, there was something that piqued my curiosity. A photograph of someone had been taped to the Monument to the Martyrs of the Revolution; however, it was too far away for me to identify the person. Moving closer to the statue, I was finally able to identify the person as Zhou Enlai. Although it was late, and the light was poor, I was determined to get close enough to take a photograph of Zhou's picture on the statue.

After I had taken a couple of shots, a young man standing next to me pointed to the picture, telling me it was a photograph of the first Premier of China. He spoke in English, as did his friend beside him who added, "It is ironic since Li Peng is the adopted son of Zhou Enlai.* The adopted father was the most revered Premier of China, loved by all the people. Now the adopted son is also the Premier, but he is the most despised man in China."

The two were graduate students at Qinghua University, and they smiled broadly when I told them that I had seen the banner the Qinghua graduate students had carried when they marched. As an American, I was especially partial to their banner since it featured a drawing of the Statue of Liberty.

I stayed to talk with the two graduate students until I was ready to leave the square. They were eager to "educate" a foreigner, and I was eager to listen to them. The first, student, Mr. L., was intent on explaining the student movement, while the second student, Mr. X., supported his classmate's explanations with clever asides.

---

*Li Peng's father, Li Shuoxun, died when his son was only three years old. Li Shuoxun had joined the Communist Party in 1924 as a student at Shanghai University, and had taken part in the Nanchang Uprising of 1927. From 1927 until his death, Li served as Party Representative and head of the Political Department of the 25th Division of the 11th Army, as a party official in Jiangsu and Zhejiang Provinces, and as Secretary of the Military Commission of Jiangsu and Guangdong Provinces. At the age of twenty-eight, Li was executed by the Guomindang on September 16, 1931, on Hainan Island. Although Zhou and his wife, Deng Yingchao, did not actually adopt Li Peng, they did take a special interest in him and in 1939 when Li was eleven, Zhou sent him to Chongqing to study.

Mr. L. explained that the students were demanding a retraction to the April 26th editorial because it had attacked the students' patriotism. With a sarcastic laugh, Mr. X. added, "To be a patriot in China, one must endorse corruption and nepotism, support inflation, defend censorship, and denounce democracy!"

Mr. L. elaborated on the corruption of the government, explaining that in order to accomplish anything in China one had to use the back door. Mr. X. said, "But now, since everyone is trying to go through the back door, it is even more crowded than the front door."

Mr. L. explained that in China the press could not oppose and criticize the Party or the Leader. Mr. X. said, "There is a trick to reading the newspapers to find out the truth of something. You don't concentrate on what is said, you concentrate on what is not said. If you read that the grain crop is going to be the best ever, you tighten your belt because you know you will go hungry."

I asked Mr. L. and Mr. X. what they thought was the most positive result the student movement had accomplished so far.

Responding immediately, Mr. L. said, "The movement has united the intellectuals and the *laobaixing* behind a common goal. That unity is the most important step that our country has taken toward democracy in the history of China. Today Li Peng said we must not confuse sympathy with support, but I think it is Li Peng who is confused. The signs that people have put up all over the city and carried to the square do not say, 'we SYMPATHIZE with the students.' The slogans that people shout do not ask for sympathy for the hunger strikers or the student movement. Li Peng should come to the square and listen to the people and read the signs and banners. Then he would know that the people are united in their support for the students' demands.

"In the past, the Party used resentment and suspicion to [pit] the *laobaixing* against the intellectuals. The Party has attacked intellectuals with political campaigns, sent intellectuals down to the countryside, and imprisoned intellectuals. All of this was done to silence intellectuals because we are the only ones who have criticized or challenged the Party. But now, the *laobaixing* are resentful and suspicious of the leadership and Party officials because they have not fulfilled the promises that were made to the people. Those who are in a position of leadership today, from the top to the bottom levels, do not fight reform because they are such dedicated socialists. They fight reform because the corruption makes their pockets and their bellies fat."

Mr. X. added, "Even if the *laobaixing* do not understand democracy, they know that our government is drowning in corruption. Corruption breeds tyranny and tyranny breeds more corruption. Only a democratic system can solve this problem. With a democracy, we can expose the corruption and depose the tyranny."

I told them about two signs, which I had seen carried by intellectuals who had marched in support of the hunger strikers on May 15th. One stated, "The Stinking Ninth is still the Stinking Ninth!" Stinking Ninth *(Chou Laojiu)* was the pejorative word for intellectuals used during the Cultural Revolution when intellectuals were added as the ninth category of bad social elements.* One had only to look at the Party's harsh treatment of Wei Jingsheng and Ren Wanding, and the ouster of Wang Ruowang, Liu Binyan, and Fang Lizhi to grasp the meaning of the sign. The other sign had issued a warning from intellectuals saying "The Stinking Ninth will not be silent again!"

Mr. L. said, "It is true. Even after the Cultural Revolution, those intellectuals who dared to challenge the Party's methods, criticize the Party and the leaders, or expose corruption have been treated like the Stinking Ninth."

With a sly grin, Mr. X. said, "Now when the leaders look down on the square, they know the people believe it is the corrupt and tyrannical officials who stink."

Bicycling back to the campus, I thought about my conversation with Mr. L. and Mr. X. Before leaving the square, I had asked them why people were now speaking out so freely. Like others before them, Mr. L. and Mr. X. had not only spoken with complete candor, but had also granted me permission to tape our conversation.

---

*The other eight categories were landlords, wealthy peasants, counterrevolutionaries, bad elements, rightists, oppositionists, enemy agents, and capitalist "roaders."

It was so unlike the China I had known before the student movement. People knew the security cameras on the square were filming and that secret police were in the crowd. Furthermore, they were aware that people had reported on each other in the past when the government clamped down with political campaigns after brief periods of openness. Yet, people from all walks of life were demonstrating with joyous abandon; students were not hesitating to give their names to journalists or say which universities they attended; and party members, public figures, prominent intellectuals, factory officials, and others were signing their names to petitions and writing open letters. It was as if the entire city had been bewitched by the truth.

It was Mr. X. who had answered my question. "There is risk, but with so many people speaking out, perhaps the risk is not as great as before. But these are things that must be said regardless of the risk. We have been silent far too long. If we truly want things to change, then we must speak out."

Still, I worried about the new trend of openness. I worried for all the people I had spoken with on the square, for the hunger strikers, the demonstrators, and for my friends. Although Hong Xin was not a hunger striker, I knew she was active in the movement on our campus. The Professor had already written a *dazibao,* and was talking about writing another. Yuanli, normally so prudent, had spent the day demonstrating and would certainly go back to the square. Wherever Shanli was, I was positive that he was cursing the Communist Party with renewed vigor. However, it was Lu Minghua that I worried about the most.

Over the weekend, I felt uncomfortable as I sat listening to Lu Minghua's comments during the student broadcast on her campus. As people gathered around the loudspeakers, they sought her out, wanting to hear her comments, laughing at her witty remarks and biting sarcasm. I told her that it worried me, and even reminded her that she had cautioned me to be careful about what I said. Shrugging, she brushed my concern aside. But still I worried.

It drizzled on and off during the night and throughout the early morning of Friday, May 19th. At 4:45 Zhao Ziyang went to the square in the morning rain. Minutes later, Li Peng also made an appearance on

Tiananmen Square. Stiff and awkward with the students, Li Peng stayed for only a quarter of an hour. Zhao, emotional and at times moved to tears, lingered on the square.

Addressing the hunger strikers through a megaphone handed to him by one of the student leaders, Zhao's voice choked with emotion as he told the students, "We are sorry we have come too late. It is correct if you blame and criticize us, but I am not here to ask for your forgiveness."

Urging the students to consider their health and their weakened condition, Zhao pleaded with the hunger strikers to end their fast. With tears in his eyes, he said, "You are young, and still have a long way to go. You must live on in good health, live on to the day when China finally realizes the Four Modernizations."

Zhao asked that the students "calmly and coolly" consider ending the hunger strike. "It is understandable that as young people you are bursting with passion. I know that. We all used to be young. We also took to the streets. Some of us even laid our bodies across railroad tracks to block trains. At the time we too did not think about what would happen afterwards." Saying again that he hoped they would end their hunger strike very soon, Zhao thanked the hunger strikers and bowed to them.

Later in the day, as the students agonized over their decision, word spread on the square and through the city that Zhao had made his final appearance as General Secretary of the Chinese Communist Party. Leaflets and *dazibao* confirmed the rumors that Zhao had proposed that the April 26th editorial be repudiated; that the National People's Congress form a special committee to investigate corruption in the government; and that information regarding officials backgrounds, salaries, and benefits be made public. All of his proposals had been overruled. Zhou no longer presided over the Politburo. Li Peng was now in charge!

Friday was the fourth day that the masses made their way down Eternal Peace Avenue to Tiananmen Square. On the square, the severe expressions on people's faces reflected the heightened urgency of the situation while their banners and *dazibao* expressed the intensity of their anger at Li Peng and Deng Xiaoping. As the cry, "Li Peng *xia tai!*" rang through the crowd, Eternal Peace Avenue echoed with the calls for Li Peng's resignation. The words *xia tai* (get off the stage/step down from office) were also coupled with the name, Deng Xiaoping. The boldness of the signs and banners was astounding. One banner showed a little bottle falling from a pedestal and a smiling crowd of spectators. Splatters of red ink represented the blood that came from the bottle. It depicted the public execution of the little bottle as a smiling crowd looked on in appreciation of the good show they were witnessing as "Xiaoping" toppled to the ground.

At the east end of the square near Mao Zedong's mausoleum, another small bottle hung from a chain. A piece of cardboard with three sets of characters written on it hung beside the bottle. The sign said, *"Jing Shan, yi jing, yici* (Jing Shan, one scene, transported)." The words were an allusion to the suicide of the last Ming Emperor.

The once golden and glorious Ming Dynasty collapsed under the weight of its own corruption. On an April morning in 1644, Emperor Chongzhen learned that the troops of the rebel Li Zicheng had entered the capital city. When he rang a bell to summon his ministers, none appeared, for Chongzhen had lost the Mandate of Heaven. Removing his Imperial robe, he went to the garden at the foot of Jing Shan,* the hill which overlooks the capital city, and wrote his last decree:

> *I, feeble and of small virtue, have offended against Heaven. The rebels have seized my capital because my ministers deceived me. Ashamed to face my ancestors, I die. Removing my Imperial cap and with my hair disheveled about my face, I leave to the rebels the dismemberment of my body. Let them not harm my people.*

Chongzhen then hanged himself. Since it had caused the death of an emperor, the pine tree from which Chongzhen had hanged himself was declared a criminal and bound by a chain.

The message to Deng was clear. The little bottle, Xiaoping, had also lost the Mandate of Heaven due to the corruption of his Dynasty. The sign also told Deng that he was undeserving of the Imperial silk cord and should use the chain of a criminal to hang himself.

Several people gathered around the display. Since the characters on the sign were written very lightly in ballpoint pen, I waited until a few of them moved on so that I could get closer to the sign to photograph it. As I waited,

---

*Jing Shan (Scenic Hill) is also known as Mei Shan (Coal Hill).

an old man in the crowd asked if I understood the meaning of the display. Nodding, I told him that I understood.

Shaking his head in awe, he said, "Whoever did this is very brave. He could spend many years in prison for making this sign." He stood staring at the sign for another minute, then as he turned to walk away, he murmured, "Truly very brave."

After I had photographed the display, I went back to the Monument to the Martyrs of the Revolution. The photograph of Zhou was still hanging from the monument, and a couple of banners had been strung across the statue with one smaller banner draped around the shoulders of the figure of a soldier on the monument. At the front of the statue, a headband had been tied around the head of one of the female figures on the monument. The headband said, "Support the hunger strikers!"

Walking back toward the hunger hunger strikers' base, I stopped to make way for a bicycle cart loaded with yogurt. As the cart pulled up beside me, a young man riding on the back of the cart leaned over to hand me a cup of yogurt. Although I felt awkward accepting food that was meant for the student guards and demonstrators and since there was not time for the three polite refusals, I decided it would be rude to refuse his generosity. When I thanked him for the yogurt, he smiled and said, "Thank you for coming to the square, honorable foreigner. Please tell your countrymen that Chinese students are true patriots." He waved to me as the cart pulled away, then motioning to me, he shouted, "Eat, eat!" Someone tapped me on the shoulder as I stood eating the yogurt. Turning, I saw Teacher Jin with two of her students who also lived in *San Lou*. I had met one of them, an English girl named Nan; the other was her roommate, a Canadian. Since Teacher Jin worked in the Administration Office in addition to teaching a class, she was the last person I had expected to see on the square.

I considered Teacher Jin a friend, but I was not eager to run into her on the square since her inquisitive manner always made me a little uneasy. I had witnessed her inspection of Jinjin's desk when she visited me in my room, and each time I saw her on the campus, she would quiz me about where I was going or where I had been. Earlier that week, she had asked me directly if I had been to Tiananmen Square. I had dodged the question by telling her that I was considering going to the square the next day. After nearly choking on a mouthful of yogurt, I greeted Teacher Jin and her students, telling them how nice it was to see them, that I was surprised they were able to spot me in such an immense crowd, and commenting on how it had turned out to be such a beautiful, clear day. Listening to myself, I realized that I was rambling like the proverbial kid with her hand in the cookie jar. Teacher Jin interrupted my monologue, telling me that she and her two students were on their way to the east side of the square where it was less crowded. Taking my hand, she insisted that I go with them.

The four of us climbed the steps that lead to the Museum of the Chinese Revolution. Teacher Jin and I stood on the first landing while Nan and her roommate sat down on the steps. Pulling out her sketch pad and pencil, Nan first drew a rough outline of the Great Hall of the People opposite us, then drew the emblem on the building with exacting detail. Flags, banners, tents, the monuments, and people miraculously appeared on her paper. Then, as her hand moved swiftly across the page, she drew in the scene below us at the foot of the stairs.

A group of students who had just finished marching were sitting beneath their two banners. Nan filled in the characters on the top banner, "Mama, I will take care of you when you are old," then wrote in those on the second banner, "Ten years of reform and who gets fat!?!"

People began to gather around Nan as she drew, commenting to each other and praising her work. Even that small crowd bothered Teacher Jin. With a look of displeasure on her face, she took my hand again, announcing that it was time for us to leave. I started to tell her I had somewhere to go or was meeting someone, but I decided against it. Perhaps we would have an opportunity to talk on the way back to the campus, and since I didn't have an inkling as to how she felt about the Pro-Democracy Movement, I assumed I would find out. However, being as adept at subterfuge as with interrogations, Teacher Jin avoided the topic by asking me questions about my children. When I tried to switch the discussion back to the student movement by telling her about some of the signs and banners I had seen on the square, her only comment was a conversation stopping "Hmmmm."

At nine o'clock in the evening, the hunger strike ended. Informed that Li Peng had ordered in troops to clear the square before morning, the students voted to end their fast but remained on the square in a sit-in protest. The heroes of the night were the vendors and other entrepreneurs who alerted the city. The midnight riders, dubbed "The Flying Tigers," mounted their motorcycles and sped about the streets of the capital, through the suburbs, and on to the outskirts of the city as they sounded the alarm and reported troop locations. Just as heroic were the citizens of Beijing. They responded to the alarm by flocking into the streets to block the roads into the city, the major intersections, and the railroad crossings.

I had already showered and put on my pajamas when Lu Minghua knocked on my door. Breathlessly, she told me that convoys of troops were advancing on the city. She had come from Fragrant Flower Road where people were gathering at the railroad crossing, lining the tracks to stop incoming trains. I asked her to wait for me to dress, but she said she was returning to her apartment to cook. She and other women throughout the neighborhood were preparing food to give to those who were standing vigil over the city, and to the soldiers as offerings of goodwill from the people of Beijing.

Dressing hurriedly, I left a note for Jinjin telling her that I would be back very late. However, on the way out of *San Lou,* I ran into Jinjin and two of her friends. They were coming to ask for my advice. A Chinese student whom they knew had asked to borrow their bicycles. Since he was somewhat vague about why he needed them, Jinjin wanted to know what I thought they should do. After telling them what was happening, I explained that some of the students didn't have bikes, so he probably wanted to borrow theirs to carry messages back and forth from the square or from one neighborhood to the other. Handing them the key to my bike, I told them that he could borrow mine as well.

There was quite a lot of activity on Fragrant Flower Road, as each large vehicle that came down the street was stopped at the railroad crossing and inspected by the students who were manning the wooden signal arm. When it was determined that no troops or weapons were aboard, the vehicles were allowed to pass. As reports came in from other parts of the city, students made announcements over the public address speaker mounted at the top of the signal pole. A signalman worked with other students to pile old rail ties and other pieces of wood by the side of the tracks. They would be used to help stop the trains. Another railroad worker helped students organize the people who lined the tracks, instructing them as to what they should do when a train approached.

Hong Xin was standing by the signal shack talking to one of the students who had been making announcements. Since she was too far away to hear me call out, I waited until she looked in my direction, then waved to her. She waved back and came over to me. Taking both of my hands in hers and squeezing them, Hong Xin told me she had missed our visits. Her hands were icy cold, and she shivered in the damp night air. The wind had started to pick up, so I scolded her for not dressing more warmly. She tugged at the sleeves of her cotton jacket, telling me she was warm enough. She asked if I had heard that the hunger strikers had ended their fast, then shaking her head sadly, she said, "The doctors told them they were too weak to flee if the troops attacked."

The public address system crackled as a student made another announcement. With all the static, I had difficulty understanding what he was saying. Hong Xin said it was an announcement that a train would be arriving in the next twenty minutes. With a quick goodbye, she went back to join the other students.

While the signalman directed them, students placed the ties and larger pieces of wood across the tracks. Using the smaller pieces of wood, they walked farther down the tracks, stacking the wood a couple of feet from the tracks and stuffing wads of paper in with the wood. As soon as the headlight of the train appeared in the distance, the pile was set afire as a signal to stop the train.

The train stopped well before it arrived at the barricade. A few of the students went aboard the train to inspect it and to talk with the engineer. It was a passenger train, but only the crew was aboard. The engineer, some of the crew, and the students who had boarded stepped off of the train and talked for a few more minutes. When they re-boarded, the engineer and crew carried with them copies of *The Liberation Daily* and other newspapers published by the students.

When the barricades were cleared away, the train slowly began to move forward. Through the windows of the train, I could see that some of the crew were already reading the newspapers. As it picked up speed, several leaned from the windows waving victory signs to the crowd.

As the hour grew later, apprehension and exhaustion combined to create some farfetched rumors. When a European student told me that he had heard that paratroopers would be dropped on the city, I began to suspect that speculation and imagination were taking over. Not long afterward, another European student topped the paratrooper story. He had heard that American soldiers were coming to Beijing. I laughed at the absurdity of that rumor suggesting that someone was either "pulling his leg," or that he had done a bad job of translating the small lane news. He was a little defensive about my comments, so I asked him which side the Americans troops were supposed to be backing. Even he had to laugh when he told me that he had forgotten to ask.

As dawn approached, the weary crowd was rejuvenated by an announcement. With the courage and passion of their beliefs, the people of Beijing had stopped the army. Troop convoys had been blocked at Fengtai, Dongaodi, Hujialou, Luiliqiao, Wukesong, and elsewhere. The human wall surrounding the city had held.

CHAPTER FIFTEEN

MANY TEACHERS, MANY LESSONS

Covering the mouthpiece of the telephone, Leslie Clark asked us to lower our voices since she was speaking to a reporter. Another American student, Paul Green, and I were standing by the front door of *San Lou,* chatting while we waited to use the phone. However, the word "reporter" guaranteed our immediate silence and absolute attention to Leslie's end of the conversation. It was a rare opportunity to overhear something more reliable than small lane news. Leslie apologized for her abruptness when she hung up the phone, explaining that the reporter was a friend who had called to let her know that martial law had just been imposed on Beijing, and to find out if anything was happening in our area of the city.

The imposition of martial law had been announced by Chen Xitong, the Mayor of Beijing. Issued by the State Council and signed by Li Peng, the order informed the citizens of Beijing that as of ten o'clock on Saturday morning, May 20th, eight of the city's districts were under martial law.* Only the two most distant districts in the 16,800 square mile area of the municipality were not included in the order.

The order prohibited demonstrations, petitioning, student and worker strikes, "the promulgation of rumors, establishment of illegal contacts, lecturing, distribution of pamphlets, [and] instigation of social unrest." It warned that the Public Security Police, Military Police, and the People's Liberation Army were under orders to "take any measures necessary to forcibly deal with the situation."

---

*The eight districts covered by the order were the Western District, the Eastern District, Chongwen, Xuanwu, Shijingshan, Haidian, Fengtai, and Chaoyang.

In addition to the same restrictions as those placed on Chinese citizens, foreign news reporters were prohibited from "carrying out interviews, photographing, videotaping, or other such activities" without prior government approval. Leslie told us that the reporter had said that Americans were being advised to remain on their compounds, to stay away from the square, and to refrain from taking photographs on the street.

While the order was being read repeatedly over radio and television, there was no coverage of Tiananmen Square. Martial law or no martial law, I was not about to sit around the campus all day long, not knowing what was going on at the square. Leslie and Paul also wanted to go to the square, so we decided it would be safer to bicycle into town together. Since we didn't know if or when we might be stopped by soldiers, we settled on two logical explanations for being out and about. If we were stopped before we reached *Xizhimen* Street, we would say we were on our way to the zoo. Once we had passed the turn off to the zoo, we would say we were going to the Beijing Hotel.

It was unusually quiet in the suburbs. Traffic was light, public buses were not running, the subways had been closed off, and most shops and vendors' stalls were closed as well. As we rode along, we could hear bits and pieces of the martial law order being broadcast over neighborhood public address systems. However, no one was enforcing the order. There were no signs of troops or armed police, and even the traffic police seemed to have disappeared from the streets. Near the center of the city, where traffic was heavier, university and high school students along with workers and unemployed youths worked together to direct the traffic.

After parking our bikes near Eternal Peace Avenue, we walked toward the square, stopping to read a leaflet posted on a wall. On our way into town, we had seen several copies of the leaflet posted on light poles and traffic signs. Signed by The Beijing Workers Autonomous Union (BWAU), the leaflet called for a strike of all workers, other than utility and telecommunications workers, as a protest against martial law. The strike was scheduled to begin at noon, and to continue until all martial law troops were withdrawn from Beijing. The BWAU also urged that workers assist in blocking troops, and "cooperate citywide with people from all sectors of society in disseminating truthful information regarding the troops who have entered Beijing."

As we turned onto Eternal Peace Avenue, a delegation of "Flying Tigers" passed by. With their girl friends sitting behind them on their motorcycles, the midnight riders were greeted by enthusiastic cheers. Beijingers were eager to express their appreciation to the "Flying Tigers," all symptoms of "Red Eye Disease" having vanished overnight.

Although the crowd was smaller than those assembled during the Four Days of Freedom, several hundred thousand people had come to the square to support the hunger strikers and to applaud the demonstrators who boldly ignored the government's orders. Added concern for the hunger strikers' safety was evidenced by the increased security around the square. Student guards and workers who lined the iron barricades around the perimeter of the square and the lane dividers on Eternal Peace Avenue stood in tighter formation than they had on previous days. We were stopped by a student guard at the lane divider who asked to see our ID before he would allow us to cross the avenue to enter the square through the emergency lane. Again, our ID was checked before we were allowed to pass through the hedges surrounding the Monument to the People's Heroes, where the hunger strikers' headquarters was located.

Looking out over the northern end of the square, I was reminded of a western movie. The dozens of city buses, which had been brought to the square for shelter, had been parked in a huge circle, as if someone had given the order to "circle the wagons" in case of attack. Students sat atop the buses, watching the sky as military helicopters made occasional passes overhead.

Although the fast had been called off and the students had eaten a breakfast of rice porridge, ambulance sirens still shrilled in the background. After almost a week of fasting, the state of the hunger strikers' health was fragile, and the unsanitary conditions on the square had contributed to their physical decline. Mountainous piles of refuse littered the square. Cooking pots lined with remnants of food sat baking in the sun adding the odor of soured porridge to the stench of urine. Scores of students had already contracted diarrhea, and without running water and adequate toilet facilities, doctors feared an epidemic of hepatitis would break out.

The crews of foreign journalists who had relayed the drama of Tiananmen Square to the rest of the world had vanished from the square. At about eleven o'clock in the morning, the government had pulled the plug, announcing that live satellite broadcasts would no longer be permitted. The Chinese media had also been muzzled. Word went out that the offices of China Central Television, *People's Daily,* and other newspapers and radio stations were now occupied by soldiers. The student broadcast system was still in operation, but its audience was limited to those who were actually on the square.

Lacking the accurate and detailed news coverage of the Four Days of Freedom, rumors had already reached epidemic proportions. With only a few confirmed, they ran through the crowd at a lightning pace, one contradicting another, adding to the sense of isolation and confusion. First it was said that troops had sealed off the subway to use the subway and the tunnels beneath the city to launch an attack on the square. Then it was said that it had been the subway workers themselves who had sealed off the subway in an effort to prevent such an attack. Announcements were made over the student broadcast system that the helicopters flying over Eternal Peace Avenue and Tiananmen Square were preparing to drop tear gas on the square. Students were first advised to use wet towels to cover their faces, but minutes later, students were told that only dry towels should be used.

While Leslie and Paul stopped to talk with a group of students, I wandered around photographing the scene. Jammed together beneath a canvas tarpaulin, several medical workers and students who were confined to cots posed for my camera, smiling, with their hands held up in the victory sign. Spotting my camera, another student flashed the victory sign from the window of a parked bus.

Four medical students rushed past me as they carried one of the hunger strikers to an ambulance parked on the square. Sadness filled my heart as I looked at his frail body and into his exhausted eyes. It had been a wise decision to call off the hunger strike. Surely, the students could not have held out much longer. Many of the hunger strikers had collapsed more than once, returning to the square to resume their fast as soon as they were able to walk out of the hospital.

Tuesday through Friday had been the Four Days of Freedom, but Saturday, May 20th, was the first day of despair. Festivity and joy had changed to bitterness and anger, while urgency had been replaced by desperation. I could hear the despair and vulnerability in the voices of the students who surrounded me, thanking me with great sincerity for coming to the square, then asking one question after another.

"Are there troops by your campus?"

"Did anyone try to stop you from coming to the square?"

"Did you see any troops on your way into town?"

"Where is the foreign press—why have they deserted us?"

"Do the American people support us?"

"Why hasn't President Bush made a statement in support of our struggle for democracy?"

The students were surprised that Western journalists had obeyed the martial law order and left the square. They were confused and disappointed by President Bush's silence. I pointed out that the Western press had no choice but to obey the Chinese government's orders; otherwise, they would be sent packing. Although I could not understand why President Bush had not endorsed their efforts to push for democratic reform, I assured the students that the American people supported them.

They seemed compelled to speak out, as if they believed it might be the last opportunity for their voices to be heard. One student expressed his anger at the Communist Party, telling me, "We have given the Party every chance to address our grievances, to solve the problems that the Party itself created. But there is no place in our government for opposing viewpoints. When the Party was founded, it represented the will of the people. The people in the Party were honest, upright Chinese who opposed the corrupt and feudal leaders of the *Guomindang*. Now it is the leaders of the Communist Party who are corrupt and feudal."

Another student stressed the importance of a free press. "With freedom of the press, democracy can evolve. The press should have the right to expose evil officials. In China, only the leaders decide who is good and who is bad. If the leaders say you are good, although you are bad, you are good. If the leaders say you are bad, although you are good, you are bad. The press should be able to write that a person is bad even if he is in the top level of the government."

Shaking his head, a third student corrected him, "No, that is not the way a free press works. Even the press should not decide who is good and who is bad. The duty of the press is to report the truth, then the people will decide for themselves who is good and who is bad."

They expressed their disgust with Deng Xiaoping, brushing him aside as an old man with an addled brain. It was Li Peng who received the brunt of their rage. Having never enjoyed the respect and admiration of the people, Li was viewed as a man who had achieved power, not through his abilities or past achievements, but rather through his connections as Zhou Enlai's "adopted son." Furthermore, as a soldier in the camp of Chen Yun, the major opponent to economic reform, Li was hardly a likely candidate to lead China in the direction of either economic or political reform. His inflexible attitude throughout the period of the student demonstrations and the hunger strike had served to further reinforce his reputation as a stodgy man, lacking in vision. With the declaration of martial law, the contempt the people of Beijing felt for Li had turned to hatred. Labeling him a criminal, the students pronounced Li Peng to be the most despised man in China. Overnight, Li's resignation or recall had eclipsed all other prior student demands, becoming the primary concern of the student movement and the people of Beijing.

While Li appeared to have gained control of the government, there were persistent rumors on the square that Li could not maintain control. Zhao was rumored to be under house arrest, but there were also rumors that he still had control of some of the media, as well as support in the military. Additionally, an announcement made over the student broadcast system claimed that the government of Shanghai had refused to accept "the illegal Li Peng government," and that approximately one third of the Ministries of the State Council had refused to acknowledge Li Peng as head of the government. While there was little evidence to substantiate the rumors, their existence alone was proof of Li's political vulnerability.

After the students had had their say, I went to join Leslie and Paul. They had stopped to talk with a British journalist who was interviewing students on the steps of the Monument. He asked what we had seen on our way into town, but we had little of consequence to tell him. We were eager to find out what was happening in other parts of the city, but his information was a repeat of the small lane news, and the rumors we had already heard on the square.

While Leslie and Paul talked to another group of students, I went from tent to tent taking more photographs. Assuming that I was a journalist, a man came rushing over to tell me that he had just returned from Liuliqiao where there had been a confrontation between soldiers and the people who were blocking the road. As he offered to arrange for a car to take me to Liuliqiao, I heard an announcement over the student broadcast system informing the crowd that over fifty people had been beaten by soldiers at Liuliqiao.

Explaining that I was a student, I told him there was a British journalist by the Monument. When he learned that I was not a journalist, he insisted that I leave the square immediately, warning me that the students expected to be tear gassed. Then, to stress the danger, he told me that the troops at Liuliqiao might have broken through the barricades, and could be heading for the square.

The panic in his voice upset me. Repeating the conversation to Paul, and adding that I had promised my family to avoid any situation where I might get shot, I suggested that we go to the other side of Eternal Peace Avenue. Although it wasn't necessary to leave the area completely, it seemed a good idea to stay closer to where our bicycles were parked, in case we had to make a run for it.

Before leaving the hunger strikers' headquarters, I looked back over Tiananmen Square, wondering if it might be the last time I would come there to talk with students. A banner hanging from a pole above one of the medical tents caught my eye. I hadn't noticed the banner before, but now it stood out among the others. The two large black characters written on the banner, *"Mei Wan* (It's Not Over)," stood as a symbol of hope amid the despair.

Leslie and Paul followed a few yards behind me as we jogged toward Eternal Peace Avenue. Stopping in the middle of the avenue, I turned to shoot a few last photographs before crossing over to the Gate of Heavenly Peace. People lining the iron barricades applauded, shouting out their gratitude as I photographed the square, and then turned my camera toward the helicopters as they buzzed Eternal Peace Avenue.

We saw another American student from our university near the Gate of Heavenly Peace. He told us that four army trucks filled with soldiers had been parked at *Yeyinglu* for a couple of hours, but the people in the neighborhood had finally persuaded them to leave. As we talked, a man in the crowd reached over Leslie's head to hand me a leaflet.

Dated May 20th and unsigned, the title of the leaflet was "A Notice to the People." The leaflet told how the people of Beijing had surrounded the troops that were moving into the city, offering the soldiers food and drink and "telling them the truth about the Patriotic Democratic Movement as well as the concerns of the people."

It went on to say that some soldiers were told by their superiors that they were coming to Beijing on military maneuvers, others were told they were making a movie, and others had not been told where they were being sent or why. For several days the soldiers were not allowed to read newspapers or to listen to the radio, but were given copies of the April 26th editorial, which they were ordered to study.

In conclusion, the leaflet stated, "At the meeting held early this morning, Li Peng and Yang Shangkun defiled public opinion and became enemies of the people. Using deception, they tricked the people as well as the troops. History will never forgive them! The people will never forgive them!"

Several people gathered around me, asking what the leaflet said, and trying to get a glimpse of it over my shoulder. One young woman standing in front of me asked if she could read the leaflet, while others in the crowd echoed her request. The simplest solution was to hold the leaflet up so that everyone could read it at once. They all laughed when one man in the group commented that I made an excellent sign post due to my taller than average height.

The young woman who had asked first to read the leaflet told me about a painting that had been taped over a public sign near the entrance to the Forbidden Palace. The student from our university had also mentioned the painting, but I hadn't had a chance to see it yet. Leading me over to the painting, the woman asked the people around it to move back so that my camera lens would have an unobstructed view.

The painting was a parody of an official portrait of Cixi, the Empress Dowager. However, this version featured Deng Xiaoping's head on Cixi's body. It had been painted by a skilled artist who was also a clever satirist.

As the power behind the throne, Cixi ruled from 1861 until her death in 1908. Born of a minor Manchu family, Cixi became the favorite concubine of Emperor Xian Feng when she gave birth to a son. At Xian Feng's death in 1861, Cixi collaborated with the late emperor's younger brother, Prince Gong, to stage a coup d'état. Although she shared the title of Regent with the childless Empress and Prince Gong, it was Cixi who actually commanded the reins of power. She even went so far as to change the name of her son's reign to Tong Zhi (Joint Reign) to emphasize that the Emperor and Empress Dowager ruled together. Sitting behind a screen, she listened to ministerial reports and whispered her instructions to the emperor.

At the death of her son in 1874, Cixi maintained control of the throne by installing her nephew, Guang Xu, as Emperor. However in 1898, Guang Xu attempted to assert his imperial authority by appointing the reformer Kang Youwei and a group of his supporters to government positions. Kang's reform policy had its roots in the earlier Self-Strengthening Movement, which sought to use the technological achievements of the west to advance China. Over a period of one hundred days, Guang Xu issued several edicts which would accomplish a comprehensive program of educational, political, economic, and military reforms. Although Cixi had supposedly retired from her duties, she responded to the reforms by placing Guang Xi under house arrest, annulling his edicts, executing six of the reformers, and issuing her own edict stating that Guang Xi had requested that she take control of the government.

Cixi's primary concern was to maintain her power and ensure the continuation of the Qing Dynasty. In order to achieve that end, Cixi tolerated extensive corruption and abuses of power by her officials, obstructed reforms which would lessen her power or weaken the dynasty, kept her officials in line by never allowing one faction to gain the upper hand over the other, and controlled imperial succession.

The obvious historical reference made by the painting dealt with Zhao Ziyang's statement to Gorbachev. While Deng ruled from behind the screen of retirement, he was still the supreme leader of China. Although Deng's words had been used in the editorial of April 26th, he had not issued any statements regarding the demonstrations, the hunger strike, or martial law. Indeed, Deng had allowed Li Peng and others to speak for the government, while he sat behind his screen at *Zhongnanhai* and *Beidaihe.**

The painting made a more subtle inference in depicting Deng as Cixi. Deng had also tolerated corruption and abuses of power, obstructed political reforms, played one faction within the Party against the other, and stripped the power from his chosen successors. Deng, like Cixi, was determined to preserve a decaying dynasty regardless of the cost.

When we left the square in the late afternoon, traffic was heavier than it had been earlier in the day as trucks and buses were being moved to major intersections in preparation for another long night at the roadblocks. In a leaflet distributed throughout the city, the ASAB advised the people of Beijing to remember that "the People's Liberation Army are our brothers and sons," pointing out that since the government had left the soldiers stranded, it was up to the people of Beijing to supply them with food and drink. Stressing that the soldiers were "ignorant of the situation and were tricked into coming to Beijing," it urged the citizens to "use reason instead of violence," and to "persuade rather than force." The leaflet also asked that the citizens allow any troops breaking formation in order to rest or retreat "to pass unhindered," and warned that citizens should "guard against undercover police attempting to use violence to start an incident."

When I returned to the dormitory, the *shiwuyuan* called me over to the office window and handed me a note. Susan had telephoned while I was out. With all that had happened, I had completely forgotten that Susan and I had planned to spend the day together. She had called me earlier in the week to tell me that Saturday was her day off, and that she wanted to go to the square with me. It was Susan that I had been waiting to call while Leslie was on the telephone with the reporter. I considered returning her call, but then thought better of it. The martial law order had made me feel uneasy about calling any of my Chinese friends. Like most Chinese, Susan's family did not have a telephone in their apartment, which meant

*Beidaihe is the seaside resort where Deng and other leaders spend their summers.

that I would have to call the communal telephone on her block. I worried that at such a sensitive time, a telephone call from a foreigner might arouse the suspicions of an "old Auntie."

Later in the evening, Jinjin's teacher, Han Ling, stopped by our room to visit. I had grown quite fond of Han Ling in the short time I had known her, and Jinjin had encouraged our friendship with enthusiastic comments to each of us about the other. Once we actually met, we found we had more in common than our fondness for Jinjin. Our shared interest in Chinese literature had given us much to talk about.

Han Ling had an aura of serenity about her which was especially soothing after the hurly-burly of the streets of Beijing. Actually, everything about Han Ling was serene; her gentle manner, her poise, her soft voice, and her beauty. Hers was that rare type of classical beauty with flawless skin and even features set on a bone structure that promised comeliness through mid-life and old age, growing more regal with the passing years.

Since Jinjin had told Han Ling that I had gone to the square, she had come to see if I had returned to the campus. Curious to hear what was happening on the square, she listened attentively as I described the scene on the square, repeated some of the comments students had made to me, and told her about the confrontation at Liuliqiao.

The report on Liuliqiao, as well as most of the rumors that had circulated around the square, had already made their way to our campus via the campus broadcast system. Messengers had carried information back and forth between the square and various points around the city. As the reports came in, they were broadcast over the public address systems on campuses and in neighborhoods throughout Beijing.

I also told Han Ling about an unsigned leaflet, which had been posted at the entrance to the pedestrian underpass by the Gate of Heavenly Peace. The leaflet was not only a response to the martial law order, but also an accusation that during the entire forty year history of the People's Republic of China, the leaders of China were the ones who had instigated and perpetuated turmoil.

Going back to the Anti-Rightist Campaign of 1957, it accused Mao of creating turmoil by first urging the intellectuals to "Let a hundred flowers bloom, let a hundred schools of thought contend," and then, damning those who responded. Although The Hundred Flowers Campaign had been devised as a means to bring the intellectuals into the class struggle, it soon developed into a program in which intellectuals were encouraged to air their grievances against the Party. However, the brief period of openness and frankness was followed by a backlash against those who spoke out. They were labeled counterrevolutionaries and ordered into exile. For many, suicide was the more desirable alternative to persecution and banishment.

The leaflet cited The Great Leap Forward as the second example of Mao's propensity for turmoil. The Great Leap Forward, which lasted from 1958 until 1962, centered around the industrialization of the countryside. Mao's ambitious but impractical plan was intended to prevent China from backsliding into capitalism, while concurrently putting the utopian dream of communization on fast forward. The results were an economic and ecological nightmare for China. In many areas of the country, soil was eroded and forest lands were stripped. Grain shortages, transportation problems, and shortages in raw materials combined with devastating floods and droughts to create a depression and famine that cost the lives of an estimated thirty million people.

The Great Proletarian Cultural Revolution, "The Ten Years of Turmoil," was the final example of Mao's reign of turmoil. The leaflet called the period from 1966 through 1978 "a disaster unprecedented in history."

It went on to denounce Deng for continuing the turmoil by launching the Anti-Spiritual Pollution Campaign of 1983-1984, and the Anti-Bourgeois Liberalization Campaign of 1987. The leaflet also charged that "the massive anxiety among the people" was due to misjudgments in the central government's economic policies," which had created an atmosphere of decline, resulting in the depreciation of the yuan; depletion of savings; and spiraling inflation, which led to panic buying. The final charge in the leaflet was leveled against Deng, Li Peng, and Yang Shangkun for "raping the will of the people" by ordering martial law and deploying thousands of troops with the intent of ordering a "bloody crackdown" to crush the will of the people.

As I spoke, there was a look of vague distraction on Han Ling's face, as if she had suddenly remembered something. Thinking that I might be detaining her and that she was too polite to interrupt me, I asked if she needed to leave.

Han Ling shook her head slightly and said, "No, while you were talking, a vision appeared in my mind. It was an image of myself when I was a child. It is something that I have never discussed with anyone, something that I haven't even thought about. I've kept it hidden away buried in the back of my mind, like an object tucked away in the back of a drawer."

As she told me about her childhood, Han Ling spoke without emotion, as if the little girl she talked about had also been tucked away someplace, and the adult had become someone completely separate and apart from the child.

"I saw myself at the age of four, standing on a chair by the window in our apartment. Our apartment had only one room, and it was dimly lit by a solitary light bulb that dangled from the ceiling in the middle of the room. Outside, it was misty and very dark. I remember how the blackness of the night frightened me. My face was pressed against the windowpane, and I watched the road, waiting for my father to appear. It was very late—around midnight, I suppose. I remember that I was crying. In fact, I had been crying all night.

"I was very angry with my father when he didn't come home to fix my supper, and at first I cried because I was angry and hungry. I waited and waited for him to come home. Around seven o'clock, I went through our building knocking on every door. There must have been fifty or sixty families living in our building, but no one answered my knock. Finally, I went back to our apartment and pulled the chair up to the window. I climbed up on the chair and stood there for hours, looking out of the window and crying. I no longer cried because I was hungry or angry. I cried because I was alone and frightened.

"It was 1967, and my mother had already been sent down to the countryside. I knew she was gone but I wasn't sure where she had gone, or why she had left. During the Cultural Revolution, class enemies were called *niugui sheshen* (ox ghost snake spirits). I had heard people call her that, but I didn't know anything about class enemies. I thought an ox ghost snake spirit must be something like a *hulijing* (fox spirit). My grandmother had told me stories about fox spirits. They were very cunning foxes who could turn themselves into beautiful women. Since my mother was a beautiful woman, it seemed a logical conclusion that an ox ghost snake spirit must be the same sort of creature as a fox spirit.

"My mother was highly educated. Until she was declared an enemy of the people and sent away to the countryside, she held a very important post as a design engineer. She came from an educated family. My grandfather was a teacher who had very little money. Grandmother was from Suzhou, and although her family was more prosperous than Grandfather's family, they were not wealthy people. However, since they owned property, her family was classified as the worst of the bad elements: a landlord family.

"Grandmother had been an extraordinarily beautiful woman. In China it is said that the most beautiful women come from Suzhou. My grandmother was a true Suzhou beauty. Her height, almost five feet six inches, made her appear even more stunning. She was in her late forties when China was liberated. After liberation, Grandmother was sent off to be re-educated through labor. Every day she worked for hours carrying stones down from the mountains. After a time, the heavy weight of the stones damaged her backbone so severely that she could no longer stand erect. She could not even raise herself above waist level. It is sad to think that a woman who had once been so tall and elegant would end up all stooped over like a hunchback.

"That night as I stood staring out the window, I worried that Father had left me, just as Mother had. When I could no longer stand the waiting, I went downstairs and stood by the road. It was so dark. The sky was starless and the moon was covered by clouds. By then, it had started to rain. I saw a man coming toward me on a bicycle. I called out to him, but he rode on past me. Not long after, I saw another man coming down the road. He was walking, but since it was raining, he walked very fast. I was afraid he might also pass me by, so I went to the middle of the road and stood there, waiting to throw myself at his feet if I had to. As soon as he was close enough to hear me, I called out to him, 'Uncle, please take me to my father.' He came up to me and asked, 'What is your father's name?' When I told him, he took me by the hand and led me to the Administration Building.

"When we entered the building, he took me down a long hallway to an office at the end of the hallway. The door was closed, so he knocked, and we waited for someone to answer. It took such a long time for someone to come to the door, I wanted to tell him to knock again. But I was too afraid to say anything. When the door finally opened, I could see Father inside the room. He was sitting in the front of the room with his head bowed. The other people in the room were seated facing him. There must have been twenty or thirty people, because I remember the room was full.

"Something made me afraid to enter the room. Maybe it was because Father looked so haggard and pale, or maybe it was because everyone else in the room had such angry expressions on their faces. Anyway, I just stood there, frozen in the doorway. I cried out, 'Papa, I have been looking for you.'

"He seemed very nervous, and he answered me very sharply. He said, 'Ling-Ling, Papa is working. Go outside and wait.'

"Then, someone took me by the hand and led me away. I don't remember if it was the man who had brought me there or someone else. I'm not even sure that I looked at the person. I just remember that someone took my hand and led me away.

"At the time, I was much too young to understand what was happening, but now I know that it was a struggle session against my father. He was a department head at the university, and all of the people who worked under him had been assembled to criticize and accuse him.

"For the next two months or so, I led a very strange life. In the daytime I was quite happy. I played with the other children who lived in our building—catching bugs, playing games. There was no one around to scold me or to tell me not to do this or not to do that. I could go outside anytime I wanted to, and stay out as late as I wished.

"At night, I was miserable. It was always very late when Father came home. I spent hours alone, and usually I cried myself to sleep. One night Father woke me when he came home to tell me that I was going away to live with my aunt. When I asked him how long I would have to stay, he looked very sad and told me, 'We will see.' The next day, my aunt arrived on the train to take me away.

"After a few months had passed, my aunt told me my mother had returned home, and that I would be going home as well. Home! It was a magical word for a magical place. I couldn't wait to go home. Everything would be the way it was before, and we would all be happy again. Mother and Father and I would be together and I could play with my friends.

"My parents met me at the train station. When we climbed into the pedicab, I was so excited I could barely breathe. However, after we had gone only a short distance, I realized that we were not heading in the right direction. I said, 'Papa, why isn't the pedicab taking us home?' Father said, 'Ling-Ling, we don't live there anymore. From now on, we will live with Grandmother and Grandfather.' At that point, I realized that things would never again be the same.

"My grandparents divided their apartment in half; half a room for them, and half a room for the three of us. That was the way we had to live. But even that did not stay the same. Not long after, Father was sent down to the countryside. Then, after a year, Grandfather and Grandmother went to live with my aunt.

"Once again, I was alone most of the time. Mother had not been allowed to return to her job as an engineer. She was sent to work at a factory, sewing clothes. Some days, she was gone from six in the morning until six at night, and other days from two in the afternoon until two in the morning. Each day, before she left for work, Mother would prepare food for me and leave it on the kitchen table. That food was all that I had to eat for the whole day. As soon as Mother left the apartment, I would open the door and all the windows. I thought with them open, I would have more ways to escape if anything happened. One morning when I woke up, I saw a cat sitting on the table. He was licking his paws and next to him was my empty bowl. When I saw the cat, I wept because I knew I would have to go hungry until the next day.

"Father had been sent away to Jilin, a province on the Russian border. Jilin is cold the year round, and the Siberian winds make the winters especially cruel. Father had to stay there until 1974. For him, it was a sentence of seven long years of bitter cold, hard labor, and loneliness. For me, it was seven long years of never hearing his voice, or seeing his face, or having my papa there to comfort me when I was afraid.

"When he finally returned, my father was already an old man. The seven years in Jilin had aged him prematurely. They had also aged me prematurely. Although I was only eleven years old when he returned, I was no longer a child. I suppose you could say that my childhood ended the night I stood looking out the window, waiting for my father to come home."

The real tragedy of Han Ling's story is that it is a common story. Millions had the same experiences, and millions more had it much worse. I had heard the students of that era referred to as "the lost generation." Yet in truth, all the generations during the Cultural Revolution were "lost generations," with each suffering the loss of something invaluable and irretrievable. The elderly lost the peace and tranquility that old age was supposed to bring. Those in their thirties and forties lost the time in their lives when efforts and achievements were supposed to blossom. Instead, as the Chinese say, they were left "half-cooked rice." Those in their teens and twenties were deprived of a beginning. Their education was abandoned, and they were denied the prime of their youth. Han Ling's story told of how the children suffered. They were robbed of the treasures of childhood: wonder, enchantment, and innocence.

As I walked with Han Ling to the main road of the campus, we could hear an announcement in the background coming from the neighborhood public address system on Fragrant Flower Road as people gathered in the streets for the second night of vigil.

When I awoke Sunday morning, I turned on the radio immediately, hoping that the news blackout on Tiananmen Square had been lifted. I moved the dial from a Japanese lesson to a French lesson to a program featuring American music before turning off the radio in disgust. Since Voice of America, BBC, and other non-Chinese stations were still being jammed on short wave, the only hope for getting any solid information was to purchase a foreign newspaper. With that in mind, I dressed and rode to the Yellow Mountain Hotel so that I could also see Susan and apologize for not calling her.

Unfortunately, Susan had not come to work. I left a note for her with one of her coworkers, then headed for the hotel newsstand intending to load up on papers. Although she gave me a copy of the *China Daily, th*e clerk told me that foreign newspapers were "not available," and pointed to the empty shelves as proof.

The *China Daily* was not exactly bulging with information on the current situation in Beijing. There was no mention of the martial law order, and the only item pertaining to the student movement was a front page article about foreigners' reactions to the demonstrations. Unlike earlier articles, which had been sympathetic to the students, this one focused on the surprise, anxiety, and concern expressed by foreigners, stressing their disgruntlement with the traffic conditions and quoting one foreigner who stated that "too many political movements pose a threat to the economy."

Instead of returning directly to campus, I rode along the Third Ring Road past two barricades set up to block troops, then cut back over to a back road that was a shortcut to the campus. There were three army trucks stopped at one of the barricades. But the soldiers seemed perfectly content to stay where they were. People from the neighborhood were chatting with them amicably and plying them with food, water, and cigarettes.

It was unthinkable to most Chinese that they could have anything to fear from the People's Liberation Army since it was, after all, the people's army. A special bond existed between the people and the PLA, and the roots of that bond go back to the period before the founding of the People's Republic to the days of the Red Army. The strength of the Red Army grew through its recruitment of peasants, its code of behavior, and its policy of land reform. Unlike the armies of warlords who had kidnaped conscripts, raped, burned, pillaged, and plundered, the Red Army adhered to the Three Rules of Discipline* and the Eight Points of Attention.** Additionally, its policy of confiscating land, property, and money from landlords for redistribution to the masses was a key factor in the popular support the Red Army received from the peasantry.

The heroics of the army—fact and fable—has served to inspire the people of China, and in doing so, strengthened the ties between the people

---

*The Three Rules are 1) prompt obedience to all orders; 2) don't take even a needle or strand of thread from the people; 3) prompt delivery to headquarters of all items confiscated from landlords.

**The Eight Points of Attention are 1) replace any articles used; 2) roll up and return the straw matting on which you sleep; 3) be courteous and assist when you can; 4) return all borrowed articles; 5) replace all damaged articles; 6) be honest in all transactions with peasants; 7) pay fairly for all articles purchased; 8) be sanitary and establish latrines an appropriate distance from people's houses.

and the army. Unquestionably, the greatest example of the Red Army's heroism was the legendary Long March. The six thousand mile long retreat of the Red Army began in Jiangxi Province on October 16, 1934, with 80,000 troops, and ended on October 20, 1935, when the surviving 6,000 reached Shaanxi Province. However, what began as a retreat was parlayed into a heroic feat, which not only preserved the Communist Party and the Red Army, but established Mao Zedong as the leader of both.

After the Long March, the Yanan base in Shaanxi Province became Mao's laboratory for a decade of political experimentation. Using a system of education by political indoctrination, which focused on uniform thought, Mao instilled the army with the "Spirit of Yanan"—unity through total dependence and loyalty to one's comrades at arms.

The Party's use of the myth of Lei Feng is another example of the bond between the people and the PLA. The story of Lei Feng, an ordinary soldier who exemplified the "Yanan Spirit" and was devoted to Chairman Mao, was conceived in 1963 by Lin Biao, then Minister of Defense. The Lei Feng myth, which capitalized on the people's regard for the PLA, was used to downplay Mao's failure, to shore up his diminishing support within the leadership by creating a personality cult, and to revive the "Spirit of Yanan" after the dismal failure of the Great Leap Forward. Whether Lei Feng was created from whole cloth or in part, he was certainly too good to be true. However, the Chinese populace eagerly took to the story of Lei Feng.

A saint, a soldier, The Good Samaritan, and an unselfish, dedicated, and energetic youth, Lei Feng had conveniently left behind a diary to document all of his good acts. In a program that inspired people to "Learn from the PLA" and to "Learn from Lei Feng," the people were taught how Lei Feng had always put the needs of others before his own, how his chief desire had been to "serve the people," and how his devotion to Mao had allowed him to achieve these goals.

From his birth to his death, Lei had to deal with every adversity, probably invented by the propaganda team. He had been born a poor peasant in 1939, and had faced all of China's enemies. His family had been victimized by landlords, Japanese, and the *Guomindang,* before he was orphaned and raised by Communist Party officials. As a dedicated revolutionary, Lei Feng had gone on to join the army and then to become a member of the Communist Party. However, as if to prove the axiom that no good deed goes unpunished, Lei met with an untimely death when he was run over by a truck while assisting a comrade in arms. The myth of Lei Feng proved to be such a successful propaganda tool that the "Learn from Lei Feng" campaign was used during the Cultural Revolution, the early 1980s, and briefly during the campaign against bourgeois liberalization.

Despite the underlying belief of Beijingers that the PLA loved the people, the presence of 150,000 armed troops could not be taken lightly. On the evening of Sunday, May 21st, there was new cause for alarm as word of Li Peng's latest directive spread around the city.

Although the government had repeated its claim that the troops had been brought into Beijing, not to suppress the students, but to assist the local police and the military police in executing the martial law order, students learned of Li Peng's Four Point Decision. In a high level meeting held Sunday afternoon, Li declared the student movement to be "a rebellion in nature," and stated that the students must be suppressed to ensure ten years of reform, regardless of the cost in lives. Finally, Li ordered "the jails in the capital to prepare to imprison more people" and "all street sweepers to clean Tiananmen Square at five o'clock, Monday morning."

Citizens rallied at the barricades for the third night, entreating the soldiers not to harm the students while reasoning with them that orders that ran counter to the will of the people should not be obeyed. Thousands of people encircled the the square in a last line of defense, determined to protect the students at all costs. Stories of the people's heroism and determination were broadcast on the square, and reported to the crowds gathered at the barricades around the city. The reports told of old people, willing to sacrifice themselves in order to save their grandsons and granddaughters, who had blocked the trucks with their bodies by lying down in front of the wheels.

At first light Monday morning, the street sweepers did arrive to clean the square. However, the scene on Tiananmen Square was not what Li Peng had desired. The students had not budged but remained on the square throughout the night, and troops had not breached the barricades. It was another humiliation for Deng Xiaoping and Li Peng: martial law had not been enforced.

Once again the streets of Beijing buzzed with rumors as the emotional roller coaster took another swing upward. The small lane news claimed that Li Peng's power was slipping, while Zhao was waiting in the wings to reclaim his position as rightful heir. Another rumor claimed that seven retired senior military officers and one hundred junior officers had sent an open letter to the *People's Daily* stating their opposition to martial law. The letter was quoted as stating, "the PLA belongs to the people and will not confront or suppress the people. It will never shoot the people. . . . To keep the situation from worsening, the army must not enter the city." But if indeed the letter was sent, it was not published.

While Beijing's Vice Mayor Zhang Jianmin warned that "the urban crisis might result in a blackout of electricity, a water shutoff, and shortages of gasoline and food," there was a substantial decrease in fires, crime, and traffic accidents as the citizens of Beijing pulled together in a united effort to protect the students and their city. Additionally, milk, eggs, fruits, and vegetables were still readily available, and some farmers even reduced their prices to show their public spirit.

As troops began to pull back from the city, spirits were boosted even higher. Thunderclouds hovered over the city on the morning of Tuesday, May 23rd, but threatening skies were not enough to prevent the people of Beijing from celebrating the failure of martial law.

As I rode past the back gate of *Zhongnanhai* on Tuesday afternoon, scattered raindrops dotted the street, and little gusts of wind formed tiny waves on Beihai Lake. Pedaling faster, I raced against the rain, heading for Eternal Peace Avenue.

Jogging from the parking lot toward the square, I could hear the now familiar chant coming from the avenue: "Li Peng *xia tai* (Li Peng resign)!" The festival had resumed in the city as dense crowds once again lined the avenue and encircled the square. Happy to see the return of gaiety to Beijing, I cheered and laughed with those around me.

Marching with brooms, dustpans, and shovels, a group of workers chanted that Li Peng must be swept out of office. In the middle of a truckload of demonstrators, a man held up a drawing of Deng and Li. Both had blood dripping from their mouths, and horns sprouted from Li Peng's head. The caption written at the bottom of the drawing was a warning to the unpopular pair, "Even if you had wings, you still could not escape!"

Squeezing through the crowd, I hurried down the avenue to the pedestrian underpass by the Gate of Heavenly Peace. From the top of the stairs leading down to the underpass, I spotted a single red rosebud pinned to a *xiaozibao* (small character poster), which had been taped to the wall of the underpass. Even before I read it, I had some idea what it said, and knew that it must be addressed to Deng Yingchao, Zhou Enlai's widow, and the "adopted mother" of Li Peng.

> *Deng Mama, discipline your son Peng. He's been very naughty. The people are extremely displeased with his governing! Strike down Li Peng! Execute Li Peng! Cut Down Li Peng! Change the color of the dragon! People of China Arise! Quickly press for the resignation of Li Peng!*

After copying down the small character poster, I walked through the underpass and up the steps to Tiananmen Square. As I started across the square, someone called out to me. Turning, I saw Professor Fang running up the stairs behind me. He told me that each day he came to the square to check on the students. Many of his students had left the square in the last two days, but Professor Fang felt a strong commitment to all of the students, not just those who were in his classes or students at his university.

Professor Fang nodded toward the Heavenly Gate of Peace and asked if I had seen what had happened to the picture of Mao. Although I hadn't noticed it before, I saw that there were six huge black splatters on the picture, one on Mao's eyebrow and the others on his throat and chest. Dozens of smaller splatters also marred the picture. Excitedly, Professor Fang told me that three men had thrown eggshells filled with ink and paint at the picture, but the students had immediately apprehended the men and turned them over to the police. Professor Fang explained that the students felt it was necessary to turn the men in since they could not risk guilt by association. He also pointed out that there was concern the men might be undercover police who were trying to create an incident that would give the police an excuse to use violence against the students.

I asked Professor Fang what he thought the students' next move might be. Exhausted after more than a month of demonstrations and almost a dozen days and nights spent on the square, many of the students from Beijing had returned to their campuses or homes on Monday. Of the thirty thousand students who remained camped out on the square, the majority were now from colleges and universities located in other areas of China.

As the exodus of students began, rumors spread that the students planned to declare a victory and leave the square. Although their demands had not been met, the students had certainly gained tremendous face, and there was justification to claim a victory. In stating their demands and staging the hunger strike, the students had communicated their point of view to the leaders and people of China and to the world at large. Their movement had received broad public support and had even drawn support from within the Central Committee. Massive numbers of people had gone to the streets to support and to protect the students and to voice their disapproval of the government.

Additionally, both students and workers had established organizations independent of government control. Regardless of the government's insistence that these organizations were illegal, the mere fact that they had been established was an incredible accomplishment. The *laobaixing* and the intellectuals had committed themselves to political reform. Furthermore, since the leaders had been unable to force the students to leave Tiananmen Square, and the army had refused to march against them, the student movement had exposed a large chasm in China's leadership.

While Professor Fang and I were talking, a man came over and stood next to us. He had been picking up pieces of cardboard and other scraps of trash nearby, but as we talked, he had moved closer and closer. Since we were standing with the wind against our backs, the man interrupted our conversation, telling us to turn around so the wind would not "blow our words away." Smiling at the man politely, we obediently turned around, and continued with our conversation. After listening to us for few more minutes, the man interrupted again to complain that he couldn't understand what we were saying. Professor Fang explained to him that he couldn't understand us because we were speaking English. The man looked at us as if we were behaving quite foolishly, then laughed, and asked us to speak Chinese.

It was impossible to tell the man's age by his appearance alone. He could have been anywhere from forty to sixty. His skin was lined and tanned a butternut brown from years spent working in the fields. Yet, his ramrod straight body was lean and muscular. His was a good face with bright, clear eyes and a pleasing smile, despite teeth stained yellow from tobacco and tea. He told us he was a peasant from a small village in Hebei Province. He had traveled to the city to come to Tiananmen Square to show his love for the students and to help them in any way that he could. With a satisfied grin, he said it was good that he had come since there was so much trash that needed to be picked up and carried away.

When we resumed our conversation in Chinese, the peasant commented to Professor Fang that it was very difficult to understand me because I spoke with such a strange accent. I laughed, telling him that I also had great difficulty understanding his accent. Professor Fang spoke up in my defense, telling the peasant that he was really quite lucky to have come across a foreigner who could speak Chinese. However, the peasant didn't find it at all remarkable that I could speak Chinese. In fact, until we told him differently, he had assumed that everyone in the world could speak Chinese since it was the only language he had ever heard spoken, before he came across the two of us.

A bolt of lightening and a deafening clap of thunder interrupted our little colloquy. Startled by the thunder, we turned toward the Gate of Heavenly Peace and saw that a massive, murky-brown cloud had completely covered the sky above the Imperial Palace. Pointing to the angry looking cloud, Professor Fang quipped that it was conclusive evidence that the "Emperor" had displeased Heaven. Suddenly, the cloud rolled toward the square, bringing with it swirling winds of sand, torrential rain, and more thunder and lightning. Grabbing my arm, Professor Fang steered me across the square, and across the street, toward The Great Hall of the People. First we headed for a large plastic tarpaulin that had been erected near the Hall. However, too many others had arrived there first. Since it appeared to be filled to capacity, Professor Fang pulled me over to the iron fence surrounding the grounds of the hall to take shelter under a tree. After a second or two, it dawned on me that leaning against an iron fence while standing under a tree was not the best place to be in a thunderstorm. Telling Professor Fang that we were an invitation to lightning, I suggested that we try to squeeze in with the crowd under the tarpaulin.

On the count of three, we made a mad dash for the tarpaulin. The people in front pressed together a little more tightly, telling those behind them to make room for the foreigner. Although we managed to get under the tarpaulin, we were standing at the very edge. When Professor Fang reached up and tugged on the tarpaulin, trying to give us a few more inches of cover, he released the buckets of water which had collected where the tarpaulin sagged. The water came gushing down the tarpaulin, splashing on my head, and thoroughly drenching me and my camera bag. Since I couldn't possibly get any wetter than I already was, I decided to make a run for the pedestrian underpass. With a quick goodby to Professor Fang, I took off running as the people under the tarpaulin laughed at the crazy foreigner and cheered me on.

By the time I had gone down through the underpass and up to the other side of Eternal Peace Avenue, the rain had stopped. Shivering violently I ran to my bicycle, but alas, even my bicycle seat was soaked through. When I climbed on the bike and sat down, water oozed out of the cloth seat cover and the foam cushion, then trickled down my legs. Nevertheless, I hoped that the ride back to the campus would at least dry my cotton shirt.

I rode at top speed, barely braking for intersections and whizzing around corners while my teeth chattered like castanets. About halfway home, just when my shirt and hair had begun to dry, the downpour started again. I pedaled furiously toward the shelter of a tunnel formed by a bridge over the bike lane. Unfortunately, everyone else going in my direction had the same idea. The tunnel was so crammed with people that there wasn't enough room left for even a single rider to pass through to the other side. Those of us left outside in the rain could only sit on our bikes, getting wetter and colder. Despite the discomfort, it was a good-natured group. When a few young men started a chant to urge those inside to make way, all of us joined in, shouting, *"Yi, er, zou* (one, two, go)!" Within seconds the chant was altered and everyone, including those under the shelter, joined in to chant *"Li Peng zou* (Li Peng go)!"

The rain was still pouring down when I pulled into the parking lot at *San Lou.* Water from my hair was streaming onto my face, and even my underwear was sopping wet. I looked like a soaked rat and felt even worse. Before entering the dorm, I shook myself like a dog, causing the *shiwuyuan* who was standing in the doorway to collapse into giggles.

Lu Minghua was having a cup of tea with Jinjin, waiting for me to return from the square. She shook her finger at me, clucking her tongue disapprovingly when I walked into the room. She told me that she had also been to the square, and had even seen me there. However, as she so eagerly pointed out, she had been wise enough to bring along an umbrella and a plastic raincoat.

For the first time in my life, I truly understood the meaning of the cliché, "chilled to the bone." I was freezing—my skin, my blood, and even my bones felt like ice. Not worrying about modesty, I ripped off my clothes and toweled myself dry, then put on my long silk underwear, a pair of jeans, a sweatshirt, and my jacket. Even that was not enough. I still shivered, and my teeth still chattered and I doubted I would ever feel warm again. Lu Minghua poured me a cup of tea while I climbed into my bed and wrapped myself in my wool blanket. When that didn't warm me, Jinjin pulled the comforter from her bed and wrapped it around me. After I had drunk three cups of boiling hot tea and Jinjin had added her wool blanket to the pile on the bed that was me, I finally ceased the shivering and teeth chattering.

Lu Minghua got up to leave, insisting that I should go to sleep. I wanted her to stay and talk to me. So much had happened that I wanted to discuss with her. Trying to persuade her to stay, I argued that it was still early and that I was finally beginning to feel warm. However, a sneeze ended that discussion.

Shaking her finger at me again, Lu Minghua opened the door and said, "See now you are sneezing. Go to sleep! If you don't rest, you will really become ill."

I moaned at that prediction. Suspicious that I had developed a new symptom, Lu Minghua stopped in the doorway, and asked if I had a pain. Assuring her that I was not in pain, I told her that I couldn't afford to get ill. I had already missed so many classes. I was certain that Teacher Wu would no longer recognize me.

Lu Minghua shook her head at my foolishness. Before closing the door behind her, she said, "Little Sister, don't you realize that over the past few weeks you have had many teachers and learned many lessons."

CHAPTER SIXTEEN

DEMOCRACY IS WORTH
THE PRICE

Life in Beijing began to take on the appearance of normalcy after the demonstration on Tuesday, May 23rd. Troops withdrew to the outskirts of the city; markets, shops, and street stalls were crowded with customers; and busloads of tourists could be seen heading for a day's outing at the Summer Palace or other scenic spots well away from the heart of the city. On Wednesday, May 24th, subways and public buses resumed their routes, and white-gloved traffic police returned to their wooden islands at busy intersections. On Thursday, May 25th, mail service was restored in the city, and foreign newspapers and magazines were again in plentiful supply in hotel newsstands.

But Beijingers knew the appearance of normalcy was a mirage and the calm as fleeting as that in the eye of a hurricane. The spans of time between the ups and downs of the emotional roller coaster shortened as whirlwinds of political activity swirled around the leaders' compound at *Zhongnanhai* and the students' encampment at Tiananmen Square. Each day, people sifted through a new collection of rumors for grains of truth and dissected news reports for subtle signs of hope or portents of doom.

In the meantime, the three top leaders of China were nowhere to be seen. Deng Xiaoping had not been seen in public since Gorbachev's visit. Li Peng had not made an appearance since his midnight speech of May 19th, and no one knew for certain what had happened to Zhao Ziyang after his visit to the students at Tiananmen Square. This vanishing act by the leaders contributed to the seesaw of emotions Beijingers had to endure, and resulted in a maze of confusing rumors.

While "inside reports" claimed that Zhao had been stripped of his power and placed under house arrest after his visit to the square, people were unwilling to count him out. But when reports of a speech made by President Yang Shangkun leaked out, hope for Zhao's revival grew faint. In Yang's address to an enlarged emergency session of the Central Military Commission on Wednesday, May 24th, he stated that it had been "necessary to make a change in the leadership because Zhao Ziyang had created dissension in the Party," causing the Party "to speak with two voices."

Yet sparks of hope that Zhao could survive were rekindled briefly when the Xinhua News Agency quoted the May 25th statement made by Li Jinhua who denied Zhao's ouster by declaring, "There is no change in the Party leadership."* On the following day, the *International Herald Tribune* quashed that hope by reporting that the Party had decided Zhao would bear the blame for the "turmoil" that the student movement had caused. Furthermore, the article cited five charges that had been made against Zhao: "creating an anti-Party clique, instigating civil turmoil, revealing Party secrets, corruption, and taking credit for Deng Xiaoping's program of reforms."

Li Peng's political future was also the subject of rumors and speculation. Although the people had never felt a rapport with Li as they had with Zhao Ziyang, Li had been disregarded more than disliked. But following his speech of May 19th and the May 20th imposition of martial law, the outcry of public rage directed against Li was as virulent as the attacks that had been made against Jiang Qing and The Gang of Four after their fall.

The public expression of hatred for Li led to the rumor that he was on the verge of losing his power. Adding fuel to the fire of speculation that Li could not hang on, all major newspapers and television and radio stations reported the public demands for Li's ouster after the Martial Law Order. While they avoided mentioning Li by name, reports such as the one in Xinhua News Agency noted that "the overwhelming majority of the protesters' slogans were directed against the Chief Leader of the State Council."

These reports led to the rumor that Li was losing support within the Party hierarchy, leading to the rumor that Li had been forced from power, which led to the rumor that Deng Xiaoping had taken personal control of

---

*Li Jinhua was the spokeswoman for the Foreign Ministry.

all military and political operations concerning the crisis in Beijing. Considering that it had also been rumored that Deng was dead, this string of rumors was all the more confusing.

While Beijingers puzzled over the confusion, Martial Law Headquarters continued to issue statements assuring the public that the PLA had not been called in to quell the student movement. In an effort to further dispel the fears of the people, articles were published in various newspapers calling for local residents to "understand and support the troops." One front page story quoted a PLA officer as saying, "We are the people's army and we will serve the people just as we did in the past. How could we shoot our own people?" But Beijingers asked why the government had deemed it necessary to amass between two to three hundred thousand troops on the outskirts of the city.

Rumors persisted that within the PLA itself, there was not complete "understanding and support" for martial law troops. Although all newspapers and broadcasts reported that the General Offices of the Army, Navy, and Air Force, and six of the seven military commands had declared their support of Li Peng and the Declaration of Martial Law, Qin Jiwei, the Minister of Defense, had not been seen since he had opposed martial law.* Furthermore, the Chief of the 38th Army, Xu Qingxian, had avoided ordering the 38th Army to march on the city by feigning illness and entering a hospital. There was also a rumor that Beijing troops were withholding food and supplies from the other troops.

After the martial law order and Zhao's apparent fall from grace on May 19th, the National People's Congress (NPC) became the wild card in the struggle for power. In theory, Article Fifty-Seven of the Constitution of the People's Republic of China declared the NPC to be the supreme national power and granted it the right to recall the State Council and Standing Committee of the NPC, as well as the power to repeal any administrative decree, decision, or order. However, throughout the history of the People's Republic of China, the true role of the NPC had been to convene once a year for the purpose of enthusiastically endorsing the decisions that had already been made by the Party leadership.

---

*The seven military commands are: *Beijing, Shenyang, Jinan, Nanjing, Guangzhou, Chengdu,* and *Lanzhou.*

Supporters of Zhao began to call on the NPC to fulfill its constitutional responsibility. Additionally, even those within the Pro-Democracy Movement, who were not supporters of Zhao, viewed the strengthening of the NPC to be a significant move in the direction of democracy.

Immediately after martial law was declared, over thirty members of the NPC Standing Committee called for a special session to rescind martial law. However, since that was far less than the necessary number of votes needed to call a special session of the NPC Standing Committee, attention focused on Wan Li. As Chairman of the Standing Committee of the NPC, Wan Li had the constitutional right to convene a special session.

Born to a poor peasant family in 1916 in Dongping County, Shandong Province, Wan Li joined the Communist Party at the age of twenty. He served first as an undercover agent in Dongping County before climbing the ladder of officialdom from the county level to the regional level, and on to the provincial level. By 1965, Wan had advanced to the central level of government, serving as the Deputy Minister of the Ministry of Construction under the Administrative Council as well as a Deputy Mayor of Beijing and a delegate to the NPC.

At the beginning of the Cultural Revolution in 1966, Wan was labeled a counterrevolutionary, paraded through the streets by Red Guards, and put through repeated struggle sessions. He was rehabilitated in 1971 and appointed Minister of the Railways in 1975. However, his close friendship with Deng Xiaoping caused him to be dismissed from office again in 1976, when Deng was purged by the Gang of Four. After the fall of the Gang of Four, Deng appointed Wan as the Secretary of the Party Committee of Anhui Province. While Zhao was introducing economic reform in Sichuan Province, Wan was implementing the Household Responsibility System in Anhui.* In 1980, Wan was appointed Minister of the State Agricultural Commission and Vice Premier of the State Council. He was elected Chairman of the NPC Standing Committee in 1988.

Although Wan was in the United States on an official visit, there was reason to believe that he would call the special session on his return to

---

*The Household Responsibility System was used to dismantle the commune system by making each farmer responsible for an individual plot.

China. A proponent of economic reform, Wan had supported Zhao Ziyang in the Politburo in the past, and he seemed to have developed a more lenient attitude toward political reform than that which he had displayed during his 1986 debate with Fang Lizhi (the debate which sparked the 1986-1987 student demonstrations). In Toronto, a few days prior to his arrival in the United States, Wan had stated that "patriotic enthusiasm should be protected," and that "all these problems should be settled through democracy and the legal system." On May 23rd, Beijingers' spirits lifted when it was announced that Wan Li would cut short his visit to the United States and return to China immediately.

While *Zhongnanhai* was immersed in political intrigue, the students at Tiananmen Square were experiencing their own leadership difficulties. On May 23rd, Wuer Kaixi was removed as the Chairman of the ASAB. Representatives of Deng Xiaoping's son, Deng Pufang, met with Wuer Kaixi and convinced him that unless the students withdrew from the square immediately, a blood bath would occur. When Wuer Kaixi ordered the students to withdraw, he was ousted from his position of leadership.

On May 24th, the Defend Tiananmen Square Headquarters was established to coordinate the occupation. Chai Ling was selected to direct the operations of the organization and named the Commander of Tiananmen Square. But there were frequent disagreements between the followers of Chai Ling, the ASAB, and the numerous student organizations that had sprung up out of the 228 schools represented on the square. As early as May 16th, students from outside of Beijing had begun arriving in the capital city. By May 23rd, over 150,000 students from universities throughout China had made their way to Tiananmen Square. Although a large number of students were returning home each day, just as many were arriving to replace those who left, and as their numbers climbed, support for the ASAB dwindled.

The majority of the students from Beijing had come to believe that remaining on the square was counterproductive. Exhausted from the occupation, they felt that the time had come to leave the square in order to concentrate their efforts on pressing for democratic reform through their publications, and encouraging workers and peasants to play a more active role in the Pro-Democracy Movement. But the students from outside of

Beijing believed the occupation of the square should continue until the government agreed to rescind martial law and recall Li Peng. The discord between the two factions weakened their organization and contributed to the conflicting rumors as to if and when the students would leave the square.

While I struggled along with everyone else in Beijing to unravel the rumors, I attempted to restore some order to my own life. With examinations scheduled the first week in June, I promised myself that I would attend the remainder of my classes, and concentrate on preparing for exams.

Since I had made up my mind to stay in Beijing instead of traveling around China, I arranged to keep my room for another month and decided to approach Teacher Wu about tutoring me after the term was over. Although we had never discussed my absences, I felt sure that he understood why I had missed so many classes and even approved of my attending the demonstrations.

The teachers who worked with foreign students had made an extraordinary effort to run our classes on a business-as-usual basis. In fact, there appeared to be an unspoken agreement between the students and teachers to avoid any discussion in the classrooms of the events which were occurring in Beijing. However, Teacher Wu had said something in an earlier class that led me to believe that he supported the students. That day we had been assigned to tell a fable as an exercise in our conversation class. One of my Japanese classmates had selected a fable from ancient Chinese folklore, "The Foolish Old Man Who Moved Mountains."

The fable concerns an old man who lived at the base of a huge mountain. The mountain was really a nuisance since the old man had to scale it each time he wanted to leave his home. Finally, the old man decided to remove the mountain. Leading his sons to the base of the mountain, they began hacking at it with their hoes. When people learned of his plan, they ridiculed the old man, calling him the "Foolish Old Man of North Mountain." One day, a man who was greatly admired for his wisdom approached the old man. Pointing out the absurdity of the old man's plan, the wise man criticized him for wasting time on an impossible task.

However, the old man replied that he did not view the task as impossible. "When I die, my sons will carry on; when they die, their sons will carry on. When my grandsons die, their sons and grandsons will carry on. The mountain is high, but it will not grow any higher, and each chunk of dirt that is chipped away makes the mountain that much lower."*

When Teacher Wu asked for comments on the fable, the Japanese students all praised the old man for being exceptionally wise since he understood the value of patience and hard work. After their comments, Teacher Wu turned to me and said, "Now that we have the Japanese perspective, let's ask Kong Kailing for an American's perspective. I suspect that Americans would think that the old man was foolish, and that he should have moved the house instead of the mountain."

I told Teacher Wu that he was partially correct, then added, "as a matter of fact, an American would move the house to the top of the mountain. That way, the house would have a spectacular view, and it could be sold for three times its actual value."

Chuckling, Teacher Wu said, "I must agree with the American solution. Patience is an admirable quality, and we Chinese have always placed a great value on it. However, there are times when patience prevents one from seeking a better solution."

Not only had Teacher Wu given his backing to a purely capitalistic solution, he had made the same complaint about patience that I had heard from many of the students. Although they were proud of the Chinese culture for its richness, they had criticized certain aspects of their culture, and "Chinese patience" was one of the traits which I had heard criticized most frequently. Many Chinese students felt that their people had been too willing in the past to sit by patiently and wait for reform instead of taking the lead and improving their situation.

When I returned to class on Wednesday, May 24th, Teacher Wu was even more open about his support for the students. The subject came up quite by accident when Teacher Wu called on me to read from the textbook. Since the vocabulary was familiar to me, I zipped through the first page without an error. However, while I was reading the second page, there were

*Mao Zedong used this fable to illustrate that only perseverance and hard work would enable the Chinese people to do away with imperialism and feudalism, which he cited as the "two big mountains which lie like a dead weight on the Chinese people."

some snickers from my classmates. Teacher Wu didn't interrupt me to make a correction, so I ignored the snickers and continued to read.

When I had finished the page, Teacher Wu nodded and said, "Very good, Kong Kailing. However, I must point out that the students in this story were not demonstrating. They were traveling."

After a few seconds of confusion, I realized that I had read the characters *luxing* 旅行 (to travel) as *youxing* 游行 (to demonstrate). It must have been a Freudian slip. Nevertheless, I was embarrassed for having mentioned the "taboo" subject and meekly uttered, "Excuse me."

When my classmates and Teacher Wu had stopped laughing, he said, "Lately, Kong Kailing has not been a very good student." Then, giving me his warmest smile, he added, "But lately, I have not been a very good teacher."

I could have hugged him for saying that. Instead, I said, "It's been very difficult to keep up with all the words I've had to learn on my own. Unfortunately, our textbook doesn't have a vocabulary list for terms that are useful in a revolution."

Teacher Wu asked which new words I had learned on my own. I replied, "For example, human rights." That started a rather interesting word association game between the two of us.

He answered back, "Freedom of the press?"

I nodded and said, "Demands."

He said, "Hunger Strike."

I said, "Express Support."

He said, "Martial Law."

I said, "Fascists."

He said, "Resign from office."

I almost said Li Peng, but decided that would be pushing it too far. After class was over, I waited to walk out of the building with Teacher Wu so that I could speak with him privately. I wanted to make certain that he knew my poor attendance record did not reflect on his ability as a teacher, or my interest in his class. As I started to explain, he interrupted, saying, "You made the right choice. It is far more important for you to witness history than to attend classes."

Asking me to come with him, Teacher Wu led me over to one of the walls where people had posted *dazibao*. He pointed to a *dazibao*, which had been written earlier in May. It supported the students and urged the government to grant their demands for political reform. The *dazibao* had been signed by several members of the faculty, including Teacher Wu.

While I kept myself busy studying, I used some "Chinese patience" to wait for my friends to contact me. Although I had stayed in touch with Lu Minghua and The Professor and Lao Pang, I had not heard from my other friends since before martial law. Susan was the first to check in. She called on Thursday, May 25th, to tell me that she had decided to apply for a job with a Western company, which was opening a new hotel in the Shenzhen Special Economic Zone. After we spent several minutes talking around the subject, Susan finally admitted that she hoped the job might offer her the opportunity to meet a handsome young foreigner who would sweep her off her feet and take her away from all of this. It was a farfetched dream, but it was the only dream around for Susan. Her only chance to improve her life was to get out of China. If she remained in China, she would never have an opportunity for advancement in her job or even the opportunity to further her education so that she might get a better job. Since she didn't have the educational background to apply for study abroad, marriage to a foreigner was her only way out of China.

On Friday evening, Hong Xin and Little Liang came to my room for a brief visit. Lu Minghua arrived a short time later, and the four of us compared notes on what we had seen and heard, trying to put the events of the past few days in perspective.

It was clear that Deng Xiaoping was gathering his ducks in a neat little row. As announced, Wan Li had returned to China on Thursday afternoon. However, instead of returning directly to Beijing, Wan had been shanghaied in Shanghai by the Municipal Party Committee. To explain this irregularity, CCTV reported that Wan's sudden return to China had been for "health reasons," and that his medical problems had been the cause of the delay in Shanghai. The general assumption among Beijingers was that Wan would make a miraculous recovery from his mysterious ailment as soon as he toed the Party line.

The other news of the day was just as bad. Martial Law Headquarters had cut off access to the satellite, which had only been restored two days earlier. Twenty-seven of the thirty provinces announced their support for

Li Peng and martial law, and an article in the *Peoples Daily* declared that the Beijing Military Region had joined the other six regions in declaring support for martial law. According to the article, after the members of the Party Committee of the Beijing Military Region had given "sufficient study to the May 19th speeches of Li Peng and Yang Shangkun," they had concluded that "the present struggle was, in essence, a serious political struggle relevant to the success of the reform and the fate of the State and the Chinese nation." The article also noted that "Troops under the Beijing Military Region, which are responsible for carrying out martial law in Beijing, are undergoing ideological education and supporting the government and cherishing the people." It went on to say that "military authorities also managed to make the voice of the central government heard by soldiers in time to quell rumors."

To top things off, Li Peng returned to the spotlight on Thursday. During a televised report of his meeting with the ambassadors from Burma, Mexico, and Nigeria, Li pointedly stated, "The chief architect of reform and opening to the outside world is Comrade Deng Xiaoping and not any other person." By denying Zhao Ziyang's contribution to the economic reforms, Li was signaling that the hard-liners on the Politburo had won out, and Zhao Ziyang was gone for good. As further evidence that the government stood firmly behind Li and martial law, it was also reported that Li had sent a letter to the martial law troops thanking them for "restoring order to the capital city."

While the hard-liners in the government solidified their power, the student movement was becoming more fragmented. Hong Xin told us that the Beijing students were pressing even harder to end the occupation of Tiananmen Square, and that fewer Beijing students were remaining on the square each day. As morale sank lower, student organizers from the universities in Beijing were having difficulty even convincing their classmates to come to the square in shifts.

Frowning, Lu Minghua said, "It's time for them to leave. It has become much too dangerous for the students to remain on the square."

She asked if we knew about the statement that had been issued by Martial Law Headquarters that morning. Although I had heard about the statement, I had paid little attention to it since it seemed nothing more than a repeat of the same old charge that the Pro-Democracy Movement had been instigated by a small number of people. However, Lu Minghua explained that I had overlooked the significance of the wording in the statement, which had called for a "grave national struggle" to be waged against the instigators of the movement.

Repeating the words, "grave national struggle," Lu Minghua said, "Don't you see what that means. The government is using these words to justify the use of military force and a purge."

Hong Xin nodded in agreement, and Little Yuan added that there were already rumors of a blacklist. I asked Lu Minghua who might appear on such a list, wondering if she or Hong Xin would be in jeopardy.

As if she were reading my mind, Lu Minghua patted my arm, saying "Don't worry about us, Little Sister. We are small fish. They would not waste their time with us. They are after the big fish. I have heard fifty names, one hundred names, as many as two hundred names, and all are prominent intellectuals like Fang Lizhi and his wife, Li Shuxian."

When I walked my friends to the front steps of *San Lou,* Lu Minghua assured me once again that if there were a purge, it would be directed against the most prominent intellectuals and political figures who were associated with Zhao. However, I kept thinking of an article in the *China Daily*, which I had read earlier in the week. Returning to my room, I searched through my stack of newspapers and finally located the article in the May 22nd issue.

Just as I remembered, the reporter had questioned an unnamed spokesman for the Beijing Municipal Government whether or not there would be "military control of higher learning institutions." The spokesman had replied, ". . . according to the demands of the order to impose martial law, some troops may carry out tasks around the schools. He insisted that the move would be taken only as a means of "assisting the maintenance of normal order around the schools." If the government did order the army to drive the students from the square and then occupy the campuses, surely they would take steps to find out which students and professors on each campus had been active in or supportive of the Pro-Democracy Movement. It was an unsettling thought that kept me from getting much sleep Friday night.

As I rode toward the square on the afternoon of Saturday, May 27th, I had to remind myself that it had only been four days since I had last gone to Tiananmen Square. So much had happened and the scene had changed so dramatically that I felt as if I had been away for months. Although there was the usual Saturday traffic on Eternal Peace Avenue, it seemed almost deserted without the throngs of demonstrators and spectators lining the street.

Tiananmen Square looked like a dismal concrete island, and the vastness of the square swallowed up the several thousand students who remained there. As I passed the square on my way to park my bike at the Beijing Hotel, I noticed the other bicyclists around me. They rode past the square without slowing, looking straight ahead as if just glancing at the square might cause them to end up on the government's blacklist. Or perhaps it was unbearable for them to look. Maybe it was just too painful for them to witness the disintegration of such an honorable crusade.

Earlier in the day, Wang Dan, Wuer Kaixi and Chai Ling had held a joint press conference. After some delay, they had issued a statement advising the students to withdraw from the square. On Tuesday, May 30th, the students planned to stage a "victory" demonstration. However, their justifications for claiming a victory seemed to be decaying like everything else on the square.

The square had become a wretched place. The piles of rubbish and the stench of urine were overwhelming. The filth upset me, which was strange since it hadn't bothered me that much in the past. Yet, as I walked across the square, I felt that even the concrete slabs were rotting away beneath my feet. It saddened me so that I couldn't stay on the square very long. Instead, I went back to the Beijing Hotel to call home and check on my family.

On my way back to the campus, my back tire began to lose air. Although I had just passed a bicycle repair shop, it wasn't necessary to turn back. With so many bicycles in Beijing, there are bicycle repairmen almost everywhere. Some work out of little shacks while others simply carry tools and a few supplies around on carts, setting up their portable shops by the side of the road. After riding another block or so, I spotted a repairman's sign propped up against a tree. There was also a pool table beneath the tree with several men standing around watching as two men played a game of open-air pool.

The repairman's cart was parked by a wall about twenty feet off the street. No one was minding the store, but I assumed that the repairman was one of the men by the pool table. Pulling off the road, I walked my bike over to the cart, and within seconds the pool game was forgotten and I was surrounded. However, I still couldn't determine which of the men was the repairman since they all inspected my bike, discussing my problem and the probable solution. I had a flat tire and would or would not need a new inner tube.

The repairman identified himself by instructing me to remove my backpack from the bicycle so that he could turn the bike upside-down to remove the tire. One of the pool players immediately designated himself as my go-between by repeating to me exactly what the repairman had just said. I attempted to deal directly with the repairman, but thereafter, all conversation regarding the transaction had to be channeled through the self-appointed go-between.

While I waited for the repairman to remove the tube and assess the damage, I sat down on a tiny stool that the go-between had taken from the cart, and placed next to my backpack. In the meantime, someone had obviously gone to the little neighborhood of clay brick houses behind us to alert the general public that the entertainment had arrived. Soon two mothers with their toddlers, a few unaccompanied children, a middle-aged woman, and one old man, who had brought his own stool, came out to join us.

The go-between squatted next to me so that he could take charge of the question and answer session. After the routine questions were asked and answered, he pointed to the other pool player and said, "My friend is smart, but he doesn't have much education. What would he do if he lived in America?"

I asked, "What type of work does he do now?"

"He's a construction worker."

"We also build buildings, so I imagine that he would do the same thing in America that he does here."

The pool player chuckled at my response, giving the go-between a good-natured jab with his elbow.

After only a few minutes of being the center of attention, I was deserted when a truck pulled up to the curb and a man started handing out leaflets. The go-between ran over to the truck, then returned with one leaflet for himself and one for me.

The leaflet, "An Open Letter to the Students From an Old Soldier," was addressed to the students and the citizens of Beijing. It explained that the old soldier had been "silently paying a great deal of attention" to the students' struggle, although he couldn't openly give his support. Congratulating the students on the "incredible victory" they had already achieved, he offered a few words of advice regarding strategy and tactics. He advised the students and Beijingers that the best tactic would be to divide and separate the soldiers so that those in charge could not "control both the head and the tail" of the troops. He also advised that any commander who gave the order to open fire or use tear gas against the public should be warned that giving such an order would result in a court-martial and a death sentence. He added that the people should not only tell the soldiers to refrain from entering the city, but also ask them to "point their guns in the other direction."

After the go-between had given me time to read the leaflet, he asked my opinion on the leaflet and wanted to know if I thought the old soldier was correct.

I told him that it made sense to me, but added that I really knew very little about military tactics. Then, I turned the question back to him.

"My opinion?" he asked.

I nodded.

Pulling out a cigarette and lighting it before he spoke, the go-between grinned slightly and answered, "I don't have an opinion."

Teasingly, I asked, "How can you not have an opinion? Either you agree or disagree."

Broadening his grin, he said, "I never have an opinion."

Shanli's father could have taught the go-between a thing or two about the hazards of never having an opinion. I wondered if he would have given me the same answer one or two weeks earlier. For a man without opinions, he certainly had been eager to get his hands on the leaflets. However, caution was beginning to come back into style in Beijing, and even more so, since the big news story of the day was the speech that Wan Li had made in Shanghai. After spending a couple of days in Shanghai, Wan Li had seen the light. In the speech, which he read word for word, he stated that after "studying the situation," he had realized that "all sorts of things [had] indicated that a very small number of people [were] plotting political conspiracy, making use of students' strikes and deliberately creating turmoil; thus seriously disrupting the normal order of society, work, production, life, teaching, and research in Beijing, and other parts of the country." Wan stated that martial law was "in keeping with and safeguarding of the constitution and absolutely necessary to resolutely stop turbulence and rapidly restore order." By announcing that the regular session of the NPC Standing Committee would be held on June 20th as scheduled, he made it absolutely clear that a special session would not be called.

While the opinionless go-between went over to find out how much I owed to the repairman, I chatted with two students who had joined us. They were returning to their campus from the square and had pulled over to get copies of the leaflet. Since their campus was just down the road from mine, they insisted on waiting until my bike was ready so that they could see me safely back to my campus. After paying the go-between who gave the money to the repairman, I said goodby to the group and rode off with the students.

On Sunday, May 28th, there was a demonstration on the square in response to the demonstrations of support, which were being staged all over the world. However, I decided to stay at *San Lou* to wait for Yuanli to call. He had called while I was out on Saturday and left a message with Jinjin asking her to tell me that he would call back on Sunday.

It was mid-afternoon by the time Yuanli called to ask if we could meet on Tuesday. There were things he wanted to discuss with me that he didn't want to talk about over the telephone, and he had another batch of newspapers that he wanted to give me. Although I had already invited Teacher Wu to my room for tea on Tuesday afternoon, I agreed to meet Yuanli at the Beijing Hotel later in the afternoon.

As soon as we hung up, I rode over to Lu Minghua's apartment. Little Heping answered the door, telling me that his mother had gone shopping, and he didn't know when she would return. He sounded a little ill at ease, but I attributed his discomfort to his usual shyness around me. However, on my way out of the building, I ran into Lao Dong who told me that Lu Minghua had gone to the square to demonstrate. She had instructed Little Heping to tell anyone who asked that she had gone shopping, and Lao Dong asked that I do the same.

Only thirty thousand people came to the square for Sunday's demonstration. Despite the poor turnout, the students overruled their leaders' decision to leave the square on May 30th. Many students were angered that Chai Ling had announced to the press that the students would leave Tiananmen Square without first going through the democratic process of taking a vote. When the vote was finally taken, 160 of the delegates representing the 228 schools on the square voted to continue the sit-in until the June 20th session of the NPC Standing Committee, in the hope that they could persuade the committee's members to use the power granted them under the constitution to rescind martial law and to recall Li Peng.

In spite of the students' determination and dedication, the movement was dying. Those within the Party leadership who had sympathized with the students' goals had either been pushed from power or pulled back in line. Most important, the hard-liners' tactics of fear and intimidation were gnawing away at the nerves of the *laobaixing*. However, on Monday evening, the movement was rejuvenated by a symbol that provided hope: a thirty-three foot high Styrofoam and plaster statue, which the students named "The Goddess of Democracy."

The Goddess was the ideal symbol for the student movement for she represented not only the philosophy of the movement but also the spirit of the movement. Even though the government had insisted that the Pro-Democracy Movement was instigated by high-level conspirators and devious plotters, there was no real evidence to support their claim. Clearly, the movement had come from the bottom up and not from the top down. The movement itself was that "small spark which ignites a prairie fire"—a student movement, not a master plan. Therefore, it was fitting that the symbol of the movement was also wholly created by the students. The Goddess was designed, financed, and built by the students. Just as the student movement had sprung up instantaneously, the Goddess appeared to have been created overnight.

On May 27th, representatives from the ASAB went to the Central Academy of Fine Arts with a request. They wanted their fellow students to build a statue to symbolize the movement, and they gave the art students a little more than US$2,000 and only three days time to accomplish the feat.

With so little time, it was necessary for the students to use a project already in progress. More than a dozen young artists collaborated to alter a clay model of a man grasping a pole so that it could be used for the statue. First, they cut off the pole, then changed the figure to that of a woman, and next made adjustments in the figure's stance. Using Styrofoam, they constructed the figure on a larger scale.

Since it was necessary for the artist to work at the Academy, they had to consider the logistics of transporting the Goddess to Tiananmen Square. Their solution was to construct the statue in pieces, then haul the separate pieces to the square by truck. However, they learned that the Public Security Bureau planned to confiscate the driver's license of anyone who agreed to drive the truck. Attacking this problem with the same creativity and determination which they had shown all along, the art students loaded the pieces on bicycle carts and headed down *Wangfujing* to Eternal Peace Avenue. It was after ten o'clock on the evening of Monday, June 29th, when the Goddess of Democracy arrived on the square. By that time, fifty thousand people who had been alerted by the small lane news were waiting to welcome her to Tiananmen Square.

Yuanli called me the first thing Tuesday morning to tell me about the Goddess. Although I was as excited as he was and couldn't wait to see the statue, I was not about to uninvite Teacher Wu to tea. However, I told Yuanli that I would try to get downtown early enough to take some photographs.

I had told Teacher Wu that I didn't take a nap, but he waited until after *xiuxi* to come to my room. To my delight, he not only agreed to tutor me during the remainder of my stay in Beijing, but seemed quite eager to get started. After we had both checked our schedules, we agreed to have our first session on June 5th, the following Monday.

It was the first time I had been able to talk with Teacher Wu at length, and to find out more about his background. I was not surprised to learn that he was originally from Shanghai, since he had that same urbane charm about him, which I had noticed in other Shanghaiese. As China's largest and most cosmopolitan city, Shanghai has historically been the center of the arts, fashion, trade, and industry in China. As a result, Shanghaiese move at a faster pace, pay more attention to the cut of their clothes, and have adapted to the economic reforms with ease.

Since Teacher Wu had mentioned his fondness for art in class, I pulled out the paintings I had purchased and asked his opinion. He wasn't all that impressed with Mr. Xu's abstract, but he approved of Mr. Pan's ink painting. I thought about mentioning the Goddess while we were discussing art, but Teacher Wu had not said anything about the student movement, so I decided to stay away from the subject.

Just before he left, Teacher Wu handed me a package, telling me that he had brought something for me that he thought I would like even more than the paintings I had bought. It was an exquisite paper cutting of a herd of stampeding horses, and the artist had captured the movement of the horses so well that I could almost hear their hoofs hitting the ground. Thanking Teacher Wu repeatedly, I told him it was a gift I would always treasure.

When I arrived downtown, there wasn't enough light left to photograph the statue, so I went directly to the hotel. Yuanli was already waiting in the bar. Telling me that he was concerned about carrying the newspapers around, he handed them to me as soon as I sat down. He said that he had considered mailing them, but I was glad he had delivered them by hand.

Despite the resumption of mail delivery several days earlier, very little mail was getting through to *San Lou*. The *shiwuyuan* had claimed that the delay was due to a backlog, but I couldn't help wondering if our mail was being held back on purpose. While it seemed a bit paranoid to suspect the delay was intentional, it wasn't a totally irrational thought since our overseas telephone communication had already been restricted. Before martial law was declared, it had been a routine service for the campus telephone office to book an overseas call in the daytime, then have it put through at night, if the caller requested an evening call. After the imposition of martial law, the office was closed. When it reopened a couple of days later, a notice was posted stating that outgoing night service had been discontinued indefinitely. As a result, it was necessary to cut class to place a call between nine o'clock and noon, or to call after *xiuxi*, between two and four o'clock in the afternoon. Either way, the time difference made it inconvenient to place a call since it was late at night or in the wee hours of the morning in the Western Hemisphere.

After our drinks had been served and we could talk privately, Yuanli told me there were more signs that a crackdown was imminent. Quoting the Chinese idiom, he said, "They've begun 'killing the chickens to frighten the monkeys.' This morning, around two o'clock, three workers and eleven motorcyclists were arrested. The workers were the organizers of the BWAU and the motorcyclists were members of the Flying Tigers. A crowd of students and other members of the BWAU went to the Public Security Bureau Headquarters to protest the arrests."

I asked Yuanli if any charges had been filed.

I haven't heard about the workers, but an official from Public Security said the motorcyclists were arrested for distributing leaflets and spreading rumors. He used the words, *'qiangjian min yi,'* to defile public opinion." Yuanli paused to write down the phrase in my notebook. As he wrote, he shook his head in disgust, saying "It's the leaders of China who have defiled public opinion!"

Telling Yuanli that I found it difficult to believe the leaders would order the PLA to use force against their own people, I reminded him that Mao had said, "Our Party commands the gun, but the gun must never be allowed to command the Party."

Yuanli replied, "Mao also said 'A revolution is not a dinner party.' I don't think the two hundred thousand soldiers surrounding Beijing are waiting to be invited to a dinner party, and it doesn't take that many soldiers to chase a few thousand unarmed students from the square."

"But the people were able to stop the troops before . . ."

Interrupting me, Yuanli said, "These troops are from distant provinces. They don't understand *putonghua* (Mandarin), so how can the people convince them not to enter the city?"

Certain that Yuanli's information was more than idle speculation since his uncle was an officer in the PLA, I asked what he thought the troops from Beijing would do.

"They are furious. They were called in and lectured to as if they were children. They were told that anyone who refused to obey orders from now on would be court-martialed on the spot. I suppose that means executed on the spot. You know that Xu Qingxian avoided ordering the 38th Army into the city by pretending to be ill. If he hasn't already been arrested, he will be."

I asked Yuanli if he had heard anything about the blacklist.

"Yes", he said. "I've heard names like Liu Xiaobu. He's a professor of Chinese Literature at Beijing Normal University, and Wuer Kaixi's friend and mentor. Dai Qing, a reporter with the *Guangming Daily* is also rumored to be on the list, and there are political figures as well. Naturally, the people who are closely associated with Zhao Ziyang are rumored to be on the list. Bao Tong, Zhao's aide, and Yan Jiaqi are certainly on the list.* Yan is one of Zhao's advisors who has taken an active role in support of the student movement. He has been very public in his support of democratic reform.

"Yan Mingfu and Rui Xingwen, two of the officials who represented the government in the meetings with students are also rumored to be on the list. Hu Qili is certainly on the list. He hasn't been seen since May 19th, and it is rumored that he was removed from the Politburo Standing Committee at the same time as Zhao. It is ironic since Hu Qili was Hu Yaobang's top aide in 1987."

I told Yuanli what Lu Minghua had said about a purge being aimed only at the "big fish." My heart did flip-flops at his response.

"Instructions have been given to all *danwei* leaders that each *danwei* will be required to fill a quota. It's the same way things were done in the past. The word is out that those who did anything before martial law was declared are okay. Those who demonstrated, gave speeches, or wrote *dazibao* after May 20th are in trouble. Each *danwei* leader will decide which of those people will be turned in to meet the quota."

---

*Dai Qing and Yan Jiaqi were members of the May 14th delegation of twelve intellectuals who went to the square in an attempt to persuade the students to leave Tiananmen Square before Gorbachev's arrival.

Lu Minghua had demonstrated on May 23rd and May 28th. I felt a wave of nausea when I thought about her name being added to a list to fill someone's quota of victims. Noticing that the color had gone out of my face, Yuanli tried to reassure me. "Lu Minghua is probably right, the government is really more concerned with public figures and the leaders of the student movement. Someone like Lu Minghua would only have to attend a few political lectures and read political works."

Despite Yuanli's reassurances, I asked him to get the check. I wanted to go back to the campus as soon as possible so that I could talk with Lu Minghua. On our way out of the hotel, I asked Yuanli about Shanli. He laughed and said, "I haven't seen him in weeks. You know how Shanli is. You can't find him, and then suddenly he appears out of nowhere. But I'll try to get in touch with him and tell him to contact you."

Instead of going back to the campus, I went directly to Lu Minghua's apartment. However, I couldn't speak openly because Little Heping was in the room. I didn't want to say anything that would upset him, so I waited until she walked with me downstairs.

As we stood in the doorway of Lu Minghua's building, I told her what Yuanli had said. Taking both of my hands in hers, she looked me straight in the eye. In a soft, calm voice, she said, "Little Sister, I saw a banner on the square Sunday. It said, 'I can die, but democracy cannot die.' It is not important if we have to suffer in the future. We have suffered in the past, and we are suffering now. We have endured the Cultural Revolution, so we know that we can endure anything. Democracy is worth the price."

15. June 1, 1989—The Goddess of Democracy stands tall on Tiananmen Square.

16. June 7, 1989—A public bus, which was jackknifed and used as a roadblock on June 3–4 is a reminder of Beijingers' attempts to stop the troops from reaching Tiananmen Square.

17. June 7, 1989—The man next to the lamppost in the center of this photograph mocks the soldiers by "directing" them as they chant, "Guard the city, protect the people."

CHAPTER SEVENTEEN

A DROP OF BLOOD ON THE FLAG

The street lights flickered along Fragrant Flower Road as a bolt of lightning cut across the sky. A blast of wind shook the poplars violently, sending a flurry of leaves sailing through the air. The thick mist turned into a steady downpour, and I pedaled harder against the wind, causing the raindrops to sting my face like a shower of tiny needles. Cursing the new telephone regulation, which had forced me out into the stormy night, I lowered my head, hunching down closer to the handlebars as I turned off Fragrant Flower Road onto the side road that dead-ends at the Great Happiness Hotel.

While one clerk went into the back office to place my call to the United States, I sat down on the vinyl sofa to wait for the other clerk to summon me to the desk phone. When the call came through half an hour later, it was nine-thirty in the evening in Beijing, seven-thirty in the morning New Orleans time. My youngest son, Michael, had just awakened. It was a big day for him: Wednesday, May 31st, his graduation day. Since I couldn't be there to see him graduate from high school, I was not about to let a thunderstorm or a stupid telephone regulation prevent me from calling to congratulate him. Besides, I knew that talking with Michael and the rest of my family would lift my spirits.

It had been a gloomy day, and my mood had been just as gloomy. The weather prevented me from returning to the square to photograph the statue, so after class I stayed in my room wondering what was going on in the city and busying myself by reading the newspapers, which Yuanli had given me. After dinner I tried to study, but it was impossible to concentrate on the textbook. My mind kept drifting back to the students on the square and to my conversation with Yuanli.

It was becoming increasingly difficult to get a sense of what might happen next. Voice of America's Mandarin broadcasts had been jammed heavily since May 22nd, and while CCTV and Chinese radio had carried a report on Wan Li's return to Beijing, the rest of the day's news broadcasts were heavy on propaganda and light on information. Usually I depended on the campus broadcasts and the *dazibao* for the most current information, but the rain made a blurry mess out of the *dazibao* and prevented the students from making their nightly broadcast.

As the government intensified its propaganda campaign and programs of intimidation, speculation increased that the leadership was setting the stage for a purge. Added emphasis was given to the "small number of people" line, first by adding one "very" to it, and then another. The new and revised "very, very small number of people" led to the rumor that China's leaders were preparing to introduce a new "Gang of Four" headed up by Zhao Ziyang.

Announcements of support for martial law from governmental agencies and officials continued to appear in the press. Various members of the old guard issued statements in support of the government's actions, and on Saturday, May 27th, the Supreme People's Court and the Supreme People's Procuratorate joined the growing list of governmental departments lining up behind the Martial Law Order. In a statement quoted in the *People's Daily,* their spokesman expressed the necessity for the government's decision in order "to stabilize the current situation and keep the social order."

Letters in support of the government from ordinary citizens also appeared in the press. One letter signed, "A citizen in the Haidian District," urged the students to "return the square to the people so that order in the city and stability in the government could be restored." Chinese television and radio broadcasts also quoted ordinary citizens who supported the government's actions; however, these supporters were never identified, and most Beijingers discounted the quotes as either fictitious statements, or statements made by people under duress.

Government propaganda messages broadcast over public address systems in the center of the city began competing with the students' broadcasts on the square. Attributing the spread of the movement to the lack of sufficient political education, the announcements urged Beijingers to keep to the socialist path and warned them to remain vigilant in the struggle against capitalist freedom and bourgeois liberalization.

The homemade signs, which the *laobaixing* had put up to express support for the students, vanished. In their place, the government's bright red cloth banners with fancy gold characters suddenly appeared on department stores, shops, hotels, and other buildings throughout the city. Despite their festive appearance, the messages on the banners were not jolly. The massive banner draped across the front of the Beijing Hotel reminded Beijingers to "Adhere to the Four Cardinal Principles of Socialism and Oppose Bourgeois Liberalization with a Clear Cut Stand." Another huge banner was hung above the figure of Colonel Sanders on the building southwest of the square on Front Gate Avenue. While the few tourists remaining in the city might have assumed that the banner advertised Colonel Sanders's Kentucky Fried Chicken as being "finger lickin' good," it actually advised citizens to "Safeguard Stability in the Capital." Several banners around the city declared, "We Want Stability, Not Chaos," while others admonished Beijingers to "Adhere to the Socialist Road," "Support the Correct Decision of the Central Committee," and "Love the Country."

The leadership's fear of a workers' revolt intensified with the founding of the two independent unions. Workers' participation in demonstrations had first been dealt with by issuing threats to fine and/or fire those who demonstrated and by promising bonuses to those who remained at their posts. However, after the founding of the unions, the government's response became much harsher. In addition to the arrest of the three workers, the "illegal" unions were ordered to disband immediately, and soldiers were stationed at some factories in Beijing.

The last days of May brought disquieting rumors that the army was on the march again and making provisions to remain in Beijing through the winter. The rumors led to some speculation that President Yang Shangkun, also Vice Chairman of the Central Committee Military Commission, was laying the groundwork to lead a military coup.

Meanwhile, I attempted to convince myself that any plans for a purge would not include the "small fish" of Beijing, but would center on the "very, very small number of people." However, just when I began to believe that I was worrying needlessly, I remembered a scene that I had witnessed in Xian.

It was in 1983, during the height of the Anti-Spiritual Pollution Campaign. The expressed aim of the campaign was to attack "individualist freedom," "rotten capitalist thinking," and other "decadent concepts" which Chinese leaders feared were filtering in from the West. Although the campaign was short-lived, over five-hundred-thousand people were accused of crimes, rounded up, and in numerous cases, tried and executed with incredible haste. This crackdown on crime was not only aimed at those who were charged with murder, theft, kidnapping, prostitution, pornography, and the like, but also at those who were accused of organizing reactionary groups for the purpose of carrying out counterrevolutionary activities.

Public notices were posted throughout the country listing the names and crimes of those who had been apprehended, along with a mug shot and a brief biography of each person on the list. A red check slashed across a person's photograph indicated that he or she had been executed. I had seen the notices as I traveled from city to city, but in Xian, I saw something decidedly more chilling than a mere list of names with red checks.

It happened at noon on my third day in Xian as I rode through the center of the city on a bus. I hadn't paid much attention to what was happening on the street until the driver shut off the engine when we became stalled in heavy traffic. Peering out of the window, I saw that each side of the street was lined with people, as if they were awaiting a parade of some sort.

Minutes later, a procession of army vehicles came into view, approaching us from the opposite lane. Two or three military jeeps led the procession, followed by a series of ambulances with sirens blaring. A long line of military platform trucks formed the remainder of the procession.

As the first truck drove slowly past us, I saw four people lined along the platform railing. With heads bowed and arms tied behind their backs, they stood facing the crowd. A dozen or more armed soldiers stood behind them, their rifles trained on the backs of the four. Each of the four wore a cardboard placard tied with string around his neck. The characters on the placard identified the criminal and his crime. As each truck filed past, I stared up into the faces of the condemned. There were three whom I remember most clearly. One was a woman who appeared to be in her late thirties. Unlike the others, she held her head and her shoulders erect, staring back at those who stared at her—defiant to the end. The second was a young man who couldn't have been more than eighteen years old. He had the look of a trapped animal, his eyes rounded in terror and his face chalky white. His whole body shook with spasms of fear. The third was an old man. He was frail, and without the use of his arms to steady himself, it was difficult for him to maintain his balance. Yet, the expression on his face was calm, and I saw only resignation in his eyes.

I could force such thoughts from my mind while I was awake, but Wednesday night they returned in the form of nightmares, haunting me through the night as I saw images of my friends with placards hung from their necks being carted away. Thursday morning when I awoke, my head ached and I felt more exhausted than when I had gone to sleep. However, the rain had stopped, and although the sky was overcast, I was determined to go to Tiananmen Square to photograph the Goddess.

Thursday, June 1st, was International Children's Day, the perfect opportunity for the government to shift its propaganda machine into full throttle. The newspapers criticized the students on the square for forcing the cancellation or relocation of all Children's Day activities originally scheduled to take place on Tiananmen Square. The *Beijing Daily* carried a letter from *Fentai* #5 Middle School which called on the students encamped at Tiananmen to "return the square to the Young Pioneers* who dreamed to see the raising of the national flag and to ask the uncles of the flag team to teach them revolutionary traditions." Despite the propaganda, many parents brought their children to the square, and the students, en-camped on the square, staged a special program in celebration of Children's Day. However, the biggest draw on the square was still the Goddess of Democracy.

Just as the design of The Goddess had been given the most careful consideration, her position on the square had not been selected in a

---

*The Party organization for young children.

haphazard manner. She had been erected in a sacred spot, the Celestial Axis between the Monument to the People's Heroes and the Gate of Heavenly Peace, and she stood face-to-face with the portrait of Mao Zedong. The crowd gathered in front of the Goddess spoke in whispers to show their respect. Many stood silent, staring up at her in awe. She was an inspiring sight, and as an American who loves China, I was deeply and doubly moved. I saw before me a symbol that represented not only the present Pro-Democracy Movement, but also the Self-Strengthening Movement of the 1860s, the Hundred Days Reform of 1898, the 1911 revolution, which brought about the fall of the Qing Dynasty, the May 4th Movement, Democracy Wall, and the student demonstrations of 1986-1987. She had been taken from an image that embodied the very best of the Western spirit, then given a Chinese heart.

The Goddess of Democracy had enraged the leaders of China who had unleashed a series of attacks in the Chinese press denouncing the Goddess as a foreign symbol and declaring her "totally against the law and against the will of the people." Nevertheless, the Goddess did express the will of the people. While the Party's propaganda machine could only crank out wooden phrases to be written on banners and meaningless tirades to be broadcast from public address systems, the Goddess had stirred the patriotism of the people and expressed their true desire for a democratic China. When she was unveiled on the square, the story spread through the city that there was a reason the Goddess held up the torch with both hands. "Democracy is so difficult to obtain in China that it takes two hands to hold it up."

After I had walked all over the square photographing the Goddess from different angles, I returned to the statue. As I looked up at her again, I thought of all the speeches I had heard on the square, the conversations I had with students, and the banners and *dazibao* that I had read. Each time I had come to the square, I had felt that I was standing on sacred ground, and that I was in the presence of greatness.

I thought about my own country and the patriots who had established a system of government, which I cherished but had so frequently taken for granted. I remembered a *dazibao* that I had seen on the square. I had read and heard the words written on the *dazibao* countless times, and although they were words that always filled me with pride, never had I been more moved by those words than when I read them on that *dazibao* at Tiananmen Square.

"We hold these truths to be self-evident, that all men are created equal, that they are endowed by their Creator with certain unalienable Rights, that among these are Life, Liberty, and the pursuit of Happiness."

Turning away from the statue, I walked toward the pedestrian underpass to cross Eternal Peace Avenue. As I walked down the steps leading to the underpass, a chill went through me. For an instant I felt a foreboding of despondency that was so strong, it brought tears to my eyes. The thought came to me that it was as if the ghosts of those who had died on Tiananmen Square in 1976 were crying out. Admonishing myself for letting my emotions and my imagination get the best of me, I walked on through the underpass.

In the evening, Lu Minghua went with me to hear the student broadcast on my campus. As we walked toward Building #8, she told me about an interview, which was broadcast that morning on Beijing radio. "A student" who claimed he had spent several days at the encampment on Tiananmen Square accused the students of "doing bad things" on the square. His remark was worded so that it inferred that the students encamped on Tiananmen Square were involved in indecent sexual behavior. The implication infuriated Lu Minghua, and with contempt in her voice, she said, "The leaders will do anything to discredit the student movement." Using the Chinese idiom, *"wa jie minxin,"* she added, "They are trying to crumble the support of the people."

However, the people's support had not crumbled. Listening to the broadcast, I was amazed at the spirit of Beijingers. With all that had been done to intimidate them and to send them cowering into the safety of silence, they laughed and joked among themselves as they listened to a comedian ridiculing Deng Xiaoping. The comedian was pretending to be an uneducated old man who had questions for Deng Xiaoping. He said, "Excuse me, Comrade Xiaoping. I am just an ignorant old peasant, not a learned man such as yourself. However, there is something that confuses me. You said that only a very, very small number of people are behind this student movement. If this is so, Comrade Xiaoping, why did I see millions of people on the streets and in the square, and why did I hear millions of voices?"

The comedian went on to joke about the awkwardness of Deng being forced into the position of appealing to the "long beards"* to make public statements in support of the Martial Law Order. The dissension within the Party had made it necessary for Deng to solicit the backing of Chen Yun, his sometime rival, and to turn to the same "Old Revolutionaries," which Deng himself had forced into retirement in 1985. During the last days of May, Deng had dusted off the old bones of the "long beards," rallying them to speak out in support of the government's hard-line stance. Yet, their antiquated political phrases and outmoded political philosophy sounded foolishly out of place in the China of 1989.

Chen Yun had addressed the Central Advisory Committee on May 26th, calling for "firm support for the correct decision and the resolute measures of the Party Central Committee." He then stressed the necessity to "resolutely expose schemes and intrigues of the very, very few people who intended to create turmoil, and to resolutely fight against them."

At around the same time, Peng Zhen, the former Chairman of the Standing Committee of the NPC, addressed a meeting of the Vice Chairmen of the Standing Committee. His speech called for "uniform thought in line with the facts and in accordance with the constitution."

On May 27th, Li Xiannian, the former President of China, spoke before the Chinese People's Political Consultative Conference. Dredging up a term from the Cultural Revolution, "a struggle between two headquarters," Li blamed "certain individuals in the leadership of the Party" for creating the current chaos.

Listening to the comedian had been good for both of us. Lu Minghua said it was the first time that she had laughed in several days, and the broadcast had eased some of my anxiety. I reasoned that the situation

---

*"Long beards" is a term used to describe the elderly, and in this case, the old men who rule China.

couldn't be all that grim if people were willing to stand around in public laughing at Deng Xiaoping.

Friday afternoon I was in a great mood as I inspected my limited wardrobe, trying to decide which of my two dresses to wear that evening. Since my class was treating Teacher Wu to dinner at the Great Happiness Hotel, I wanted to look my best for the occasion. I had almost decided on the pink dress when Paul Green knocked on my door. Pulling him into the room by his elbow, I demanded to know which dress he liked best.

Pointing to the blue dress in an offhand manner, Paul told me that he had not stopped by to act as my fashion consultant but to tell me about a conversation that he had just had with one of the American advisors on our campus. The advisor had told Paul that inquiries were being made about the American student from our university who had been observed photographing the Goddess of Democracy the day before. Although the advisor didn't know the name or the gender of the student, Paul thought that I should know that questions were being asked.

Putting down the dresses, I uttered a predictable expletive. Division Thirteen had such a strong presence on the square that people joked about it, saying there were now more undercover police on Tiananmen Square than there were students. With fewer foreigners going to the square, those who did go were highly visible. I had walked all over the square taking photographs, then stopped in the pedestrian underpass to read small character posters on the wall. I had also bought a copy of the student newspaper, paying for it with a ten yuan bill, and leaving the change as a donation. Any one of those actions could have attracted the attention of someone from Division Thirteen. Lumped together, they were as obvious as wearing a neon sign that said, "Follow me."

Furthermore, my previous trips to the square had hardly been clandestine operations. Even the fruit vendor by the back gate of the campus knew that I went to the square frequently. I usually stopped to buy fruit from him on my way to or from Tiananmen, and once he had pointed to my tape recorder and camera equipment, commenting that I must be on my way to the square. Not knowing exactly how to respond, I had mumbled something about going sightseeing. Teasingly he had answered, "Yes, you go sightseeing almost every day."

It occurred to me that neither Mr. Jiang nor Mr. Liu had contacted me since our banquet at the Beijing Hotel. In fact, my telephone call inquiring about the white card had been our last contact. It was strange since they were my hosts and had promised to keep in touch with me. Paul suggested that I telephone Mr. Liu to see if I could sense a change in his attitude.

Mr. Jiang answered, telling me that Mr. Liu was out. Our conversation was brief, polite, and not all that friendly; however, Mr. Jiang didn't mention that I was on the verge of being expelled from China. I decided to "Scarlet O'Hara" the issue. If need be, I could worry about it at a later date. In any event, I wasn't going to let inquiries stop me from going to the square.

The dinner at the Great Happiness Hotel was a smashing success. Through the weeks, our class had developed into a close-knit group. After breaking the house record by "polishing off" three bottles of Chinese liquor, we became even closer-knit. The colorless liquor was served in tiny glasses that held about a third of an ounce since it was so potent that it could remove the patina from a Shang Dynasty bronze. At the beginning of the evening, we hoisted our glasses in loquacious toasts. But as the evening progressed, we shortened the preliminaries to an unadorned "*ganbei* (empty cup)!"

Six *ganbei* later, I returned to the dorm to discover that *San Lou* was no longer orbiting around the sun in the same direction as the planet Earth. Pointing out that phenomenon to a giggling Jinjin, I ejected myself from both orbits by diving into my bed and saying good-night to all of the Jinjins standing before me.

The final bars of the Chinese national anthem blared out over the campus broadcast system, rousing me from a heavy sleep. Unwilling to open my eyes and face the morning sun, I reached over to the nightstand, groping around for my alarm clock. Thinking that it had to be a couple of minutes past seven since the anthem had just ended, I intended to set the alarm for nine o'clock so that I could get a little more sleep before Han Ling came to meet me. I waited until the clock was right in front of my face before opening my eyes. The clock said 9:16. Assuming that it must have stopped the night before, I held it to my ear. It was ticking. Reaching over to the other side of the night table, I turned Jinjin's clock around. It also said 9:16. Although my brain was still fuzzy, I knew it was highly unlikely that both of our clocks would have wound down at the same minute of the same hour. Therefore, it had to be 9:16.

As I dressed, I tried to come up with a logical explanation for the anthem being played at 9:15 instead of seven o'clock sharp. I speculated that the anthem player had also indulged in a few too many *ganbei;* however, I became concerned when the anthem was repeated at 9:30, and then again at 9:45. Something was going on. Since the anthem had also awakened Jinjin, I asked her to tell Han Ling to wait for me, then left to take a quick ride around the campus.

On Saturday, June 3rd, the campus looked the same as it did on any other Saturday morning. There was the normal foot and bike traffic on the roads as people went about their daily routines. A few joggers were running laps around the track, some students were shooting baskets on the large concrete game court, and a small group of people were standing by the side wall of Building #8, reading the *dazibao*. Since it wasn't quite ten o'clock, I decided to take a quick look at the *dazibao* before returning to *San Lou* to meet Han Ling.

A lot had happened on Friday, June 2nd, while I was lolling around the campus and going to dinner with Teacher Wu and my classmates. There had been some disturbing incidents during the night. Hou Dejian and three well-known intellectuals had begun a seventy-two hour hunger strike, and someone had attempted to kidnap Chai Ling.

The Commander of Tiananmen Square, Chai Ling, and her husband, Feng Congde, had been sound asleep when four people crept into their tent around four o'clock, Friday morning. Feng had managed to escape when the kidnapers tried to gag the couple and returned with help before the kidnapers could carry Chai away. The three students and one worker who were involved in the plot were apprehended immediately. After the four kidnapers were interrogated, Chai and several other student leaders were convinced that the Public Security Bureau had masterminded the kidnapping.

The new hunger strike had been announced on Friday during a rally at the square. The brief fast was planned as a symbolic gesture to show the unity of students, intellectuals, and workers in opposing the declaration of martial law and the use of troops against the students. The most famous of the four hunger strikers, Hou Dejian, a pop singer and composer in his mid-thirties, was no stranger to controversy. Having been born in Taiwan, Hou had defected to China in 1983, becoming one of the PRC's most popular entertainers. The other three participants were Liu Xiaobo, Wuer Kaixi's mentor and a lecturer at Beijing Normal University; Gao Xin, Editor of the Beijing Normal University newspaper; and Zhuo Duo, Director of Strategic Planning and Public Relations of the Stone Corporation, the largest corporation in China.

After reading the next *dazibao,* I was certain that I had discovered the reason that the national anthem had been playing on the campus broadcast system all morning. The three-sheet poster told a story, which both intrigued and distressed me. It began with the report of a puzzling traffic accident, which had occurred the previous evening, approximately four miles west of Tiananmen at the intersection of Eternal Peace Avenue and *Muxudi.*

Sometime between 10:30 and 11:00 Friday night, eight police jeeps were speeding down Eternal Peace Avenue when the last jeep in the convoy veered off the road, mowing down three cyclists and one pedestrian. The three cyclists, all workers, were killed, and the pedestrian, a twenty-seven year old teacher at Beijing #2 Foreign Language Institute, was seriously injured.

The driver jumped out of the jeep, attempting to run away from the scene, but he was surrounded by approximately two hundred angry bystanders who became enraged when he denied that he had caused the accident. The driver's refusal to accept responsibility for the tragedy and his indifference toward the victims seemed symptomatic of the drastic deterioration in relations between the *laobaixing* and those in positions of authority.

The incident triggered a spontaneous protest march down Eternal Peace Avenue, and by the time the marchers arrived at Tiananmen Square, at least a thousand people had joined the march. Shouting that "blood must pay with blood," the protesters demanded that the proper authorities accept responsibility for the deaths and threatened to carry the bodies of the three workers in a procession through the city.

The *dazibao* went on to report even more disturbing news. Troops had re-entered Beijing and soldiers by the tens of thousands had attempted to make their way to the square. Friday night, columns of soldiers and convoys of military vehicles had advanced on the city from all directions, with the largest concentration of troops, 5,000 soldiers from the 24th Army, moving in from the east.* Motorcyclists again sounded the alarm that troops were advancing on the heart of the city; rousing half-dressed Beijingers from their beds, sending them into the streets to throw up barricades and confront the troops before the square could be penetrated.

There were certain aspects of the army's attempted assault on Beijing that were genuinely perplexing, if not outright suspicious. License plates had been removed from all military vehicles involved in the advance. Even the plates on the jeep involved in the traffic accident at *Muxudi* had been removed. Additionally, troops were dressed in plain clothes and most were unarmed. Wearing white shirts and khaki paints, they had entered the city jogging ten abreast—most carrying only canteens and backpacks. Furthermore, the troops from the 24th Army seemed an unlikely choice to lead the primary assault on the square. They were young, inexperienced soldiers who were unfamiliar with the city and ill-prepared for the hordes of angry Beijingers who confronted them.

Between two and three o'clock Saturday morning, approximately a thousand Beijingers blocked the advance at the intersection of *Wangfujing* and Eternal Peace Avenue. Surrounding the soldiers in front of the Beijing Hotel, the crowd had taunted and berated them for marching against their own people. Finally, the soldiers broke rank in a confused retreat, dropping their gear and wandering off in small groups.

With equal ease, Beijingers had captured three army buses at *Xidan, Liubukou,* and *Hengertiao*. The buses had each been stopped by crowds who surrounded the vehicles, then slashed the tires when it was discovered that the buses were loaded with a few AK47s, some rifles with bayonets, clubs, daggers, butcher knives, and ammunition.

As I rode back to *San Lou,* the story about the buses nagged at me. It just didn't add up. It wasn't logical for soldiers to allow three buses loaded

---

*The 24th Army is based in *Chengde, Hebei* Province, which is approximately 300 kilometers from Beijing.

with weapons to be confiscated by an angry mob. It amounted to arming the enemy. Although the troops were under orders not to fire on the people, they could have drawn their weapons to frighten the crowds, or if necessary, fired into the air. Moreover, butcher knives are not standard military issue for most armies. It made me wonder if the army had purposely allowed the weapons to "fall into the hands of the enemy," and included butcher knives because they were weapons Beijingers might easily have obtained on their own.

Han Ling was waiting on the steps when I returned to *San Lou*. After parking and locking my bike, we took off for the bookstore at Yeyinglu. Earlier in the week, Han Ling had offered to help me run a couple of errands. I wanted to buy some Chinese novels and to stop by the restaurant at the Great Happiness Hotel. After almost a month of planning and trying to get a date everyone could agree on, I had settled on Wednesday, June 7th as the best date to give a dinner party to repay my friends for their hospitality. Since the restaurant required a few days notice, I needed to set the menu and pay the deposit.

Han Ling thumbed through every novel in the Yeyinglu Bookstore. Normally, I would have been just as thorough, but I was eager to leave in order to take care of my business at the hotel and head for Tiananmen Square. Finally, she selected two books for me, and we were on our way.

It took even longer to make the arrangements for the dinner party than it had taken to buy the two books. The manager was not in any hurry to write up the order, and she refused to be rushed. When she finally finished with the order, she informed me that payment in full was required since there would be more than a dozen people at the party and special food had to be purchased. Unfortunately, I had brought only enough money to cover the deposit, so I had to run back to *San Lou,* grab some money, and then return to the restaurant. By the time we left the hotel, it was after one o'clock.

My original plan had been to return to the campus with Han Ling, then ride my bicycle to the square. However, the bus stop was only a block away from the hotel, and a bus was pulling up just as we reached the stop. Telling Han Ling that I wanted to go downtown to see what was happening, I joined the queue for the bus. Much to my surprise, she boarded with me.

The sun was shining brightly, but a slight haze made it appear as though we were seeing Tiananmen Square through a mist. The fog-like quality only accentuated the undercurrent of uncertainty that I sensed on the square. Everyone appeared to be a little skittish, including Han Ling. Drawing closer to me, she tightened her grip on my hand as we waded through the litter, and she steered me around a jumbled heap of bicycles.

A helter-skelter duet blared around us, as the students and the government broadcast discordant messages. Everything and everyone looked disheveled and spent: the square, the students, their tents, and even the flags and banners. One student who was resting inside a battered tent stared out at us with that same hollow hopelessness that one sees in the eyes of refugees. His expression disturbed me. I had wanted to see reassurance in his eyes.

As we made our way across the square, my head started to throb and I suddenly felt queasy. Although I was uncertain if it was the effects of Friday night's liquor or that I hadn't eaten anything all day, I suggested to Han Ling that we get some tea or soup or something at the Palace Hotel near *Wangfujing*.

An announcement caused a stir on the square as we went down the stairs of the pedestrian underpass; however, I wasn't able to make any sense out of it. The floor of the underpass was lined with people stretched out on cardboard and pieces of newspaper. Most looked like workers, not students. Exhausted from the predawn standoff with the army, they slept soundly, undisturbed by the constant noise of voices and footsteps echoing through the underpass.

The sterile, sparkling-clean, marble lobby of the Palace Hotel belonged to another world. A massive cascade of glistening water gushed up from the fountain below us, then came splashing down behind us as we entered the coffee shop on the mezzanine. The hostess seated us at a back table, and before I could pick up the menu, Shanli sat down across from me. However, I was not all that surprised to see Shanli. He had a special talent for appearing and disappearing at the most unlikely times and places.

Since I was a little peeved with Shanli for not getting in touch with me, I greeted him with "Where have you been?" instead of saying hello.

Giving me an exaggerated look of innocence, Shanli asked, "Aren't you happy to see me, Lao Ban?"

Scolding him, I said, "Of course, I'm happy to see you. I'm absolutely wildly delighted to see you! I just want to know where you've been. I haven't heard a word from you. Yuanli hasn't been able to get in touch with you, and I've been waiting for weeks for you to call me."

Lowering his voice, Shanli told me that he had been working independently as one of the interpreters for _____, a foreign television network. With typical immodesty, he said, "It's a good thing they have me working for them because the f------ Communists are doing their best to make things impossible for the foreign press."

No doubt Shanli was a big help to the network since foreign journalists had been slapped with a stack of new media restrictions on June 1st. In a seven point statement, a spokesman for the Beijing Municipal Government had announced that journalists would no longer be allowed to invite Chinese citizens to their apartments, offices, or hotel rooms for interviews concerning the demonstrations, and that advance approval had to be granted for any coverage of events in Beijing. Moreover, journalists were barred from reporting in the central part of the city or filming, photographing, or reporting on troops.

Shanli laughed sarcastically, then said, "The f------ Communists don't want us to film anything but their phony demonstrations."

I told him that I had seen CCTV's coverage of the pro-government demonstrations on Thursday.* The demonstration that I had seen was a pretty poor excuse for a demonstration. The people looked listless and ill at ease, and after an obvious off-camera cue, they chanted "Oppose chaos in Beijing" a couple of times, then stood silent again, waiting to be dismissed.

Shanli nodded and said, "We filmed the demonstrations at Changping. Officials passed out six hundred new straw hats, then as soon as the demonstrations were over, they took the hats back." With a chuckle, he added, "Those peasants were really p----- off when they didn't get to keep the hats."

After another Chinese man came over and whispered something to Shanli, he excused himself, saying that he needed to go back to his table for a few minutes. That gave me a chance to find out what Han Ling

---

*Demonstrations had been staged at *Daxing* County, *Hairou, Sunyi,* and *Changping.*

thought about Shanli. She hadn't said a word while he was with us, and I wondered if she might be put off by his manner. After all, Han Ling came from a rather sheltered environment, and Shanli's English was not exactly the textbook version that she was used to. However, when I commented on Shanli's tendency to use some pretty colorful language, I realized that I had underestimated his charm. If anything, Han Ling was smitten. She smiled and almost gushed, "Yes, he's very exciting. I've never met a Chinese quite like Shanli."

Shanli returned, telling me that he had arranged to have a network car drive us back to the campus. Thanking him, I told him that would work out perfectly. The car could take Han Ling home, and I could go back to the square without worrying about deserting her. However, he didn't seem to care for my plan, so I changed the subject, asking if he had been on Eternal Peace Avenue the night before when the 24th Army moved in.

"Yeah, we got it all on film. There was a lot of pushing and shoving, but that was about it. Once the people surrounded the troops and started yelling at them, the soldiers didn't know what to do. There was a great deal of confusion and the soldiers just started wandering off. People were shouting at them, telling them that the PLA was no better than the *Guomindang.* Everyone was yelling, 'Go Home! We don't want you here!' "

I told Shanli that it had all been too easy—too easy to capture the buses and too easy to push back the troops.

He shrugged and said, "I don't know, Lao Ban, but everyone thinks the s--- is really going to hit the fan tonight."

There was no reason to ask Shanli why he felt that way, or what he thought might happen. For days, Beijingers had been expecting the troops to march in with tear gas and riot equipment. Since everyone knew the troops would hit at night, each day they had assumed it would be that night. With the troops closing in on Beijing, there was even more reason to believe that an attack was imminent.

While I paid the check, Shanli went over to his table to tell the driver that we were ready to leave. I was still determined to return to the square, but I waited until we were outside before I brought it up again.

In a tone that left little room for discussion, Shanli said, "You might have trouble getting a bus or a taxi later. Anyway, I'm going to escort you back to your campus." As he spoke, the car pulled up, and before I could protest, he ushered Han Ling and me into the back seat, closing the door behind us.

Shanli pushed a tape into the cassette player, and when the music started up, he gave me a broad smile, saying, "Isn't this much nicer than taking the bus?"

I shrugged and said, "Of course it's nicer than the bus, but I'd like to see what's going on at the square."

Ignoring my comment, he turned to Han Ling, focusing in on her as if he had just noticed her existence. While Han Ling and Shanli chatted away in Chinese, I watched the people on the street as Waylon and Willie blared out at us from the cassette player. There was something a trifle bizarre about cruising down the streets of Beijing while Waylon and Willie cautioned mothers not to let their sons grow up to be cowboys. It occurred to me that there was also something a trifle bizarre about the people on the street. Most of the foot and bicycle traffic was heading toward the center of the city. It should have been just the opposite since it was about five o'clock.

The route the driver chose was also strange. It was convoluted at best: first taking us too far in one direction and then the other. I pointed it out to Shanli, but he shrugged saying that the driver didn't know his way around very well.

That seemed odd as well. I said, "A driver, who was born and raised in Beijing, doesn't know his way around the city as well as I do?"

Shanli replied, "He's new."

We let Han Ling off at her building, then drove on to *San Lou*. When we pulled up at the dorm, I asked Shanli to see me to my room since I wanted to talk with him in private. As soon as I had closed the door behind us, I gave him a mild lecture. "You really have to be more careful what you say and whom you say it to. Just because someone is with me, it doesn't mean you can say anything you want to about the Communist Party."

Shanli asked, "You don't trust Han Ling?"

"Yes, I trust Han Ling, but there are other people I know whom I don't trust. One of them could have been with me today instead of Han Ling. Besides, that's not really the point. You're taking enough risk working with _____; please don't complicate that risk by talking about the 'f------ Communists' in a place where undercover police might overhear you."

After promising to be more cautious, Shanli told me that the network needed couriers to get their videos out of China. He wanted me to find a foreign student who would agree to take videos out. Telling me that he would check with me Sunday evening or early Monday morning, he jotted down the number of the network's hotel suite, in case I needed to get in touch with him before then. I had a strong desire to hug my dear friend and tell him how much I care for him. However, since that isn't done in China, I simply said goodby and cautioned him again to be careful.

A short while later, Jinjin opened the door. She let out an exaggerated sigh of relief when she saw me, then started chattering away in Japanese. I waited for the Chinese version to follow.

According to small lane news, at three o'clock soldiers had clashed with the students at the Great Hall of the People. Jinjin had heard that several thousand soldiers had rushed out of the rear of the Hall in an attempt to block off Eternal Peace Avenue. Students and *laobaixing* by the tens of thousands held them back, but not without violence. When the soldiers struck the people with belts, the people retaliated by throwing stones and bottles. At around the same time, there had been a confrontation at *Zhongnanhai* as well. The troops there had used tear gas and electric prods on the crowd. The rumor made me uneasy, but I refused to believe it.

Just as I was telling Jinjin that there must be some mistake, Joan knocked on the door. Obviously, she had heard the same rumor. As soon as I opened the door, she said, "Great, you're back. I want to know what's happening out there?"

"There weren't any troops on Eternal Peace Avenue when Han Ling and I left the square a few minutes after three. Besides, I was just with a friend who works for _____. He would have known if there had been trouble, and he would have said something to me if the situation was critical."

As I said the words, I thought about the way Shanli had insisted on taking us back to the campus, and the serpentine route the driver had taken. I also remembered the announcement that I hadn't been able to understand as Han Ling and I were leaving the square. Still, I reminded Joan and Jinjin that we had heard so many rumors over the past two months and a great number of them had proven to be inaccurate.

Joan was not so easily convinced. "Have you heard the statement the government has been running on radio and television all day? They're saying 'a counterrevolutionary rebellion' took place early this morning, and that 'hooligans and students' seized military vehicles and weapons."

I had to admit the statement sounded like a justification for a no-holds-barred assault. Yet, I didn't want to believe there would actually be bloodshed. Joan pointed out that four people had already been run down by a police jeep.

I reminded her that CCTV had traced the jeep and identified it as one they had been renting for several months. However, I didn't mention that the *dazibao* had reported that the jeep didn't have a license plate. If the *dazibao* was accurate, CCTV's claim was certainly questionable.

Although my assurances did little to alleviate Joan's anxiety, I did manage to convince Jinjin that everything was okay. Having done that, I went about trying to convince myself. After Joan left and Jinjin went to join some of her friends who were preparing a Japanese meal in their room, I decided to take a ride over to Great Knowledge Boulevard.

If anything, the boulevard was quieter than usual. After riding only a couple of miles, I circled back and returned to the campus. When I walked into *San Lou*, the TV room was open, so I stopped to listen as the announcer read a statement that had just been released by the government. The statement repeated the charges that had been made earlier in the day and warned people to stay away from the square, stating that "Beijingers would bear the responsibility for their own fate if they went into the streets." The statement cautioned that "all means necessary" would be taken to "remove resistance."

It was a grave warning, but the government had been issuing grave warnings for days. I reasoned that before launching a full-scale attack on the square, the Martial Law Forces would erect barricades and set up checkpoints to prevent people from entering the area. I felt certain that since there were so many universities in the area, they would barricade Great Knowledge Boulevard and every other major thoroughfare in the Haidian District.

I decided to push it all from my mind and go back to my room to catch up on my journal. However, it was more difficult to keep my head in the sand after Paul came bursting into my room a little after eleven o'clock. Both frightened and excited by what he had seen, he collapsed in my chair, telling me that he had just come from the center of the city.

At half past seven, Paul and a Chinese friend had gone to the Beijing Tea House to watch the evening performance. Dusk was fading to darkness and the city was quiet when they arrived at the tea house around seven-thirty. When they left, a couple of minutes after nine o'clock, they heard shouts and screams coming from the direction of Front Gate Street. Although he was a little alarmed, Paul was even more curious, so he and his friend decided to walk to Front Gate Street, about forty meters away from the tea house, to investigate the commotion.

Still astounded by what he had witnessed, Paul said, "People came running toward us, scattering in fear. When we reached the southwest corner of Front Gate Street, there was a sea of green helmets stretching down the boulevard to the west. The soldiers were in full uniform and armed with AK47s. They were ripping up the metal barriers that run along both sides of the street, and I thought they would first storm the sidewalk, then head for the square.

"Within minutes, hordes of people surrounded the soldiers and pinned them in. A bus was driven lengthwise across Front Gate Street, and parked facing north to south, so that it obstructed the entrance to the square. Several people climbed atop the bus and joined in with the rest of the crowd, shouting at the soldiers, yelling at them to go home. The press was all over the place, flash bulbs were popping and TV cameras were rolling. I was relieved to know the whole world was watching.

"I realized it was the first time that I had actually seen an armed soldier face-to-face, much less a thousand or more. However, after I was calmer,

I could see that they were only eighteen or nineteen years old, and definitely not killer-soldier types. One soldier looked especially stunned and frightened. I thought that he might have been pushed down in the crush of people or bumped on the head. Several people were gathered around him, patting him on the back and wiping his forehead. They led him over to the curb and sat him down, continuing to comfort him while they tried to convince him to go home.

"My friend and I crossed Front Gate Street and went to the square. There were at least a hundred thousand people there, and probably hundreds of undercover cops. Although the square was calm, we stayed clear of the bright lights around the monument. A little after ten, we headed home."

Half-disbelieving what his own eyes had seen, Paul put his head in his hands and said, "It was positively surreal. There are no other words for it! Positively surreal!"

I had a thousand questions for Paul, but he was too exhausted to deal with them. He just wanted to go to his room and crash. Only minutes after Paul left, Joan appeared at my door. Her face was flushed and she looked startled. Jabbing at the air as if she were stabbing it, she pointed toward my window.

"Did you hear that noise? Were those gun shots?"

I had heard the noise, and it did sound like gun shots; however, I told Joan it was probably thunder. I knew the sounds had come from off-campus, somewhere south of us. I suggested that instead of speculating, we walk over to the south gate by Fragrant Flower Road to check it out. Although the gate was locked at night, if there were troops in the area, I thought that we might be able to see or hear something from there. We were still several yards away when two trucks filled with students sped past the gate. The students were shouting, but there was such a jumble of voices, we couldn't make out what they were saying. Anyway, we had grown so accustomed to seeing truckloads of students, that we didn't give it much thought. We stood by the gate for several minutes, but there was very little traffic on Fragrant Flower Road and all was quiet after the students passed.

When I returned to the room, Jinjin was already in bed. She was sound asleep when there was another round of noise. This time, I also saw flashes of light in the sky. Jinjin turned toward the window and murmured, "What was that?" I said, "Thunder and lightning," and she went back to sleep. I wasn't certain if it had been gunfire or an explosion, but I knew damn well that it wasn't thunder and lightning. I had never seen lightning leave behind a strange orange glow in the sky.

When I was certain that Jinjin was sleeping soundly again, I crept out of the room and walked down to Paul's room. He said he hadn't heard anything, but his room was on the north side of the building. Apologizing for disturbing him, I went back to my room.

The glow was dimmer, but it was still visible. I poured a cup of tea and pulled my pillows to the foot of the bed. Lighting a cigarette, I lay down facing the window, watching as the glow began to fade.

A few cups of tea and several cigarettes later, there was another clap of noise and a series of popping sounds. An even brighter glow hung in the sky. I went to the door and looked up and down the hallway. It was empty, and the entire dorm was still. Like Jinjin, everyone else seemed to be sleeping peacefully. Wondering if my imagination had played a trick on me by making me think I had heard the same sounds again, I walked to the window and stared out at the glow. I certainly hadn't imagined that.

There were more noises, but they were distant and muffled. Afterward, there was only silence. I smoked more cigarettes and sat propped against the pillows, watching as dark became dawn. The sky outside my window had already turned lighter, with glittering dabs of pink and orange cutting through the blue. I knew that I should sleep, but I didn't want to sleep. I didn't want to awaken to hear what had happened during the night. I thought it would be easier to face wide awake.

No longer able to deny or rationalize or stick my head in the sand, I knew the crackdown had come, and that there had probably been bloodshed. Perhaps the square had already been cleared, and thousands of students and *laobaixing* had been carted off to jail.

I tried to picture the square as it had been before the demonstrations, before the hunger strike. The image seemed cold and sterile and grim.

I wondered what would happen to the Goddess of Democracy. She had become so much a part of Tiananmen Square that it would look bare without her. The students had constructed her so that she wouldn't be easily destroyed. Yet, I knew the government would take her down as soon as they controlled the square. I remembered a poem I had seen on Thursday when I photographed the Goddess. It was in the pedestrian underpass, only a few characters on a small sheet of paper.

> *"I gaze in the square*
> *At the bright five star flag.*
> *A drop of blood has appeared on the flag."*

PART THREE
THE AFTERMATH

"I'll be judge, I'll be jury, said cunning old Fury:
I'll try the whole cause, and condemn you to death."
Alice's Adventures in Wonderland

CHAPTER EIGHTEEN

STREET OF BLOOD

A long, black limousine pulled up beside me. Michael and a group of Chinese students were in the back. They were all dressed in tuxedos and carrying protest signs. Michael stuck his head out of the window and said, "Hi Mom! We're going to the graduation party." Before I could say anything, the limo picked up speed. I struggled to keep up with it. I had to warn Michael not to go to the square. I tried to scream out, but I couldn't make a sound. Frantic, I started pounding on the limousine.

I awoke in a panic. Someone was pounding on my door. I recognized Lu Minghua's voice calling out my name. Something was wrong. She always tapped lightly on the door, and she hadn't called me by my name for ages. Jinjin sat straight up in bed, pulling the covers to her chin. I jumped out of bed and started forward, but I was facing the window instead of the door. As I turned, my foot hit the ashtray that had been left on the floor. The ashtray flew across the room, scattering cigarette butts and ashes everywhere.

As soon as Lu Minghua heard the lock click, she pushed the door open. Her hair was uncombed and her face looked gray. I stared down at her shirt. She hadn't tucked it into her skirt and she had skipped a button, making one side of the shirt a couple of inches longer than the other. She was telling me there had been a bloody massacre, that the soldiers had slaughtered people. I just kept staring at her lopsided shirt tail, thinking I should point out that she had missed a button.

My head cleared or maybe I allowed myself to hear her. Yet, when she began telling me what had happened during the night, I was certain I had lost all ability to comprehend Chinese. The words couldn't possibly mean what I thought they meant. I kept stopping her, asking her to speak slowly and making her repeat what she said. I thought if she repeated the words, I would understand that they meant something else. Finally, I realized that it wasn't the Chinese that was incomprehensible, it was the senselessness and inhumanity of what had happened.

The killing began at Muxudi around 10:30. The 27th Army had moved in from the west and arrived at *Muxudi* Bridge around ten o'clock. The crowds pulled up the lane dividers on *Fuxingmen* Avenue and used them to barricade the street.* Immediately, there were random flashes of violence. The people were armed with stones, wooden sticks, and pieces of iron pipe they had torn from the lane dividers. They faced an army equipped with AK47s, machine guns, truncheons, tear gas, and armored personnel carriers.

Unlike the timid 24th, the soldiers of the 27th Army did not weep at the pleas of the *laobaixing* or retreat in humiliation at their insults. It was an army comprised of men, not boys. Many were illiterate peasants and most were unable to understand the Beijing dialect. Some had joined the army to avoid prison; some had fought in China's war with Vietnam. All were hard-faced, hard-eyed, hard-hearted combatants who didn't flinch at shedding Chinese blood.

People shouted "Fascists!" The soldiers responded by opening fire. First they fired tear gas canisters. The bullets followed; first high, then low, then aimed to kill. Everyone thought the guns were firing rubber bullets, until people fell dying and blood and brains splattered through the air.

The soldiers shot at anyone and everyone. They fired at people on the street and into buildings along the avenue. They cut down students, workers, children, old people—men and women alike. Those who tried to flee were shot in the back, and the wounded shot pointblank. Ambulances were sprayed with machine gun rounds and people who dragged the wounded away made easy targets. Those who stood in front of the tanks were pulverized. A head on one side, feet on the other, and in between just tracks over pools of blood, clumps of flesh, and splinters of bone.

Fuxingmen Avenue is the western extension of Eternal Peace Avenue.

The slaughter continued as the troops pressed east, past *Muxudi,* on to *Xidan,* then to *Liubukou.* At the same time, another detachment from the 27th Army headed west down *Jianguomen* Avenue.* They began killing at *Dabeiyao,* roughly four miles east of the square. Just as in the west, Beijingers tried to stop the troops with barricades. Trucks were pulled across *Jianguomen* overpass, but as the lead tank flicked the trucks aside, the people who had stood atop them went flying through the air. To the south of Tiananmen, troops surged past the Temple of Heaven, killing people as they headed north up Front Gate Street.

Shortly after midnight soldiers closed off the eastern perimeter of the square. By two o'clock, the detachments moving east and west along Eternal Peace Avenue had converged on the northern perimeter at the Gate of Heavenly Peace. The troops on Front Gate Street sealed off the southern perimeter while the western perimeter was closed off when soldiers swarmed out of the Great Hall of the People. After four hours of carnage, Tiananmen Square was surrounded.

Thousands of students clung to each other at the Monument to the People's Heroes, vowing to die for democracy. Around them, sounds of chaos filled the heart of the city: screams of terror; shouts of rage; bursts of machine-gun fire; reports of automatic weapons; shrieks of ambulance sirens; and the drone of tanks and APCs. Canisters exploded, spewing tear gas into the air. Thick, black smoke billowed from the APCs that Beijingers had set afire with Molotov cocktails. Banners and tents made smaller fires that glowed orange on the stone slabs of the square. A scratchy recording of the "Internationale" played over the students' one remaining loud-speaker, while over the other loudspeakers, a shrill voice repeatedly an-nounced that an insurrection led by counterrevolutionaries and hooligans was occurring on the square. The four hunger strikers pleaded with the students to leave the square and with army officers to allow the students to withdraw. At 4:00 a.m. the lights on the square were doused and red flares shot up through the blackness. In the dark, with bayonets fixed and machine guns aimed at the students, soldiers encircled the monument. Forty minutes later the lights came on again and the students saw that they were surrounded.

Jianguomen Avenue is the eastern extension of Eternal Peace Avenue.

Gunfire grew heavier as tanks, APCs, and soldiers surged in toward the monument. The students finally began their exodus from the monument, singing the "Internationale" through their sobs as they filed toward the southeast corner of the square. As they withdrew, machine guns fired around them and rows of riot police beat them with clubs. Behind them, tanks toppled the Goddess of Democracy, then crushed forward over tents and bedding, without concern that students might be inside. By 6:00 a.m. the troops had secured Tiananmen Square, but the butchery was not over. As students ran through the streets heading north to their campuses, many were felled by bullets or run down by tanks.

The battlefield of Eternal Peace Avenue was embedded with tank tracks, dotted with corpses, and slick with human blood. The morning sky was heavy with smoke, tear gas, and the stench of burning flesh. Along the avenue, crushed bicycles; smoldering vehicles; shards of glass; pieces of iron; and chunks of concrete, bricks, and stones lay in mute testimony to the valor of Beijingers.

I could hear the bitter anger and grief in Lu Minghua's voice. There was also shame. At first, the shame confused me. It was not a reaction I had expected. Yet, I came to understand. Everything she had been taught and had believed in since childhood was wiped out in one bloody night. She had loved the Party; she had loved the People's Liberation Army. She had been taught that they were the "Soul of the Country." Although she knew there was corruption in both, she had still believed in their basic goodness. Now, she felt betrayed by her beliefs and shamed by what the soldiers had done. Chinese had massacred their own. As a Chinese, she shared their shame.

I wanted to reach out, to comfort Lu Minghua. I wanted desperately to say something that would make her understand my deep sadness. Yet, as the images she had described filled my mind, no words would come. I waited for the tears, but I couldn't cry. I felt numb and hollow inside. Lu Minghua promised she would return later in the day and insisted that I must not leave the campus. Then she was gone.

Jinjin had not moved from her bed. When I looked over at her, I saw she was terrified by what she had heard. I told her that everything would be all right and assured her that we were safe. Nodding, she got out of bed, dressed hurriedly, then went to wash her face.

Not long afterward Lao Pang came to my room. Little Ma stood behind her. Subdued and red-eyed, Little Ma's chin trembled as she fought back tears. Lao Pang was breathless and winced in pain as she sat down. Knowing the walk to *San Lou* had been difficult for her, I thanked her for coming and told her I had already heard. She muttered, "It's terrible, terrible!" and then could say no more. Warning me not to go to the square, she rose to leave. At the door, as she squeezed my hand and looked into my eyes, I knew that she understood what was in my heart.

When they had gone, I went to my armoire and pulled out a clean shirt. I was still in the same clothes I had worn the day before, but I didn't have the energy to change. Instead, I sat staring at the shirt until Jinjin came back to the room with one of her friends. They had decided to go to a hotel to try to call home to Japan. It was dangerous for them to go out on the street, but Jinjin promised they would turn back if they saw any sign of troops. I went outside with them and watched as they rode away.

I started up the stairs to *San Lou* but I didn't want to go back inside. Instead, I walked around the campus, feeling as if I were walking through a dream. It was as though I could move invisibly from place to place, seeing, but unseen. Chinese funeral music droned from the campus broadcast system in a mournful wail. Other than that, there was a silence of horror. People moved about hurriedly along the campus road, passing each other without speaking or even making eye contact. Everything around me seemed strange, distorted, almost unreal.

Outside Building #8, a wreath of white flowers had been placed against the wall beneath the *dazibao*. A huge banner in honor of the dead hung above the wreath, and a memorial and an eyewitness account of the massacre were posted nearby. Farther down the wall, two students moved from one *dazibao* to the next, checking for signatures and tearing up those they found.

I sat on the curb across from Building #8 watching the door for several minutes hoping that I might see Hong Xin or one of her roommates. I wanted to go inside to look for Hong Xin, but I knew if she felt it was safe, she would contact me. Chinese students were already leaving the campus.

Those who lived in Beijing were the first to go. Some students were going home to be with their families; others were going into hiding. Some were too frightened to return to the campus, and most who did return only took time to pack backpacks or small suitcases.

I watched as one father piled all of his daughter's belongings on a child's wagon. Half-running, they took off for the back gate. With one hand, the father pulled the overloaded wagon, while with the other, he held his daughter's hand.

I walked to the back gate to see if the fruit stand was open. There wasn't any food in our room and it seemed wise to have something on hand to eat in case there was a shortage of food. As the vendor stuffed bananas into my bag, he said, "Stay away from Tiananmen Square. The soldiers have orders to shoot foreigners who take photographs."

Returning to my room, I switched on the radio as an announcer was reading the official version of the massacre. The government claimed that the People's Liberation Army had crushed a counterrevolutionary rebellion. The report stated that over a thousand soldiers and riot police had been killed or injured. While it was acknowledged that there had been "some civilian deaths," the report justified the actions of the PLA as "necessary to preserve lives and property."

Paul banged on my door, shouting for me to come outside. A body had been brought to Building #8 and he thought we should see it. I cringed at the thought of viewing a body, but I knew Paul was right. As witnesses, it was our responsibility to look at things we didn't want to see. I knew that I should bring my camera along, but couldn't bear the thought of photographing a body.

As we rushed toward Building #8, Paul told me the body was that of a nine-year-old child. He had been killed near *Muxudi,* shot twice; once above the eye and once in the chest. It had been a hot, humid night, and he had gone outside to get a Popsicle. Certainly his parents had heard the warning, but there had been so many warnings and nothing had happened. Why believe that this warning was any different from the rest?

Now he was dead, and his parents were risking their own lives by bringing their son's body from campus to campus, from neighborhood to neighborhood. It was the only way to show what the PLA had done to the people. Others had to know the truth of the brutality. The government was trying to cover-up the massacre with vague statements about the number of casualties. There were rumors that the bodies on the square had been burned and bodies from the streets and the hospitals had been hurriedly gathered and rushed to the crematorium. If the survivors didn't tell the world what had really happened, who would?

A crowd was gathered by the side of Building #8. Certain that the crowd had gathered around the child's body, I stopped at the curb, unable to go closer. My knees began to shake. No matter how hard I tried, I couldn't force myself to walk over to the crowd. Turning away from them, I convinced myself that I didn't have to go any closer. I could say I had seen him from a distance. As I turned, a small truck pulled up to the curb and stopped right in front of me. When I looked down, I saw the child.

He lay in a bed of white paper flowers. His body had been washed and his hair neatly combed. He was a beautiful child. The only thing that marred his beauty was a small black mark above his left eye. It looked like a little glob of paint or a smudge of ink. I fought back the urge to wet my finger against my tongue and wipe away the mark. But then, a wet finger cannot wipe away a bullet hole.

I stared down at his little face and saw him as my own child. I felt his mother's pain. He was her life, her purpose. There was so much of him in her and her in him. She could remember his smell as a baby. She could still hear his first words. She knew which foods he disliked and which he preferred. She had made plans for him, dreamed for him. She had loved him with a fervor that she hadn't known existed in her until he was born. She had scolded him, praised him, laughed and cried with him. And, when he bled, she bled with him. His pain was over, but hers had just begun.

The truck pulled away, but I could still see his face. I knew the image would fade with time, but it would always be there. Feeling lost and alone, I went back to my room. There was no place else for me to go. Although I needed to talk with someone, I didn't know with whom or what I would say. I sat on my bed shivering; wanting to sob, waiting for tears which wouldn't come.

Someone tapped on my door. When I opened it, Han Ling was there. Softly, she said, "Kong Kailing, I have a Chinese idiom for you. *'Yu ku wu lei; yu yu wu sheng.'* It means, you want to cry, but you have no tears; you want to speak, but you have no words." Her voice quivered and she asked, "Kong Kailing, why can't I cry? Why can't I express the pain in my heart?"

I was so grateful for her words. They made me understand my own agony. I took her hands in mine and said, "Han Ling, perhaps there are things too horrendous for tears or words."

We sat with each other, comforting each other in our silence. Finally, she asked if I would have to leave. I had tried not to think about it. I didn't want to leave my friends. I also felt the presence of foreigners on campus might prevent the police or soldiers from storming the campus to arrest Chinese students. I knew I would eventually have to leave, but I told Han Ling I would stay as long as I could.

By early afternoon the rumor mill was running at full speed. Some said the 27th Army was a warlord army, loyal to President Yang Shangkun and under the command of Yang's nephew, Yang Jianhua. Others claimed that the 27th Army had been injected with amphetamines or some mysterious mind-altering drug that had turned them into hopped-up, glazed-eyed, bloodthirsty killers.

No one knew how many had died. According to the Chinese government "some" civilians had died in the melee, but none on the square. According to the people, ten thousand Beijingers and students had died in the slaughter. Whatever the number, it must have been in the hundreds at the very least. When the massacre occurred, between two to three hundred thousand people had been on the streets of Beijing.

There were rumors the massacre was a prelude to civil war. People talked of a rebellion in the military, and as sporadic gunfire continued around the city, reports came in that soldiers were firing on soldiers. There were stories that caches of weapons had been turned over to students and that soldiers from the 40th Army had gone to Beijing Normal University and volunteered to join with the students in a fight against the the 27th Army.

While rumors were plentiful, facts were hard to come by. We were in the middle of it all, yet we couldn't get accurate information and we felt cut off from the world. Voice of America and BBC were being jammed in both English and Chinese. Jinjin and others who had gone to hotels in the area to place overseas phone calls had been unsuccessful. Students had been calling their embassies for advice throughout the day. However, their conflicting advice added to the uncertainty. Some embassies told their nationals to stay put. Others either evacuated their nationals immediately or advised them to prepare to leave.

The word was out that all campuses in Beijing would be occupied by troops. The anxiety around *San Lou* increased with the threat of an occupation. A few of the students were becoming panicky, but I felt we were safe. The Chinese government might force us to leave, or our own governments might tell us to leave, but the Chinese would not provoke an international incident by attacking foreigners or holding them hostage.

Later in the afternoon I decided to ride to Lu Minghua's apartment. I wanted to know if Lao Dong had news of his niece, a student at Qinghua University. It had started to drizzle, but I didn't care. I had to get away for awhile, to see what was happening outside the campus walls.

As soon as I turned onto Great Knowledge Boulevard, I knew where the noise and bursts of light had come from during the night. A military jeep and five truckloads of soldiers were stalled less than a block from the front gate of the campus. The tires had been slashed on every vehicle in the convoy and the engines had been sabotaged. With the windows shut tight and the doors locked, the four soldiers inside the jeep were dripping sweat. They sat stiff-backed with eyes staring straight ahead, ignoring the people who lined each side of the jeep.

The trucks were just ahead of the jeep, parked more or less in a row, but turned at odd angles in the road. I circled each of the trucks and stopped at the last one. The soldiers inside were armed and in full uniform. Those in the other four trucks were dressed in white shirts and fatigues. Groups of people stood at the back of each truck, telling the soldiers that their comrades had murdered their own people. The soldiers sat stone-faced, betraying no emotion at their words.

Several yards south of the lead truck in the convoy, two trucks, which had been gutted by fire, blocked the street. Little wisps of smoke curled up from the engines and the rain drops sizzled as they hit the hot metal. As I rode past the blackened trucks, I saw a crowd of people gathered around a pickup truck that had stopped at the intersection. The body of a man in his thirties was on display. Turning the corner, I rode on without stopping.

Lu Minghua was alone in the apartment when I arrived. Although she scolded me for leaving the campus, I knew she was as glad for my company as I was for hers. Lao Dong had finally made contact with his niece. He and Little Heping had gone to Qinghua to bring her back to the apartment. Lu Minghua insisted on making tea for me. While she was in the kitchen, she asked me to check the shortwave radio. The only foreign station that wasn't jammed was Radio Moscow. It was coming in loud and clear in English, Chinese, and Russian. Little was said about the situation in Beijing. The newscaster stated that twenty-three people had received minor injuries when hooligans attacked the government compound at *Zhongnanhai* on Saturday afternoon. The massacre was not mentioned.

When Lu Minghua brought the tea in, she sat down beside me. I wanted to tell her how much I loved her, how much our friendship meant to me, and how worried I was for her safety. I knew she would pay for what she had said and done, but I couldn't say those words just yet. They were words to be saved for later, when I had to leave Beijing.

I told her I had seen the body of a child. She nodded and said he had also been brought to her campus. She asked if I had photographed him. I told her I couldn't. At first, she misunderstood and told me his parents would have allowed it because they wanted the world to know. I realized I should have photographed him and felt guilty that I hadn't been strong enough. When I told her again that I couldn't, the words came out in a half sob. Tears welled in her eyes and she said, "It's all right, Little Sister. You will tell about it and people will see it through your words."

One of Lu Minghua's cats crawled into her lap and curled into a tight ball. She stroked its back gently and sighed. "My poor country, what will happen to China? What will happen to the people? We've had so much pain, and now this."

The kitten mewed and stretched as she continued to stroke it. Her voice heavy with bitterness, Lu Minghua said, "Eternal Peace Avenue! Beijingers will never call it that again. Now, Beijingers are calling it the 'Street of Blood.'

With her free hand, she wiped away the tears that had started to trickle down her cheeks. Softly, she said, "So many dead, so many good and brave people dead. The leaders are already trying to hide the truth. We may never know how many died."

One thing was certain, the dead and the wounded were not the only casualties. The suffering would continue. There would be reprisals and even those who escaped arrest or a purge could never erase the horror from their minds.

Lu Minghua told me about a student from Qinghua University who had returned to her campus Saturday evening to urge her friends to return to the square. They had remained on the square until early morning when Chai Ling led the students from the monument. The tanks came after them near Liubukou. She escaped, but her friends were crushed. After daylight, she was found wandering around in a stupor; her clothes soaked with the blood of her friends.

It had started to drizzle again and although it was not yet six o'clock, the clouds had darkened the sky. There would be an early nightfall, and Lu Minghua said I should return to my campus. She walked me to my bike and told me she would come to check on me Monday afternoon.

I rode down Great Knowledge Boulevard without stopping. It was raining a little harder, but people were still standing around the trucks. I turned off at Fragrant Flower Road and rode to the back gate. As I neared Building #8, I saw a large crowd had gathered by the side of the building for a memorial service. The paper wreath had been draped with black ribbon and placed in a wooden and glass case to protect it from the rain. A large black cross, which had been made by foreign students, stood next to the wreath.

People had pinned white paper flowers to their shirts and most wore black armbands. Weeping quietly, they huddled together in the rain, umbrella touching umbrella, their grief too deep to bear alone. In a trembling voice, a female student read a tribute to the dead, until she could no longer choke back her sobs. The last words came out in mournful gasps, and when she had finished, the funeral music started.

A young man walked out of the darkness in front of Building #8. Staggering and moaning in anguish like a wounded animal, he came toward us. As he passed, I could see his face. It was distorted with emotion; wild-eyed, his mouth open and rounded, frozen in an internal scream. He stood motionless for a few seconds, then flung his arms around himself. It was as if he had to hold on to something or someone, even if it was only himself. With a final moan, he turned and staggered back into the darkness.

All the while, the people in the crowd stood silent, refusing to intrude by seeing him or hearing him. It was a kind thing to do. It gave him privacy in his pain.

CHAPTER NINETEEN

THE CALL TO LEAVE

Sunday night I slept, but it was an exhausting sleep filled with grim dreams of soldiers, tanks, and mangled corpses. I spent the night alone in the room. Jinjin and the other Japanese students all slept together, crowding their bedding into one room on the top floor of *San Lou*. At midnight, we were asked to turn off our lights since some students feared soldiers would shoot into lighted rooms, just as they had done on Eternal Peace Avenue Saturday night. During the night, there were bursts of gunfire in the distance. On the campus, there was an eerie quiet.

I had not expected Teacher Wu to keep our appointment Monday morning. We had agreed to meet on June 5th, before we knew what the 3rd and 4th would bring. I realized it might be dangerous for him to bicycle to the university since he lived at his wife's *danwei* near *Muxudi*. However, he appeared at my door at 9:45, apologizing for being late.

Teacher Wu had not come to tutor me, but to talk with me as a friend. The heaviest killing had taken place at *Muxudi* and he had seen much of it. He had wept when he saw a four year old child killed in a hail of gunfire and a pregnant woman hit in the stomach with a rifle butt, then shot dead as she lay withering on the ground. Tears came to his eyes again as he described the scene, and his whole body shook with rage. "They are not human beings," he said. "They are mad dogs!" Shaking his head in despair, he repeated the words, "Mad dogs, mad dogs!"

I thought of him as I had seen him last; holding his glass up in a toast, laughing and teasing me as he challenged me to another *ganbei*. It hurt to see his pain. There was nothing I could do to console him, except to promise I would tell what had happened when I returned to America.

It surprised me when he said, "You must not do that, Kong Kailing." I had already decided if one person asked me to remain silent, I would honor that request. I said, "Teacher Wu, if you are afraid you will suffer if I speak or write about this, you must tell me."

His voice hardened. "No, Kong Kailing, I'm not afraid. They took away the fear. When they killed the people, they killed the fear. He paused, then said, "If you talk about this, the Chinese government might come after you." I assured him that the Chinese government would not bother me in America.

I told Teacher Wu I might have to leave much sooner than I had hoped. An official from the U.S. Embassy was coming to the campus in the afternoon to meet with the American students. If he advised us to leave, I would have no choice. I wanted Teacher Wu to know that I appreciated his friendship and his help with my studies. I told him how excited I had been when he had agreed to tutor me. He smiled and said, "Even if you return to America, I can still help you. We will write to each other so you can keep up with your Chinese."

I didn't think that would be advisable. All along, the government had made statements attacking bourgeois liberalization and blaming the turmoil in China on the corrupt influence of foreigners. After the massacre, the statements were a strong indication that those with foreign contacts would be in for a very rough ride during the coming months. Expressing my concern to Teacher Wu, I asked him to write first, so I would know that it was safe for me to write.

After Teacher Wu left, I went downstairs and sat on the front steps of *San Lou*. I couldn't stay cooped up in my room, but I needed to be near the dormitory in case Shanli called. As worried as I was about him, I didn't dare call the suite at the hotel. It would be necessary to ask for him by name and I suspected that the phones were being monitored. There had already been a rumor that plainclothes policemen had searched the rooms of journalists in the Beijing Hotel and confiscated videos and film. Once again, I would have to practice Chinese patience and wait for my friends to get in touch with me.

Outside, I watched as one embassy caravan after the other arrived to pick up their nationals. The Italians came first; then the French, Dutch, and British. When the Australians came, Joan gave me a big hug and handed me the keys to her room. We had hidden my film in her room when we first heard the rumors about an occupation. She didn't have a camera, so it was unlikely her room would be searched as thoroughly as mine.

At noon, I gave up on hearing from Shanli and took Little Heping's Flying Pigeon to the bicycle repair shop on Fragrant Flower Boulevard for a minor overhaul. I wanted to return it to him in A-1 condition. After dropping off the bike, I decided to walk over to the Great Happiness Hotel to cancel my dinner party. Even if I were able to remain in Beijing, my friends would not be in the mood for a dinner party.

Near *Yeyinglu,* I noticed a man on a bicycle behind me. Something about him made me ill at ease. He didn't look like he belonged in the neighborhood, and he was riding his bicycle in an odd manner. He was meandering, an extremely difficult thing to do on a bicycle without losing one's balance. I stopped to see if he would pass me. He did, but staring at me as he rode past. It was not the typical benign, curious stare that I was accustomed to in China. He rode ahead a few yards, then turned around and slowly rode back toward me. Again, he looked straight into my eyes. I stared back at him, thinking that he would look away. Instead, he locked in on my eyes in a hard, cold stare. It gave me goose bumps and I remembered that Lu Minghua had cautioned me to be careful since "spies" had been sent to the campuses to watch the students.

When I came out of the Great Happiness Hotel a half hour later, I had forgotten all about the man. At Fragrant Flower Road, however, the man was standing by his bicycle a few yards past the turnoff to the hotel. It was as if he had been waiting for me. I pretended not to notice him and went on about my way.

I walked directly to the campus gate instead of stopping to get my bicycle. At the gate, I stopped abruptly and turned around. He had followed me, but this time he rode by with only a glance in my direction. After waiting by the gate for several minutes, I walked back to the repair shop.

On the way to the meeting with the U.S. Embassy official, I told Paul about the man. While I attributed my suspicions to creeping paranoia, Paul didn't agree. There had been a man watching *San Lou* on Sunday night and Paul had also been tailed after helping a Chinese friend sneak into a foreign residential compound. Paul told me that he had encountered a man on the stairs of the compound as he was leaving the building. They had a brief, hostile verbal exchange; with the man insisting he had seen a Chinese woman enter the building and Paul denying it. Paul took the offensive and demanded to know the man's name and *danwei*. When he refused to answer, Paul reminded the man that the building was a residence for foreigners and asked him to leave. The man gave Paul a vicious glare, then turned and stomped out of the building.

When Paul left the compound a few minutes later, the man was waiting in the shadows. He followed Paul across the campus, but Paul lost him by ducking into another dorm and hiding there until the man finally left.

Very little was accomplished at the meeting. After we had waited for the official for almost an hour, the embassy called to tell us that their caravan had been turned back at a barricade by a group of men wielding Molotov cocktails. Although the embassy told us the men were dressed in plain clothes, I suspected they were either Division Thirteen or soldiers. It didn't make sense for the *laobaixing* to threaten Americans. However, it did sound like a tactic the government would use to discredit the students and *laobaixing*.

Jim, the senior American foreign expert on campus, told us the meeting had been rescheduled for ten o'clock Tuesday morning. In the meantime, the official wanted to know how many of us would be willing to leave the campus on Tuesday. The embassy was offering to relocate us to a hotel, which they considered to be a "safer location." We assumed they were referring to the Lido Hotel since it is in the northeast suburbs of Beijing, near the airport. There were murmurs of astonishment when Jim told us the embassy planned to move us to either the Jianguo Hotel or the Jinglun Hotel. The hotels are located between *Dabeiyao* and *Jianguomen* overpass on *Jianguomen* Avenue, the eastern extension of Eternal Peace Avenue. People had been killed in that area Saturday night. Furthermore, we knew the Jianguo Hotel had been machine-gunned at least once since the massacre, and *Jianguomen* overpass, approximately two blocks from the hotels, was lined with tanks. It seemed ludicrous to suggest that we leave a campus where there had not been a single gunshot fired to go to a hotel that had been machine-gunned. When I asked Jim why the embassy considered those hotels to be "safer locations," he just shrugged and asked for a show of hands. Only four of the thirty-two Americans on campus agreed to relocate to the hotels. More than half agreed to leave if the embassy would relocate them to the Lido.

Despite our dissatisfaction with the embassy's recommendation, I did receive good news from Jim. He had arranged for my film and the leaflets I had been given to be "relocated" to the American Embassy on Tuesday. When the meeting was over, I went straight to Building #8 to see if there was anything else the students wanted me to take out of China. The students' headquarters were on the top floor of Building #8. Lu Minghua had taken me there one night in May to meet some of the students. That night, they had given me a *dazibao* to bring back to the States so their American counterparts could see an example of China's "alternative press."

The only students remaining in Building #8 were those who had nowhere else to go or nothing to fear since they had not been active in the movement. Still, I felt a responsibility to make the effort to go there and offer my assistance. I was aware there was some risk involved in approaching a student I didn't know and offering to smuggle Pro-Democracy literature out of China. However, it was a risk I was willing to take.

The echo of my footsteps on the concrete floor was the only sound I heard in Building #8 as I climbed the steps and walked down the dark hallway. It was so different from the night Lu Minghua and I had been there. That night, the hall had looked like a *dazibao* assembly line. Long sheets of red paper stretched halfway down the floor of the hall. A dozen students with brushes in hand and cups of ink at their feet squatted by the paper, composing the messages on the *dazibao* from notes they had scribbled on scraps of paper.

The headquarters had been located in a small room, crowded with students and supplies. The walls were covered with snapshots of the students on the square, paper banners with democracy slogans written on them, leaflets from other universities, a sign-up sheet, and the portrait of Hu Yaobang, which had hung in the dorm entrance right after his death. On one side of the room, piles of overcoats and bedding were heaped on a table. On the other side, two tables were cluttered with rolls of brightly colored paper, cans filled with brushes, pots of ink, and stenciled leaflets that had been stacked and bound with plastic twine. Several students were seated at a small table in the middle of the room, discussing the wording of their next leaflet. Other students wandered in and out, stopping to listen to the discussion and adding their own suggestions. There had been an electric atmosphere in the small room; charged by the enthusiasm of the students.

The door to headquarters was ajar. I tapped lightly on the door, not expecting anyone to answer my knock. Pushing the door open, I walked in. The walls were bare and the room was empty except for a small table and two chairs. A thin shred of red paper, which had stuck to the wall, was all that remained as evidence that the room had been the campus headquarters for the Pro-Democracy Movement.

I walked out of the room and collided with a student in the hallway who was even more startled than I. He hadn't expected anyone to come out of that room, much less a foreign woman. We both apologized, then he asked if he could help me. When I told him why I had come, he took me to his room and asked me to wait there. After a few minutes, he returned with four friends. They smiled, nodded to me and said hello, then huddled in conversation by the door. One by one, the students left the room, smiling and nodding at me, asking me to wait. I wondered if it had been a good idea for me to come. The students didn't seem to know what to do with me and they were obviously uneasy. However, when they returned several minutes later, they had five copies of the June 4th Memorial and one copy of a leaflet, which was dated June 2nd and signed, "Eight Art Institutes of the Capital."*

One of the students handed me the papers and said, "This is all we have left."

Taking the leaflets, I assured the students that I would make certain the papers got out of China, then shook hands with each of them wishing them

---

*See Appendix.

luck. When I reached the first floor, one of the students called out for me to wait. He came running down the stairs and handed me a folded sheet of paper. In a whisper, he said, "I found this. Please take it out with the other papers." Putting it in my bag without looking at it, I nodded and said goodby.

After returning to my room, I took the papers from my bag and rolled them up in the *dazibao* together with the other leaflets I had saved. I was about to put the package away when I remembered the folded sheet of paper. I unwrapped the package and unfolded the sheet of paper, expecting to see another leaflet. Instead, it was a photocopy of two photographs that had been taken on Eternal Peace Avenue. Bodies lay in the street, bicycles scattered around them. My hands shook as I looked at the pictures. They were only blurred black and white images. Yet, until that moment, the massacre had been a vague, clouded vision in my mind, formed by other people's words. I put the paper back, rewrapped the package, and lay down on my bed to wait for Lu Minghua to come. It was dusk and *San Lou* was quiet. I was grateful for the quiet.

When Jinjin returned from dinner, she gathered her bedding and went to join the other Japanese students. Not having to worry about inconveniencing Jinjin, I decided to tackle the unpleasant task of packing. After emptying out my suitcases and armoire, I spread everything out on the beds and the floor. Having created absolute havoc in the room, I sat down on the floor to figure out the best system for getting it all back together again.

There was a knock at my door. I knew it was Lu Minghua as she had come by earlier and left a message that she would return in the evening. Since the door was unlocked, I shouted for her to come in. When she opened the door, she put her hand to her mouth in surprise. The room did look like a tornado had come through. Apologetically, I looked up at Lu Minghua and said, "I'm packing."

She started to giggle. It began as a soft giggle but turned into a full-fledged laugh. If I could have gotten up from the floor and made it through the maze of books, tapes, camera equipment, and suitcases, I would have hugged her. I had begun to believe we had both forgotten how to laugh. Through her laughter, she said, "Little Sister, I thought your room had been searched."

"Perhaps I should leave my room this way. If Division Thirteen comes to *San Lou,* maybe they'll think the same thing and leave it alone."

Her expression changed to a frown because she thought I had decided to leave. I told her I had decided to stay, even if the embassy agreed to take us to the Lido. However, it was necessary for me to prepare to leave in order to be able to grab the things that were most important to me, if I had to leave in a hurry.

Lu Minghua offered to help, so I briefed her on my system. My backpack was for the film and leaflets that would go to the embassy. I had thought about putting my notes in it as well, but Jim had said that his friend at the embassy might want to look through the papers. My notes were a strange mixture of English-Chinese shorthand, which I doubted anyone else could decipher, but the idea of someone else going through them bothered me.

I designated my carry-on as Bag #1. If it didn't leave China, I wouldn't leave China. It was for my notes, tapes, camera, the *dazibao,* gifts from my friends, and the backpack when I got it back from the embassy. Everything else would be split up according to importance and packed in my two suitcases.

We were a great team. Lu Minghua would hold up an article, I would call out the bag number, and she would stuff it into the appropriate bag. As we worked, she asked me what would make me decide to leave. It was strictly a matter of semantics as far as I was concerned. If the embassy ordered an evacuation or issued a strongly worded advisement, I knew my family would not understand if I remained in Beijing. However, if the embassy said anything short of that, I could stay.

When we had finished packing and put the suitcases away, I sat down on the bed and told Lu Minghua once again that I was worried about what might happen to her. I wanted her to tell me what she would do if she were interrogated or arrested. She came over and sat next to me on the bed.

"Little Sister, we are very much alike. We are both strong women and we don't frighten easily. If they come to me and ask, 'What did you do?' I will tell them I did nothing. If they asked, 'What did you say?' I will tell them I said nothing. If they ask what other people said or did, I will say, 'What do I know of other people? I didn't hear anyone say anything and

I didn't see anyone do anything.' If they arrest me, I will go to jail. If they send me off to the countryside, I will go." She paused, making a zipping motion across her mouth, then said, "But, I will tell them nothing."

I told Lu Minghua it would be best if we didn't write to each other for awhile. She patted my hand and said, "We can write to each other. That won't cause trouble for me. We will write about ordinary, everyday things: our families, the weather, things that no one can criticize."

Just as I had done with Teacher Wu, I asked that she write to me first. Despite her assurances, I wasn't convinced it would be that simple for us to keep in touch. Although it was early, Lu Minghua had to leave. She had promised Lao Dong she wouldn't stay out late. I wanted to walk with her to the campus gate, but she wouldn't allow me to go any farther than the door of *San Lou*. She said I looked tired and told me that she knew I hadn't been sleeping or eating as I should. With great sadness, she said, "No one sleeps or eats in China anymore."

She was right. I had barely eaten anything since Sunday and felt as if I might never sleep deeply again. It was a calm, quiet night with no sounds of gunfire to keep me awake. There was only the faint rustle of leaves; the soothing sound of a gentle breeze. And yet, sleep didn't come easily.

I left *San Lou* at half past six Tuesday morning to go see The Professor and Lao Pang. I knew they would be awake and wouldn't mind my stopping by that early. They were eating breakfast when I arrived and insisted that I join them. I tried to beg off, telling them repeatedly that I was not hungry, but they thought I was only being polite. I sipped a cup of tea to appease them, and broke a bun into little pieces, moving the pieces around my plate in hopes they wouldn't notice my lack of appetite.

Lao Pang was relieved to see me. She had worried that I didn't have enough to eat. Food was getting scarce in some parts of the city, and it was rumored that the situation would become worse since Beijing had been sealed off by troops. Lao Pang opened her refrigerator and cupboards to show me they were full, and insisted I come to them if the food shortage got worse.

The Professor looked especially tired and had little to say other than to call Li Peng an idiot and Deng Xiaoping and Yang Shangkun foolish, senile old men, no longer fit for leadership. Never mind that both Deng and Yang were younger than he. The Professor still had clear vision. He could see the China of tomorrow.

On the way back to *San Lou,* I saw Little Ma across the courtyard talking with a woman from the neighborhood. I started to call out to her, and then decided not to interrupt her. Anyway, I would see her on Wednesday. Lao Pang and The Professor had insisted that I check in with them each day.

Mr. M., the embassy official, took his seat at the conference table and cleared his throat. His statement was brief and to the point. The embassy was not issuing an evacuation order or an advisement, merely an offer of transportation. We would be taken to the Jianguo Hotel or the Jinglun Hotel, but not the Lido. When I asked why the hotels were considered "safer locations," Mr. M. replied that they were convenient to the embassy. He grimaced at my comment that they were also convenient to two dozen tanks and repeated that the embassy would transport us to the Jianguo or Jinglun.

I asked, "Take it or leave it?"

Clearly losing his patience, Mr. M. sighed in exasperation and replied, "Yes, to use your words, take it or leave it." Only the four students who had previously voted to relocate decided to "take it." The rest of us decided to stay. The caravan arrived a little after one o'clock. While Leslie and the other three students loaded their luggage, the rest of us chatted with the people from the embassy. We were eager for accurate information, but we were willing to settle for fresh rumors. One of the men from the embassy told us the freshest: Deng Xiaoping had died of cancer of the prostate and Li Peng had been shot in the thigh by a guard at the Great Hall of the People. The story was that Li's wound was not serious. Supposedly, the guard had been executed on the spot.

I waved to Teacher Jin who had come to see one of her students off. We had seen very little of each other since the day we met on the square. She came over to say goodby, but I told her I had decided to stay. Frowning, she said, "You should leave, Kong Kailing. It may not be safe for you to stay."

Before I could answer, Paul came over to tell her about Deng and Li Peng. Teacher Jin jumped up and down and clapped her hands, saying "Is it true? Is it really true?" I was startled by her reaction. It was the first time I had seen any spontaneity in her or known how she truly felt.

Lu Minghua came rushing up as the vans were pulling away. She was out of breath and gulped for air between her words. "I heard the Americans were leaving and I thought you had gone."

Squeezing her hand, I said, "Elder Sister, you can't get rid of me that easily. I told you I have decided to stay."

I tried to persuade her to come up to my room to catch her breath and drink a cup of tea. She put her hand to her chest as she took another deep breath and said, "No, I'm very tired. Now that I know that you are still here, I can go back to my apartment and rest. Tonight I will come for a long visit."

I started walking with her, but once again she stopped me at the main road and ordered me to go take a nap. I stood watching her until she grew smaller and smaller in the distance, thanking whatever whimsy of fate had brought us together to become beloved friends.

I tried to take a nap. I even took off my jeans and put on my nightshirt, thinking the appropriate costume would trick my body into sleeping. It didn't work. Instead, I put my jeans on again and rode to Great Knowledge Boulevard. Han Ling was riding ahead of me, near the front gate. She stopped to wait for me. As I pulled up beside her, she said, "There is something I must do right now, but later I will come to see you." In a tiny voice that made me think of the four year old girl standing on a chair by the window, she said, "Kong Kailing, I'm frightened. I am afraid to stay in my room tonight."

I told her to come to my room, hoping to sneak her into the dorm for the night. She nodded and said, "I'll try, Kong Kailing." Then, with a wave, she crossed Great Knowledge Boulevard and disappeared through the gates of the campus across from ours.

White wreaths hung from the campus gates along the boulevard. Six blackened iron skeletons were all that remained of the jeep and trucks I had seen on Sunday. The two trucks, which had been smoldering, were little more than chunks of metal and piles of ashes. I rode past them, further than I had gone on Sunday. There was little to see and very few people were out in the street. By then, it had started to rain.

I circled back and rode slowly, not letting the rain bother me. It felt good against my face, and its smell was clean and fresh. Turning off on Fragrant Flower Road, I rode past *Yeyinglu*. The ride gave me time to think. I felt good about my decision to remain at the university. With my film and the leaflets tucked safely away in Mr. M.'s office, there was no longer any reason to worry about my room being searched.

Paul and Jim were waiting inside the door of *San Lou* as I pulled up. Paul said, "Great, you're back." They looked anxious and I thought perhaps they were upset that I had left the campus.

Jim waited until I was inside to break the news.

"The embassy just called to tell us another caravan is on its way. We were afraid you wouldn't get back in time."

I looked at Paul and my questions came out in a rush. "Why are they coming back today? What did they say? How soon will they be here?"

Paul knew what it would take to make me leave. He said, "I'd rather you hear it from them and then decide what you're going to do."

It had stopped raining, but the street was still wet and we could hear the splash of tires on the asphalt before we saw the caravan. The lead car pulled up to the entrance to *San Lou* and a woman got out of the back seat. Jim took me to her and said, "Tell her what you told me."

In a cold official tone, she said, "The Ambassador wants all U.S. citizens to leave China."

She had said the secret words. Sadly, I asked, "Is this an evacuation notice or an advisory, or what?" She repeated the exact words, and that was that. She had even said China, not just Beijing. I looked at Paul, hoping he would say something to convince me that her statement was not as serious as it sounded. But there was nothing he could say. I knew I had to leave.

As she repeated the statement once more to other American students who had come outside, I asked another member of the embassy staff how long they would give us to decide. Answering me in a brisk manner, he said, "You have about two minutes to get your luggage."

My first thought was Lu Minghua. I had told her I was staying. I couldn't leave without telling her. I had to say goodby. I turned back to the man and asked, "Please, can't you give us a little more time? I have a friend who is expecting me to be here. I have to tell her I am leaving."

When he answered me, his tone was not official nor brisk, but sympathetic. "I'm sorry. We have to leave before it starts getting dark. If you are coming with us, you'll have to come right now."

I asked, "How many bags can we bring?"

"One bag."

"One bag and a carry-on?"

He pointed to the first van and said, "Okay, but put it in there."

Paul said, "Come on, I'll help you get your things."

Several of the Japanese students had also come outside. As Paul and I walked back into the dorm, I glanced around looking for Jinjin, but she wasn't there. Spotting one of her friends, I shouted, "Go find Jinjin! Tell her I'm leaving!"

While Paul got my suitcase and carry on, I wrote down Lu Minghua's address. He promised that he would go to her apartment to tell her that there hadn't been time for me to say goodby. I dropped the keys to Little Heping's Flying Pigeon into the ceramic jar on my desk, then took one last look at my room before closing the door.

As she ran up the stairs, Jinjin screamed my name from the first floor to the third floor. At the landing, her voice convulsed into a sob, and she flew into my arms. Holding me tightly and weeping, she said "I'll never forget you—never forget you!"

Nor would I forget her. That first night in Beijing, Lu Minghua had predicted Jinjin would become my substitute daughter, and I her substitute mother. It was true. We had adopted each other immediately. So many nights we had sat up talking when Jinjin came to me for motherly advice. We had shared our thoughts and feelings, finding passage through our different cultures by forming a common bond.

I hugged her, telling her she was my Japanese daughter. Gently tugging on my arm, Paul said, "It's time to go." As I pulled away, Jinjin fell to her knees, covering her face as she sobbed. I realized that I was also crying. My tears had finally come.

Paul loaded my bags in the back of the van. We hugged each other and promised to keep in touch. I climbed into the van and shut the door. Jinjin came running after me, crying so hard she could barely speak. Reaching in through the window, she sobbed, "Picture . . . picture." Frantically, I rummaged through my wallet until I found my ID photo. It was the only picture of me that I had. She took it, then held it to her chest, hugging the tiny picture as the driver pulled away from *San Lou*.

People stopped in the street to watch as the caravan went by. It was not idle curiosity that made them stare. Foreigners were leaving their country by the thousands. What would happen to the Chinese if the doors of China were shut tight again?

Along the Second Ring Road, there were the same signs of violence that I had seen on Great Knowledge Boulevard, and the government's banners calling for stability hung in tatters from the buildings. On some, the *laobaixing* had written their own message over the government's propaganda. They wrote the slogan "Blood for blood."

Crowds had begun gathering at the intersections, waiting for the cover of darkness to come. Several men standing by one of the barricades waved to us. In response, I held my fingers against the window in a "V." One man put his hands to his mouth, blowing me kisses, while the others cheered and raised their hands high, returning the victory sign. They were *laobaixing*, but never again would I think of them as ordinary people.

CHAPTER TWENTY

THE SPRING WIND IS CRUEL

Yuanli answered the telephone before the second ring. I said, "I'm at the Jinglun Hotel." He said, "I'll be there first thing tomorrow morning." Then we hung up. Just two sentences—that was the extent of the conversation. At least I knew Yuanli was okay. He probably knew that I would be leaving China. Otherwise, I wouldn't have risked calling.

The room had all the expected amenities of a Western joint venture hotel: a thick, firm mattress; a console with a TV and mini-bar; a terry cloth robe and an enormous bathroom with perpetual hot water. I felt displaced, as if I had been uprooted and deposited in a posh refugee camp. This was definitely not the way I had planned to spend my last days in Beijing.

Now that I had left the campus, there were things I needed to do. I had to call my family, contact the airline, get myself to the airport and on a plane. Yet, I knew I would just be going through the motions, hoping all the while that things would change. It was too early in the States to call my family, and too late in Beijing to call the airline. I could stall a few hours, so I decided to go eat.

A man was at the other end of the corridor. He looked vaguely familiar, but it took me a few seconds to realize it was Stephen Hanks. We had studied together at the university in 1987, and Stephen had stayed on in Beijing to take a job with an American computer company. We had run into each other early in April when Stephen came to the campus to visit a friend. We had said then that we would get together before I left China; however, this was not what we had in mind.

Stephen had an apartment near the Temple of Heaven, so I was surprised that he was staying at the Jinglun. While we ate dinner, he explained that he had moved to the hotel because he wanted to be closer to the embassy. He was also concerned about the food shortage in Beijing. He had already run out of food, and the shelves in his neighborhood market were bare. To make matters worse, the water in his apartment had been shut off not long after the massacre. He suspected that the electricity would go next.

Stephen had driven himself to the Jinglun that afternoon, and his trip had not gone smoothly. Armed soldiers had stopped him at a checkpoint near *Jianguomen* overpass. Although he had heard the soldiers were allowing all foreigners to pass, Stephen was afraid he would be arrested because he didn't have a driver's license. The soldiers were belligerent and a little jumpy, but after a few tense minutes, they waved him through.

After we finished dinner, there was still faint light in the sky. I told Stephen that I wanted to walk to the embassy to pick up my backpack. I had overheard Mr. M. say that he would be working late, so there was a chance he was still in his office. Always the southern gentleman, Stephen insisted on walking with me.

I had only glanced at *Jianguomen* Avenue when the embassy van arrived at the Jinglun. When Stephen and I walked outside, I took a long look in both directions. I had expected it to be deserted, but small clusters of people dotted the median, the bicycle lanes, and the courtyards of the tall buildings on the other side of the street.

West of the hotel, a dozen tanks lined *Jianguomen* overpass with their cannons aimed down the avenue in our direction. At the opposite end of the overpass, another dozen tanks were parked facing Eternal Peace Avenue. To the east of the hotel, less than a block away, two charred tanks and three burned military trucks stretched across the width of the avenue. Just behind them, two buses blocked the foot of *Dongdaqiao* overpass. A few yards from the overpass, another bus was jackknifed in the bicycle lane.

About twenty Chinese were standing in the westbound lane of the avenue, directly in front of the hotel. They were staring at the tanks on the *Jianguomen* overpass, and one man had a pair of binoculars. Since the American Embassy had afforded me the opportunity to see the tanks, I decided to get a better look. The man with the binoculars graciously handed them over and asked if I were an American. My response received an even more positive reaction than usual. The owner of the binoculars said, "Your radio speaks the truth." Others around him nodded in agreement and expressed their gratitude for the in-depth report on the massacre that Voice of America had broadcast earlier. Although Voice of America was still being jammed, their reports were being repeated frequently enough for people to piece them together.

Unconsciously, I took a few steps in the direction of the tanks as I looked through the binoculars. The owner of the binoculars said, "We can walk closer if you like." Stephen was not thrilled with the idea of walking in the middle of the street. Laughing nervously, he said, "If you don't mind, I'll stick to the sidewalk." His apprehension was certainly understandable after his experience that afternoon. As the crowd walked along with me, I asked if they had heard the rumor about Li Peng. They nodded and a middle-aged man wearing an undershirt spoke for them all. "We heard, but the bullet was wasted. Li Peng was only wounded in the leg."

Without stopping to think, I answered, "The guard didn't shoot him in the head because he knew Li Peng doesn't have a brain. He didn't shoot him in the chest because he knew Li Peng doesn't have a heart. He shot him in the leg because it's the best way to stop a coward."

The people around me laughed, and I could hear those behind me asking, "Did you hear what the foreigner said?" then repeating my words through the crowd. Immediately, I regretted having spoken so carelessly. If a "spy" happened to be in the crowd, those who laughed at my comments and repeated them might be turned in to Public Security.

After we had walked about a block, Stephen shouted over to me that we had gone close enough. He was worried that someone was watching us from the overpass, and it might appear that I was leading an advance on the tanks. The man who owned the binoculars stopped and said, "Your friend is right, this is as close as we should get." I took one last look and returned the binoculars to the man. Saying goodby to the crowd, I shook hands with the people standing nearby. As I shook his hand, the man in the undershirt asked, "What do you think of the people of Beijing?"

It was not a question I took lightly. When I answered him, I spoke loudly so that everyone in the crowd could hear. "The people of Beijing are the bravest and the best!"

I called Mr. M.'s office from the embassy gate telephone, but he had gone for the day. It was quite dark when we left the embassy, and the people had vanished from *Jianguomen* Avenue. Feeling eyes watching us from the overpass, imaginary or not, Stephen and I quickened our pace to a trot on our way back to the hotel.

As soon as I returned to my room, I telephoned my family. Then I called *San Lou.* I could hear Jinjin's footsteps as she ran to the telephone. A flood of Japanese poured out of her when she recognized my voice. This time, I did not wait for the Chinese translation. Instead, I asked if Han Ling had come to our room. Jinjin told me Han Ling had stopped by, but had only stayed until dark.

Paul came to the phone to tell me he had seen Lu Minghua. He had taken my "Long March" suitcase to her apartment and explained why I hadn't come to say goodby. He told me that Lu Minghua had understood, and wanted me to know that she would go to my room the next day to get the rest of my things.

I heard machine-gun fire coming from *Jianguomen* Avenue and quickly hung up the phone. Shouts and the sounds of people running to the side street were coming from the back of the hotel. I looked out my window, but there were only shadows. I ran across the hall and knocked on the door opposite mine. It faced *Jianguomen* Avenue, and two American students from *Beida* were staying in the room. We quickly turned out the lights so we wouldn't be targets, then opened the drapes wide. A convoy of tanks and trucks was heading east on *Jianguomen* Avenue. We watched the convoy from the dark room until the last truck had disappeared over *Dongdaqiao* overpass and the avenue was quiet again.

A young American woman was standing in the hallway near my room, shaking in terror. I went to her and told her that she was safe in the hotel, explaining that the soldiers had fired the machine guns to frighten people away so the avenue would be clear when the convoy came through. Although my explanation made sense to her, she continued to shake. I couldn't leave her standing there frightened and alone, so I took her to my room and made a cup of tea for her.

Hope was a college student from South Carolina. She and three friends had been traveling through China alone. They had arrived in Beijing the day before the massacre and checked into the *Minzu* Hotel. Neither Hope nor her friends could speak Chinese, and since they had been traveling from place to place, they hadn't kept up with the news. When they arrived in Beijing, they didn't even know the city was under martial law, much less that things were about to erupt. On the night of June 3rd, they found themselves in the midst of the killing as the 27th Army stormed past the *Minzu* Hotel. Hope shuddered as she told me the lobby floor had been covered with blood from the wounded and dead who were brought into the hotel that night.

When she had calmed down, I suggested that she go to the embassy early the next morning and ask for their assistance. Her chin started to quiver, "It won't do any good. I've already called the embassy, and they told us to go to the railroad station since all of the flights out of China were already filled."

It was bad advice, and I warned Hope to stay away from the train station. Soldiers had been bivouacked there for days and troops were all around the area. There was also the language problem. She might be able to find an English speaker to assist her, but it was too much of a chance to take. Hope started to cry again and told me that she and her friends had already gone to the station that afternoon. She had fallen and nearly been trampled by the crowd when soldiers charged into the station. She had a nasty collection of bruises and abrasions, but felt that she was lucky to be alive.

It just didn't make sense to send four young women who couldn't speak the language into an area where there were large numbers of troops under such volatile conditions. Furthermore, even if she had escaped without a scratch and been able to purchase tickets, it wouldn't have done much good. A train would take her into China, not out of China. They could have gone to Shanghai and then flown out of China or gone to Guangzhou and then on to Hong Kong by train, plane, or boat. However, it is seventeen hours by express train to Shanghai and thirty-six hours to Guangzhou. With rumors of civil war and reports of incidents in other cities, the last thing they needed to do was travel thousands of miles through the country. I walked Hope back to her room and told her to take a taxi to the airport the next morning, advising her to camp out in the terminal until she could get a plane to the United States, Tokyo, or Hong Kong.

Since Stephen's room was just a few doors from Hope's, I went to tell him I was going to the roof to take a look around the city. There was a full view of Beijing from there, and I wanted to see if there were any signs of fighting in the suburbs. It seemed odd that tanks had been moved from the center of the city, unless the 27th Army was retreating or they were being sent out to reinforce other troops. Once again, Stephen's southern chivalry got the best of him. Although he was hardly enthusiastic, he insisted on going with me.

We walked behind the gigantic neon "Jinglun," stepping over guy wires and around pipes. I went to the southwest corner of the building and looked through my zoom lens, but the overpass was just a dark blur in the distance. I walked back to the center of the roof and panned the city, looking for fires or smoke. In the distance, there was only the yellow haze of city lights and stark quiet all around us.

Stephen called a little after seven o'clock Wednesday morning to suggest we go downstairs to the Japan Airlines office in the hotel. He wanted to be there as soon as the office opened. At least a dozen people had the same idea. We stood in line for more than an hour before a JAL employee announced that only those holding tickets for the flight that day would be served. The crowd groaned when he added that the tickets for the June 9th flight were only available at the airport and would be sold on a first come, first serve basis.

A burst of machine gun fire came from *Jianguomen* Avenue as Stephen and I walked back to the lobby. Stephen headed for the elevators. I headed for the front doors. People were running into the hotel and ducking behind the lobby furniture for cover.

I saw Leslie do a swan dive from the front of the lobby to the back. People outside the hotel were crouching behind buses and cabs. I knew I could get outside without being shot and wanted to see what was happening. I had almost reached the door when Stephen shouted my name. I looked back and saw him standing, spread-eagle in the elevator; holding the doors open with both hands and both feet. He shouted, "Get in the elevator right this minute!" As we rode the elevator up to our floor, he said, "That's it! I've had it! We're getting out of here today, and I'm not letting you out of my sight until we leave."

Stephen went to pack his things and called the embassy to try to persuade them to send vans to transport the Americans in the hotel to the airport or the Lido. I went back to my room to wait for Yuanli.

There was gunfire again, but it sounded like single shots instead of machine guns. Grabbing my camera, I ran to the room across the hall, but no one answered my knock. The maid's cart was down the corridor, and the doors to the rooms on both sides were open. I ran into the first room and pulled the drape back. The 27th Army was moving east.

I squatted by the window and started photographing the convoy. I had taken only two shots when the floor manager and the maid came into the room. He panicked when he saw me, insisting that I leave the room immediately. It was pointless and a waste of precious time to argue with him. I ran out into the corridor, intending to go into the room next door, but the door was shut and locked. The maid came out behind me and motioned for me to follow her, then led me to another open room several doors away. However, the floor manager found me again. He allowed me to take a couple of quick photos, then shooed me out of the room, telling me that it had been announced that people who took pictures of the soldiers would be shot immediately.

Yuanli was in the hallway when I came outside. With the 27th Army on the march, I was relieved he had made it to the hotel. As we walked down the corridor, I saw the room across from mine was open. The students had moved out and an older couple had moved in. They said they didn't mind if I took photos, as long as I squatted on the floor and held my camera down low in the window.

The tanks had already gone past, but below us there were hundreds of military vehicles. The line of trucks stretched up and down the avenue as far as I could see. There were open jeeps and closed jeeps; open trucks and closed trucks; trucks filled with soldiers; trucks filled with equipment; trucks filled with crates and boxes; trucks pulling artillery weapons; and even a mess truck with cooking gear inside.

The open trucks were filled with soldiers who had their guns pointed up in every direction at the windows of the buildings that line the avenue. The foot soldiers followed, dozens walking point; in the middle of the street, on the sidewalks, and in the bicycle lanes. Behind them, several hundred soldiers marched ten abreast in the eastbound lane. Those to the outside held their rifles ready.

As they marched, the soldiers chanted. Their fierce voices boomed and roared through the canyon of tall buildings, echoing down the passageways between. As the first squad marched by, the soldiers chanted "Oppose the Rebellion!" Next they chanted, "Guard the city, protect the people!" As the last squad passed us, they chanted "Long live the people!" Doubting my own ears, I turned to Yuanli and asked him to translate the last two chants. We could only stare at each other in dismay at the cruel irony of their words.

A few people returned to the streets after the last soldiers reached *Dongdaqiao* overpass. Yuanli and I went back to my room and opened two bottles of beer to toast the departure of the 27th Army. After listening to rumors of civil war for three days, we wondered if it was a forced retreat or if the 27th was being moved to the east to fight with incoming troops. Yuanli flipped through the channels on the TV to see if there were any news reports that would give us a clue. Three Chinese officials, Yuan Mu, a general from Martial Law Headquarters, and a representative from the municipal government were holding a press conference. There were no foreign journalists present; only Chinese journalists had been allowed to attend.

The three officials were giving the Chinese government's version of the massacre. It was the story the people of Beijing were calling "The Big Lie." According to their statements, the most vicious attacks of June 3rd and June 4th had been against soldiers, not the citizens of Beijing. The general became quite emotional as he told how soldiers had been stoned and beaten by hooligans with iron pipes and wooden sticks that were studded with nails. In fact, he seemed more disturbed by the destruction of 568 vehicles than the loss of civilian lives. Changing his tone to anger, he charged that several hundred guns had been stolen from the PLA and were believed to be in the hands of "hooligans."

Praising the PLA, the general claimed that "many more people would have been killed had the PLA not shown restraint in their actions." Dramatically, he stated, "We are the people's army! We serve the people, we do not shoot the people! However, we could not distinguish the normal people from the hooligans." I wondered how anyone could possibly mistake children, pregnant women, and old people for "hooligans."

The city official droned on about the 202 public buses and trolleys that had been disabled or destroyed, complaining that they could not be moved from the streets. Once again, the focus was on public property instead of the lives of the people in his city.

Yuan Mu blamed the victims for the massacre, stating that "some people are not satisfied with our socialist system and used their dissatisfaction to incite violence." There was another moment of irony when he said, "I sincerely hope for the sake of the country, for the sake of the nation, for the sake of the people that the truth is known by the whole society."

The government's version of the truth, as stated by Yuan Mu, was that one thousand civilians and six thousand soldiers had been wounded. He said about three hundred had died; one hundred of them soldiers and twenty-three students. While he admitted that some bystanders had been killed, he claimed that most of those who died were "criminals who deserved to die."

The maid came to clean the room while Yuanli and I were watching the press conference. When I got up to get a tissue, she followed me into the bathroom. She was worried I would take photographs of the soldiers from the street. She told me that it was one thing to take a photograph from the hotel where I could conceal myself, but if I took photos from the street, I would surely be shot. When I replied that I would be careful, she wasn't satisfied with my answer. She thought I hadn't understood her and despite my assurances that I had, she insisted on calling Yuanli in to translate her warning into English.

Stephen came into the room to tell me that he had given up on trying to reach the embassy by phone. I remembered that he had driven himself to the hotel and asked why we couldn't use his jeep. He explained that a Chinese friend had taken the jeep. Stephen thought we should go to the embassy immediately and ask for transportation to the Lido or the airport. Since I had to pick up my backpack anyway, I agreed.

It was hard saying goodby to Yuanli, but at least I could say it to him in person. He promised he would contact Shanli and tell him that I had left. I gave him a list of names and addresses of a few other friends and asked him to contact them when it was safe. He told me he would write and call me, when and if he could.

Stephen and I were less than a block from the hotel when we heard the familiar rumble of tanks. It was a sound we had come to recognize immediately over the past few hours. There hadn't been the customary rounds of machine-gun fire to announce their impending arrival, and the tanks were bearing down on us from the east. As he ran into a narrow alley, Stephen shouted for me to follow him. There was a lamppost to use for cover, so I stayed on the street where I could see. After the first tank raced by, Stephen insisted that I make a run for the alley. We waited there until the last tank had passed, then took a back street the rest of the way to the embassy.

The embassy was in an uproar when we arrived. The tanks had gone to the Foreign Diplomatic Residential compound and surrounded it. Troops had also surrounded the compound and fired on the buildings with assault rifles. A PLA officer claimed a sniper inside the compound had fired on a convoy of soldiers moving west and insisted on searching every building in the compound. Ninety minutes later, the troops finally pulled out, but only after they had arrested a Chinese man they had dragged from one of the buildings. United States Ambassador James Lilley, responded to the confrontation immediately by ordering all embassy dependents to evacuate China.

Despite the confusion, we located Mr. M. and retrieved my backpack. Stephen tried to arrange transportation for all the Americans staying at the Jinglun, but his request was refused. Mr. M. and another embassy officer, Mr. D., told us that the evacuation of dependents was the embassy's first priority, and explained that all embassy vehicles were needed for the evacuation. I asked if we could stay at the embassy until we had made arrangements to leave the city, but Mr. M. told me there wasn't enough room. However, he did agree to let us stay at the embassy until the "all clear" was given, and then offered to escort me to the Jinglun on foot.

In the meantime, Mr. D. offered the use of the embassy telephone and suggested that Stephen call business contacts to arrange transportation through one of them. It was easier said than done since many offices were closed; however, Stephen finally reached a friend at Occidental Petroleum who agreed to send a car over to the hotel immediately to take us the Lido.

Since Stephen was only able to provide transportation for the two of us, he convinced Mr. D. to come to the Jinglun to talk to the other Americans in the hotel. As soon as he returned to the Jinglun, Stephen and I went from door to door on our floor, telling all of the U.S. citizens that a representative from the embassy was on his way. After everyone had assembled in the corridor to wait for Mr. D., Stephen and I went to get our luggage.

The maid greeted me in the hall, politely asking if I had eaten yet. I answered that I had eaten my fill, then inquired about her. A couple of minutes later, she saw me dragging my suitcase, backpack, and carry-on out of my room. She rushed over, took the suitcase from me, and brought it to the elevator. While I waited for the elevator, she went to her cart and grabbed a pack of matches. Hurriedly, she wrote something inside the cover and handed the matches to me as I stepped into the elevator. She said, "You must tell the world!" and as the elevator doors closed, she wished me a smooth journey home. Stephen was already downstairs, waiting for me by his friend's car. We loaded my luggage, hopped into the car, and the driver peeled out of the hotel parking lot. After I caught my breath, I pulled the matches from my pocket and opened the cover. Inside, the maid had written, "The leaders of China are murderers."

We were worried that we might run into the 27th Army on the way to the Lido, but we only saw troops from the 40th Army. Their trucks were parked in a field and the soldiers seemed quite harmless. They were sitting in the shade of their trucks eating lunch and relaxing, as if they were on a summer picnic.

The lobby of the Lido was a madhouse. The U.S. Embassy dependents were arriving, and there were people and piles of baggage everywhere. While Stephen went to the reception counter to arrange for our luggage to be stored until we could check in, I went to cash a traveler's check to get FEC for cab fare to the airport.

The taxi driver demanded $200.00 FEC for the round trip. Several bystanders from the neighborhood came over to listen as Stephen told the driver the price was too high. While we were aware that fares had escalated because of the crisis, $200.00 was several times the regular fare. Stephen offered the driver $100.00 and the driver countered with $150.00. Since

Stephen's Chinese was better than mine, we had decided to let him handle the practical matters. During the first round of bargaining, I kept my mouth shut. However, I quickly lost patience with the bargaining game, and marched over to scold the driver. "You should help foreigners get to the airport, not take advantage of us! We are trying to get out of China so that we can tell the world what the *feng gou* did."

As soon as I had spoken, I was sorry I had lost my temper. The driver was only worried about making enough money to feed his family after the foreigners were gone. Besides, I really wasn't that angry with him. It was the whole situation that had me upset. However, the bystanders immediately criticized the driver, telling him that I was right and urging him to help us. Bowing to public pressure, the driver agreed to our price.

As we climbed into the taxi, Stephen whispered, "What's *feng gou?*"

"Mad dogs!" I replied.

Stephen told me to wait in the cab while he made a quick tour of the airport to see if any of the airlines had tickets for Hong Kong or Tokyo. He took a few steps, and then came back to the cab. Sticking his head inside the window he said, "If I can get a ticket for a flight right away, we won't have time to go back and get our luggage. Will you still go?"

My backpack was with me, but I didn't have my carry-on. I shook my head adamantly and said, "No way!"

As I watched Stephen disappear through the doors of the terminal, I finally realized that I was really leaving Beijing. Until that moment, I had managed to convince myself something would happen that would allow me to stay. Now, I could no longer pretend and I started to cry.

The driver didn't know what to do with a weeping foreign woman. He was munching on a cracker, so he offered me one, hoping that would appease me. I shook my head and continued to cry. He tried a cigarette, but that didn't work either. I told him that I only wanted to stay in Beijing with my friends. He stopped munching on the cracker for a minute, clearly trying to think of something to say that would stop my tears. Finally, he turned and spoke to me in a comforting voice. "It's okay if you leave Beijing. Foreigners eat too much and there isn't enough food."

His statement didn't stop my tears, but it did make me laugh. As for the driver, he went back to munching on his cracker, content that he had thought of the perfect thing to say.

There were no tickets available, but Stephen found out that the State Department had chartered a jet for their dependents. It was scheduled to leave the next morning and if there were any seats left over, the State Department would sell them to U.S. citizens.

Before I went to bed, I walked down the hotel driveway to *Jiangtai* Road. It was my last evening in China, and I wanted to smell the pungent odor of a China night one more time before I left.

As I walked, I realized the taxi driver had thought of the perfect thing to say. It wasn't his words, it was his meaning. Leaving China was the best thing for me to do. I could no longer help my friends by staying. Actually, I might become a detriment to them. Just being with me would become more difficult and more dangerous for them. As much as it hurt me to leave, it could hurt my friends more if I stayed. The best way to help them was to do what the maid at the Jinglun had said, to tell the world.

There was a heavy mist in the air when Stephen and I arrived at the airport early Thursday morning. After we had signed a blank promissory note payable to Uncle Sam, we were issued tickets to Tokyo. From Tokyo, we would have to find our own way home.

Just before we were ready to leave, Ambassador Lilley came aboard the plane for a couple of minutes to shake a few hands. Then, the cabin door was shut and we taxied to the runway. People cheered as the plane lifted from the ground. Although I understood their joy, I felt only anguish. I closed my eyes to hold back the tears. I had started to cry again, and I knew it would be a long time before I stopped.

The massacre was not the end of the story, just the end of a chapter. I wondered what would happen to China, to the students, to the *laobaixing*, and to my friends. I wondered how long it would be before I could return. As the plane climbed higher and we flew farther away from Beijing, the words of Li Bai, the Chinese poet, ran through my mind:

> . . . *I just stared at clouds to the south,*
> *heart sick for my home folk, eyes full of tears,*
> *feeling that the spring wind is cruel . . ."*

EPILOGUE

For you no monument is raised.
For you no plinth for statue laid.
Yet the monuments to you are legion,
deeply rooted in the people's hearts.
Nine thousand strokes of lightning
cannot strike them down.
Nor a twelve-force typhoon topple.
Deeply rooted in the people's hearts,
Your monument more enduring then any man-made!
                                 Unidentified Chinese Poet

EPILOGUE

FOR YOU NO MONUMENT . . .

How many people died on June 3–4, 1989? The Chinese government finally settled on a figure. In the official account of the massacre, *Report on Checking the Turmoil and Quelling the Counterrevolutionary Rebellion*, authorized by the State Council and delivered by Beijing Mayor Chen Xitong at the eighth session of the seventh NPC Standing Committee on June 30, 1989, it was stated that over 200 civilians were killed. How many is "over 200"? Is it 201, 2,000, 10,000?

According to *Punishment Season: Human Rights in China After Martial Law*, published by Asia Watch in March 1990, "Several hundred and perhaps as many as a thousand of these 'counterrevolutionaries' were killed on the streets of Beijing by the PLA as it converged from all directions on Tiananmen Square on the night of June 3-4. . . ." The United States Department of State concurs. *Country Reports on Human Rights Practices for 1989,* published by the Department of State in February 1990, states, "At least several hundred, and possibly thousands, of people were killed in Beijing on June 3-4."

As another anniversary of the massacre approaches, China appears to be back on the track of economic reform.* On a sweep through southern China in January, 1992, Deng proclaimed his commitment to one hundred years of economic reform, endorsed the use of capitalist economic methods, and encouraged other areas of China to exhibit the same accelerated development as in the south. It should be noted, however, that he made it perfectly clear that political reform was not in the picture.

*Written in May 1992.

The State Council of China has granted Shanghai the authority to open Economic Development Zones in Minghang, Hongqiao, Caohejing, and Pudong. A new Special Economic Zone has been declared in northern China in Hunchun, Jilin Province. On the outside, the Chinese appear to be prospering as the economic reforms allow more and more people to achieve the "Eight Bigs"—a motorcycle, a color television, a stereo, a matching sofa and chairs, a VCR, a refrigerator, a washing machine, and a camera. Underneath the shiny surface of this middle-class prosperity, there is apathy, disillusionment, misinformation, and distrust.

Despite the appearance of normalcy, the massacre has left deep scars in China—on the Party, on the economy, on the PLA, and most especially on the people. Deng Xiaoping finally retired from his last remaining official post in 1990, although he remains as China's "helmsman." It is said that he regrets the massacre, which cost him the affection and respect of his people, as well as his place in the world as a statesman. He is too old and too ill, and there is too little time left for him to wash the blood from his hands or to rewrite history. Instead, he will go to his grave remembered as much for this bloody act of tyranny as for the economic reforms that came before and after.

Zhao Ziyang was stripped of all Party posts and subjected to the policy of the "three nos": no prosecution, no verdict, and no work. On July 18, 1990, the *Los Angeles Times* reported that Zhao had been released from house arrest, and that there were rumors that Deng had "authorized Zhao to make provincial 'inspection' tours to study the state of China's economic reforms." The rumors proved to be unfounded, and Zhao remains in political purgatory. Beijingers say that he lives at #3 Fuqiang Alley, the house where Hu Yaobang once lived. The story goes that frequently an official black sedan belonging to Deng Xiaoping arrives at #3 Fuqiang Alley to fetch Zhao for a visit with his former mentor. But, of course, that is only small lanes news.

Premier Li Peng remains the most despised man in China, and since the massacre, rumors have persisted that he will be replaced as Premier. He continues to head up the Chen Yun faction on the Politburo and has repeated his stand that "China will adhere to the socialist road." In the spring of 1992, Deng Xiaoping issued the warning that "Whoever is opposed to reform must leave office." Li responded with halfhearted support of economic reform. During the 1992 session of the NPC, deputies drafted a resolution requesting the Premier to revise his report to the NPC to include criticism of the "leftist" faction in the Party. As further evidence of his political vulnerability, numerous NPC delegates attacked his power base, the State Planning Commission, referring to it as a haven of "Stalinist economics."

Sixty-five-year-old Jiang Zimen was plucked from his post as Party Leader of Shanghai and named by Deng to replace Zhao Ziyang as the Party General Secretary, as successor to Deng, and as a member of the Standing Committee of the Politburo of the Chinese Communist Party Central Committee. In addition, Jiang was named as Chairman of the Communist Party Central Military Commission when Deng retired from the post. However, Jiang would be well advised to look behind him. His two predecessors did not fare well.

The struggles within the Party continue, and as the winds of change swept across Eastern Europe, the Soviet Union, and even neighboring Mongolia, leaders of the Chinese Communist Party slept with one eye open. Even before the massacre, the Party had taken steps to silence the voices of opposition in the press. Since the massacre, censorship has escalated, and other methods of constraint have been used to tighten control on the press and the arts.

On October 14, 1989, the editors-in-chief of forty-five major newspapers were required to participate in a twenty-day "Document Study Session" directed by the Party's Ideology Unit for Coordinating Thought Education. As of February 1990, every publisher in China had to go through the process of reregistration. One-hundred-and-ninety newspapers and periodicals had been shut down by April 1990 in a campaign of economic austerity and ideological purification. To date, the government has also banned hundreds of thousands of books and movies in an attempt to dam the flow of contamination from Western ideology.

In January 1991, at a meeting of the All-China Journalists Association, a professional code of ethics was adopted for China's 420,000 journalists. While the code is supposedly aimed at truthful coverage of the news, it requires journalists to "safeguard national interests and state policies" and to avoid reporting on the negative aspects of society such as crime, sex, violence, and superstition.

Since the massacre, hard-liners in the Party have launched continual attacks against bourgeois liberalization, capitalism, and western-style democracy. The influence of the Old Revolutionaries was obvious in the earlier attacks, which lambasted John Foster Dulles. Mr. Dulles has been dead since 1959.

Who will win control of the Party in the long run, the reformers or the hard-liners? Much depends on who dies first—Chen Yun or Deng Xiaoping. Neither can live too much longer. It is rumored that the eighty-seven-year-old Chen suffers from leukemia, while Deng, also eighty-seven, suffers from cancer of the prostate. Even with the renewed emphasis on economic reform, if Deng goes first, the balance of power could rest with the hard-liners. Most Chinese pray that Chen dies first.

As to the long-term effects on the Chinese Communist Party, the leadership has pledged to strengthen the bond between the Party and the masses. Only time will tell if that bond has been irrevocably severed.

From June 1989 to June 1990, China's economy floundered under the weight of the economic sanctions that were imposed on China by the Western community as well as the Party's own reflexive retreat toward centralized planning. The Hong Kong *Monthly Mirror* reported that by June 1990, inflation had risen 18.5 percent, the cost of living index had risen to 20.7 percent, and the the real income of all households had dropped by 34.9 percent. In an effort to control inflation, the government devalued the Renminbi in 1989 from 3.72 RMB per US dollar to 4.71 RMB per US dollar. As a result, the people found that their salaries no longer stretched through the month's end. There were rumors that salaries would be increased, but that was a nonsolution that could only result in higher inflation. On October 17, 1990, the Renminbi was again devalued by 9.35 percent to 5.209 RMB per US dollar, and the Chinese people wondered how they could possibly make ends meet.*

Since June 3–4, the People's Liberation Army has had its own problems—the people no longer love the PLA. On returning to their villages,

---

*The rate as of October 1992 is 5.50 RMB per US dollar.

many soldiers who participated in the massacre found that they were not welcomed as "Guardians of the Republic," as they had dubbed themselves, but were shunned as butchers of unarmed civilians. With respect declining some soldiers and their families have been the victims of verbal and physical attacks. The military has also experienced difficulties in recruiting while draft dodging is on the rise. To ensure that those who are recruited have the correct political viewpoint, voluntary enlistees of the PLA are now subjected to a program of stringent political and ideological training as a matter of course.

When it came to the matter of settling accounts, the leadership of China acted swiftly and unsparingly. It would appear that the men at *Zhongnanhai* altered Deng's black cat/white cat quote to read, "It doesn't matter if the fish is big or small, as long as we catch him."

After the massacre, plainclothes police and soldiers scoured campuses, neighborhoods, and *danwei* in pursuit of suspected "counterrevolutionaries" and "hooligans." On June 13, 1989, the Ministry of Public Service began a nationwide search for the big fish by issuing a list of Twenty-One Most Wanted Students, followed by subsequent lists naming three leaders of the Beijing Workers Autonomous Union (Han Dongfang, He Lili, and Liu Qiang), as well as prominent intellectuals such as astrophysicist Fang Lizhi; Fang's wife, Li Shuxian; Wan Runnan, head of the Stone Corporation; political scientist Yan Jiaqi; Su Xiaokang, a co-writer of the documentary "River Elegy"; and Bao Zunxin, a researcher at the China Academy of Social Studies. The mug shots and biographical sketches of the big fish were televised nationally, along with the telephone numbers of special hot lines that were set up to accommodate the expected onslaught of calls from "patriotic citizens" eager to report on each other.

Although there were a few highly publicized cases of people turning in friends, neighbors, or relatives, the government learned that the Chinese people are not as easily manipulated as they once were. Throughout China, people aided and sheltered the wanted, and scores of people dialed the televised telephone numbers just to jam the lines. Some brave souls even called the hot lines to report on the whereabouts of China's "two most infamous criminals"—Deng Xiaoping and Li Peng.

Nevertheless, thousands of people have been apprehended since June 4, though it is impossible to state an exact number since statistics in the People's Republic of China historically have more to do with the science of politics than with the science of mathematics. The Chinese government acknowledged that about 2,500 people had been arrested by the end of June, 1989, and in December 1989, the *Beijing Youth News* reported that the exact number was 2,578. But these totals did not agree with the total of the government's other figures, stating the number of those tried and sentenced, released, or still awaiting trial.

The consensus among independent sources such as Amnesty International, Asia Watch, and Western journalists is that tens of thousands have been arrested as a result of the crackdown. According to Asia Watch by the end of July 1989, 6,000 people had been arrested in Beijing and 10,000 had been arrested nationwide. The aforementioned United States Department of State's 1989 report on human rights violations states that some sources have estimated as many as 100,000 have been arrested.

The first public executions of those charged with crimes relating to what the Chinese government referred to as "the turmoil in Beijing" took place on June 22, 1989, when three workers charged with burning a train were executed in Shanghai. *Repression in China Since June 4, 1989*, published by Asia Watch in September, 1990, states that forty-nine people have been executed as a result of the crackdown while three have been given suspended death sentences. However, these numbers reflect only those executions that can be documented. As there have been persistent and credible rumors of secret executions, it is likely that the number is much higher.

Despite the government's efforts to seal every border, some of the big fish escaped. Wuer Kaixi, Yan Jiaqi, Wan Runnan, and Chai Ling were among those who made it to the West. Fang Lizhi and his wife, Li Shuxian, were granted sanctuary in the United States Embassy in Beijing where they remained for 386 days.

On June 25, 1990, Fang and Li were finally allowed to leave China after issuing a statement in which they acknowledged their opposition to the Four Cardinal Principles of Socialism, requested approval to travel abroad "to visit relatives and friends and to obtain necessary medical treatment," and promised to "refuse to participate in all contrary activities whose motives lie in opposing China."

For those who were apprehended, the government initially allowed a series of speedy public trials for the little fish, but the majority of trials have been closed to the public. Defendants have been denied the right to select their own attorneys and have had to rely on state-appointed attorneys. In violation of the Chinese Constitution, many prisoners were held in prison well over a year before being tried. While in prison, they were subjected to isolation, torture, continual interrogations, and deprived of their visitation rights.

Yu Zhijian, Yu Dongyue, and Lu Decheng, the three men who splattered Mao's portrait over the Gate of Heavenly Peace with ink, were brought to trial in July, 1989, and sentenced to life, 20 years, and 16 years, respectively. The three students who on April 22, 1989, knelt on the steps of the Great Hall of the People with a petition listing the students' demands were all arrested. Zhou Yongjun was arrested in June 1989 and sent to Qincheng Prison. According to Asia Watch, he was released without trial on January 16, 1991. Zhang Zhiyong was also arrested in June 1989 and released in January 1991. The third, Guo Haifeng, was arrested on Tiananmen Square on June 4, 1989. He was tried in January 1991 and sentenced to four years imprisonment and one year's deprivation of political rights.

Student leader, Wang Dan, #1 on the Ministry's 21 Most Wanted Students List, was arrested on July 2, 1989, and held in Qincheng Prison before being brought to trial more than a year and a half later on January 23, 1991. Wang was convicted on the charge of instigating counterrevolutionary propaganda and sentenced on January 26, 1991, to four years in prison.

Bao Zunxin, the noted intellectual who participated in the May 14th Delegation of Intellectuals and was a signatory of the May 17th Declaration, was arrested in June 1989 and sentenced to five years imprisonment on January 26, 1991. According to Asia Watch, Bao shows symptoms of mental illness, and has repeatedly attempted suicide after learning that statements, which he made in prison, were used as evidence in the arrests of several other activists.

Wang Ruowang, the seventy-three year old Shanghai writer who was expelled from the Party following his activities during the 1986-1987 student demonstrations was arrested in the fall of 1989 for listening to Voice of America and writing letters in support of the hunger strikers, including his open letter to Deng Xiaoping. After sixteen months in detention, he was released on October 29, 1990. However, he remains under investigation, and was detained overnight in April 1991. Wang's telephone line was disconnected; he was forbidden to travel outside of Shanghai; and he was ordered to make frequent reports to the Shanghai police. But in the late summer of 1992, he and his wife were allowed to come to the United States. His friend, Qin Benli, the former editor of the *World Economic Herald*, was investigated, but never arrested. He died on April 15, 1991, at the age of seventy-three.

One of the saddest cases is that of Ren Wanding, the bespectacled forty-six year old accountant who is a longtime activist and human rights advocate. Ren was first jailed for four years in 1979 as a result of his activities during the Democracy Wall Movement, and his protests against the arrest of fellow Democracy Wall activist, Wei Jingsheng. Asia Watch reports that Ren sought sanctuary in the United States Embassy in Beijing following the massacre; however, he was turned away. He was arrested on June 9, 1989, and sent to Qincheng Prison. On January 26, 1991, Ren was sentenced to seven years imprisonment and three years deprivation of his political rights for counterrevolutionary propaganda and incitement. Following his sentence, he was transferred to Beijing #2 Prison. Xinhua News Agency reported that due to Ren's lack of repentance, he received the longest sentence of the twenty-five defendants who were tried in January 1991. Following Ren's arrest, his *danwei* evicted his wife from their apartment. According to Asia Watch, she and her thirteen-year-old daughter live in the apartment's 15 square meter yard.

The *laobaixing* have received the harshest treatment. Workers and peasants have been executed while intellectuals have escaped the ultimate punishment.* Furthermore, far more workers have been arrested than intellectuals. Those who have been tried have been charged with nonpolitical crimes, which allows the government to give them longer prison terms and prevents groups such as Amnesty International from monitoring their treatment.

---

*This is in reference to the forty-nine executions that can be documented.

Those who have escaped prosecution have not escaped persecution. In the clamp down which followed June 3-4, the Chinese returned to the days of close supervision with their actions being monitored by soldiers, secret police, hidden cameras, *danwei* leaders, and "Old Aunties." The "turmoil" of June 3-4 revived the old Party custom of the *biaotai.** The definition is "to declare where one stands," but Lu Minghua's explanation defines the practice more clearly.

> *Everyday they violate our human rights. They make us do things which we do not want to do, and they make us say things that we do not want to say. If anyone speaks the truth, they will suffer. We can only keep the truth hidden in our hearts.*

People were forced to write journals, detailing accounts of their actions during the "turmoil," as well as the actions of their friends, co-workers, and neighbors. For several months following June 4, police interrogated people in their homes, at their *danwei,* and at police stations. Political meetings and ideological study sessions were held regularly, and citizens were required to carry their identity cards with them at all times. Although the tensions have eased, telephone conversations are still monitored, mail opened, people followed, and their homes raided. Chinese who associate with foreigners, both officially and unofficially, are subjected to special scrutiny and mistrust.

A national law on demonstrations was enacted on October 31, 1989. It is more restrictive and comprehensive than the 1986 law which only restricted demonstrations in Beijing.

Martial law was lifted on January 11, 1990, but it was an illusion and a ploy for the sake of appearances. The Chinese people call it *"nei jin wai song* (tight on the inside, loose on the outside)." The government renamed the players and dressed them in different costumes, calling soldiers paramilitary police and outfitting them with police uniforms. Then, they could claim that there were fewer soldiers in Beijing, even if the number re-

---

*In a final insult to the Student Democratic Movement, the Chinese government uses the term *dongluan* (turmoil) to refer to the massacre.

mained the same. They could state to the world that things in Beijing had returned to normal and declare that tensions had eased.

As I expected, it has been difficult to maintain contact with my friends in China. Some have not been able to contact me at all, while others can only do so indirectly. As to those few with whom I have direct contact, we cannot say what we want to say, or ask what we want to ask. For their protection, we must rely on allegories and allusions, referring to the weather or their health when we discuss conditions in Beijing.

I have not heard from Hong Xin, Professor Fang, Teacher Jin, or Mr. Pan. Nor did I expect to. I received my first letter from Susan less than two months after the massacre. Obviously her disinterest in politics has served her well, for she doesn't appear to have had any difficulties. However, I have not heard from her in over a year. I attribute her silence to the official warning issued to employees of hotels and restaurants, advising them not to have close contact with foreigners. I will not write to her until I hear from her again. I often think of the words in her last letter: "Mama Gail, please do not forget your China daughter Susan. She very miss you!"

It was not until August 1990 that I heard from Wei Wenfu. His letter from Luoyang was brief. He wrote that he and his family were well and that he missed hearing from me. However, he politely requested that I not reply to his letter since it might cause him some "inconvenience." In August 1991 he was sent abroad on business. Since then, it has been "convenient" for me to reply to his letters.

While The Professor and Lao Pang do not write to me directly, I have received letters from them through their son in the United States. The Professor was questioned about the *dazibao,* which he wrote concerning the seventieth anniversary of May 4th, but he is too old to be easily intimidated. When his interrogators criticized his poem as being supportive of the Pro-Democracy Movement, The Professor responded that they were free to interpret his poem in any way that they wished.

Teacher Wu went abroad to do research in 1990. We correspond frequently, and he has been a source of encouragement and support to me in my writing. We have made plans to meet over a bottle of Chinese liquor when we both return to Beijing. We hope that things will have changed by then.

I received my first letter from Han Ling in July, 1989. She wrote,

> *It is more than two weeks since you left China, my dear friend. We parted from each other so unexpectedly and quickly that I could not believe the truth and could not come back from the dream. That last evening I went to visit you, but I returned to my room with tears in my eyes and the gifts that I would like to have given you in my hands.*
>
> *Although it is very hot here and makes you feel stifled, you can still smell a little fresh air in the early morning or in the late evening. However, as the Chinese proverb says, "xinjing ziran liang." The translation is, "if you have a quiet mind, you don't really feel the heat." In my mind, to gain a quiet mind is to sublimate your feelings of unease, sorrow, and hopelessness through music, literature, art, and all of the good things, which have been created by human beings and are the best of humanity. Beautiful things live forever, and in this spiritual world, you can regain your confidence, your courage, your belief, and your hope.*

I have only received two letters from Han Ling since then. In her letter of December 1990, she asked if I had received the letter which she wrote to me that summer. Unfortunately, it never arrived.

Yuanli called me just days after I returned home from Beijing. Since his participation in the demonstrations was limited, he did not have much difficulty. We have been able to keep in constant contact since I left Beijing. He is my lifeline at times, for he brings me back to China through his letters, his phone calls, and news of friends whom I cannot contact. It would be a smaller and lonelier world for me without Yuanli.

I did not hear from Shanli until a few months after the massacre. One quiet morning at four o'clock, as I struggled to put his devilish and irresistible manner into words, the phone rang. I couldn't believe my ears when I heard, "Hello, Lao Ban, this is Jack!" Once again, he had appeared at the most unlikely moment, but his timing was absolutely perfect. Although thousands of miles away, I could see him so clearly, it was as if he were actually here.

Knowing that I had been worried about him, he apologized, explaining, "Things have been very tight in Beijing." Alarmed that the phone call was being monitored, I interrupted and said, "SHANLI, talk to me about the WEATHER!" There was a slight pause, followed by a chuckle. Then, he said, "Okay, Lao Ban, the weather has been very tight in Beijing!"

Since June 3-4, Shanli had been hauled in for questioning, followed, investigated, and hassled in a dozen different ways. I can always tell when the Chinese government has a new campaign of harassment in the works, because Shanli will call to tell me that I shouldn't expect to hear from him for awhile, and that I shouldn't call or write. Later, I will receive a phone call or a letter, telling me "the coast is clear."

Despite his irrepressible spirit, things almost got the better of Shanli. As the winter of 1990 came to an end, he wrote to tell me that there would be another period of silence.

> *In the winter, the weather here seemed "back to normal"; however, people had to wear masks to hide from the cold. Now life is only mama huhu (so-so). I think that I might die soon. I am too tired. I need a good, sound sleep.*

I cried when I read his words and the poem, written by Wang Wei, which he had enclosed.

> *No dust is raised on pathways wet with morning rain.*
> *The willows by the tavern look so fresh and green.*
> *I invite you to drink a cup of wine again.*
> *West of the Southern Pass, no more friends will be seen.*

I waited and prayed for his safety until he called to tell me that, once more, he had survived the ordeal. There was another long period of silence beginning in September 1990. In late January 1991, I received an early morning phone call, and rejoiced when I heard those wonderful words, "Hello, Lao Ban, this is Jack!"

In August 1989, I received a letter from Lu Minghua, which had been written only days after I left Beijing. However, it had gone through many hands and traveled many paths before making its way to my door.

Lu Minghua has found a way to reach me, with letters which are as open and honest as she. While her letters are infrequent, and usually they are written weeks before they arrive, my letters to her are even more infrequent. They must travel through channels, which are far more complex than those which she uses, and unlike her, I must write with extreme caution. However, our correspondence has brought us even closer than we were before, for it has given Lu Minghua someone to reach out to, and it is through her words that I have come to understand the true meaning of freedom.

I have noticed her handwriting steadily deteriorate, mirroring her deteriorating health, and while each letter has been a treasure to me, each has brought with it the burden of her torment. I can only hope that it gives her some slight comfort to share that torment with me.

On June 14, 1989, she wrote,

> Since the night of June 8th, soldiers have been patrolling every intersection checking identification. Small skirmishes are still taking place. More than 500 people have been arrested. Two people from our school have been arrested. One is a teacher from our department who made speeches at the square. The other is a worker. We don't know what will be done to them. I am prepared. I am not afraid.
>
> By now you have seen Western news coverage of June 3-4. . . . How many really died? Who knows? In China, if you don't know anything at all, you may be able to live happily. But, the more you know, the more pain you feel. We are suffocating here.
>
> If I haven't been arrested by the time summer vacation begins, I will clean your things and put them in your suitcase. There were still many things that you like and need in your room. I will take care of them.

Her next letter was written in December 1989, and it terrified me. She wrote,

> Little Sister, do you know what it has been like this last half year? I have held my indignation inside until I am truly crazed. Sometimes I think that if I am pressured again, I will go to my leader's home and kill myself. But I want to see victory, victory for democracy in China. I believe that we can achieve a victory for democracy, and I want to be there for that victory. This conviction encourages me to live on. It is the reason that I am still alive.
>
> I feel that I am living in a prison. During this half year, investigations have been carried out in the universities and factories. 'Who demonstrated, collected donations, wrote big/small character posters?' They

want everyone to incriminate themselves. Very few have confessed. We are told to write down what we did. Write it one time, it is not accepted. Write it again, write it ten times. The majority of people do not admit their own actions. Even fewer expose the actions of others. The Haidian District has informed the least. However, someone said that I demonstrated, that I did such-and-such. Of course, I will not admit it. Nor, will I report on other people. Time after time, they have come to interrogate me. Right now, I don't know how I will be treated in the future.

I was relieved to receive her letter written a month later, for I knew that she was still clinging to hope. She told me that the Chinese people felt they had contributed to the changes in Eastern Europe, and when they learned about Rumania, they were happy for the first time since June 3-4. She said people were dancing and singing at their work units, claiming that they were celebrating the Chinese New Year early, when in reality they were celebrating the fall of another tyrant.

However, there was bad news in the letter. She wrote that she had been experiencing dizzy spells, shortness of breath, and chest pains. She said the doctor told her that she was suffering from a coronary disease. I knew that she was suffering from a broken heart.

I got a letter to her as soon as I could, telling her that although the winter had been cold, gray, and bitter, she must guard her health so that she could enjoy the warm days of spring. I received her answer in June 1990. After telling me that she understood what I meant, she added, "The weather in Beijing is still quite harsh. I have been attacked by the cold winds of winter."

She wrote that she had wept when she received my letter, that now she cried much of the time. I could see the tear stains on her letter, and as I read it, I wept with her.

I am a person of very strong character. I do not like to cry. I cry because inside there is such sadness. I have many friends who are kind to me and admire me. They give me great happiness, but that happiness is fleeting. The depression and sorrow endure.

Little Sister, I have been so wronged. I don't understand why good people should be bullied. I have worked hard at my job for over twenty years. What mistakes have I made? I only opposed corruption and evil people. Yet, I am criticized for that. . . . It is all right for the *laobaixing* to wish the Party well and to love the Party, but we cannot discuss their evil deeds. . . . What is the sense of all of this?

Sometime later, I received a letter, which had been written in June 1990, describing the conditions in Beijing one year after the massacre. She wrote,

> Beijing is tightly controlled. There are many soldiers and security police on the streets, and Tiananmen Square. . . . The leaders try to give the appearance that all is normal. They say the right things to convince the world. However, every university and college is severely restricted. Many *danwei* leaders are hard-liners, and the people in these units are especially unlucky. People just can't understand. It is not only me who is unhappy. . . .
>
> The students who went to Tiananmen Square last year cannot find good jobs. They have been assigned to remote places and told that if they work hard and improve their ideology, they can return. Otherwise, there is no return. This is done so that other students will know the consequences and remain silent.

Later in 1990, she wrote,

> Little Sister, I truly feel that I am tired of living. From my outside appearance, I look cheerful. Inside, I feel despondent. During this last school year, I tried to overcome my sadness by throwing myself into my work. From morning until afternoon, I taught my students diligently. Now, I am tired, and I am angry, and my health is getting worse. I truly feel that the days drag on like years, and my life is really meaningless. . . .
>
> The conditions are the same here. They are very strict with intellectuals, but many people have already grown accustomed to it. The official propaganda tells a convincing story. It sounds like nothing happened. Newspapers and broadcasts rarely mention corruption. Instead, they appeal to the people to "Learn from Lei Feng." The *laobaixing* respond, "You leaders should first show us how you have learned from Lei Feng. You send your children abroad and deposit your money in foreign banks." Is this learning from Lei Feng?
>
> I have always loved my people and the soil under my feet. I have always felt grateful to the Party for saving me from a bitter childhood.

However, the leaders of the Party are all corrupt and depraved—they only add to our suffering. They speak of the need for tranquility. All Chinese desire tranquility, but the *laobaixing* must live without it. All Chinese long for the day when we have tranquility in our hearts.

The Chinese people believe that this situation cannot last forever. Things will get better someday. Inside our hearts, we are no longer obedient. We are just waiting for someone to die.

APPENDIX

Author's Note

When I visited Building #8 for the last time on Monday, June 5, 1989, I was given two leaflets by the Chinese students with whom I spoke. I promised the students that I would bring the leaflets back to the United States so that others might read them. Including the translations of the leaflets in this book is my way of fulfilling that promise.

Since the first leaflet was unsigned, I have no way of knowing who wrote it. The "Memorial," however, was signed. Although the name is probably a pseudonym, it might put that person at risk to give credit to him or her at this time.

NOTICE TO THE PEOPLE FROM EIGHT ART INSTITUTES OF THE CAPITAL

June 2, 1989

These past few days, we have suffered so many attacks. Deng Mama did not lead her son Peng back home. Several old generals did not stand up and speak justly. Wan Li did not hold a meeting of the National People's Congress. We still hail the slogan, "Xiaoping, how are you?"

In fact, from "Xiaoping, how are you?" until today, it was inevitable that a dictatorship would occur. Although there are several cases in Chinese history of people arising and overthrowing feudalism and corrupt governments, it only happened when people had no way out, no food to eat, and famine was everywhere. As long as they had a steamed bun in hand, no matter how much they suffered, they waited for the "upright official" to appear and speak justly. That is the basic characteristic of the Chinese people; to rely on an "upright official" instead of law. If the "upright official" stood up for justice, people felt grateful. As a matter of fact, today's tragedy goes back to the time when the students of Beijing, overjoyed, raised the banner when passing the rostrum on Tiananmen and hailed "Xiaoping, how are you?" There has never been a savior in the world; yet, we always cherish too much illusion over a particular person.

Hasn't the Cultural Revolution created enough disaster in our Motherland? Yet, we still focus only on the disaster itself and that influences our fate. Rehabilitation is only a kind of medicine for easing the pain of our souls and bodies. However, we did not think of what caused the Great

328 Spring Winds of Beijing

Cultural Revolution. Therefore, just thirteen years after this disaster, we have a bureaucratic system, bribery, corruption, and the establishment of a personality cult. This despicable cloud developed under a dictatorial political system. We have not found a political system to prevent this from happening. After the unforgettable Cultural Revolution, who could have thought a system with a supreme ruler could avoid mistakes. The legacy of this Cultural Revolution is that tens of thousands of people and thousands of hunger strikers could not win just a few words. The tragedy lies in the fact that there are still no just laws to combine the will of the people with the position of government officials.

No matter if the Democracy Movement wins or not, we should remember a lesson of blood. We must establish a system supervised by the people on the basis of law and order to avoid the government's mistakes. Don't cherish any illusions regarding any one person. Don't hope that there will be an "upright official" to voluntarily stand up to establish a system to supervise himself. The history of reform shows that the ruler will not point the spearhead of reform at himself. People can only safeguard the system if it is a system established by people themselves.

Law should be established by the people, for the people's benefit. It should not be established by any party. The country is the people's country. The system is meant to serve the people. The party in power should be the spokesmen of the people. People have a right to reject a party which holds power against the people's will. They have a right to abolish a system that is against the will of the people; no matter who established it or for what objective or ideal.

It is up to us ourselves to obtain human happiness! People of China arise! Let us fight for democracy and freedom for ourselves as well as our descendants!

MEMORIAL

June 4, 1989

Among those who died were students and ordinary citizens, adults and children, pregnant women and loving couples. They were all peaceful, conscientious, and kind people. Until the last moment of their lives, they never expected the reactionary soldiers and police to inflict upon them a catastrophe of death. Unyielding souls, come back to us! We who are still alive must rise to further action. . . .

The movement which we are engaged in is a national political struggle through which dictators shall be overthrown, corruption uprooted, and freedom secured for the people. This is a life and death struggle for the people. This is a life and death struggle for the masses against a handful of demagogues, tyrants, and traitors. It is a war of light against darkness. For a long time, the dictators and tyrants have sensed their final days. They have fought like cornered animals. For the last hope of life, they have even resorted to killing thousands of their own people. . . .

A new China shall stand tall in the Orient: democratic, free, civilized, strong, wealthy, unified, and peace-loving.

We resolutely believe that there will be a day when we can cheer and sing in victory for those who died yesterday, for those who are dying today, for those who will be dying tomorrow, and for those who are today meeting in the world and will meet in Heaven tomorrow. Unyielding souls, come back!